UNRULY SPEECH

Unruly Speech

Displacement and the Politics of Transgression

SASKIA WITTEBORN

STANFORD UNIVERSITY PRESS
Stanford, California

For my parents who support me in all of my journeys
For my brother who gives me peace of mind

STANFORD UNIVERSITY PRESS
Stanford, California

Printed in the United States of America on acid-free, archival-quality paper.

Cataloging-in-Publication Data available upon request.

Library of Congress Control Number: 2022012262

ISBN: 9781503633391 (cloth), 9781503634305 (paper), 9781503634312 (ebook)

Cover design: Rob Ehle

Cover background: paper patterns from pxhere and Flickr | Renee, via CC 2.0 license.

Typeset by Newgen in Minion Pro 10/14.4

Contents

Preface

I am writing the last sentences of this book in Hong Kong Special Adminis-trative Region (SAR) in early 2022, in a city that is coping with the Covid-19 pandemic and with creating a sense of normality after the 2019–2020 polit-ical unrest and the introduction of a national security law. The law declares subversion, secession, terrorism, or collusion with foreign entities as crimes and regulates freedom of speech and the press.[1] As a woman born in East Germany, I did not think I would find myself in a rapidly changing system that replicates some of my early experiences with censorship of speech and thought. Yet here I am, finishing a book on unruly speech that I started writing in Hong Kong during intellectually and politically more open times with seed grants from The Chinese University of Hong Kong, followed by a General Research Fund grant from the University Grants Committee in Hong Kong (2008–2010). When I began my research journey, little did I know that this project would become a long-term observation of shifting geopolitical relations between China, Europe, and the United States. Like many of my students from across the border in mainland China, I have been a witness to the economic growth of the country during my visits to academic insti-tutions and travels from urban to rural areas. Every time I have gone, I have been moved by the hospitality and curiosity of people and their eagerness to travel and study abroad. This was also true for the many Uyghurs I met, whose physical and digital mobility has been heavily regulated over time but who found ways to connect with the outside world.

This book traces communication practices like naming place and testimonio to explore how those practices transgress established political and social limits and create spaces for change. It illustrates what happens when not only people move but their unruly speech as well. Two of the largest Uyghur diasporas in the West—in the United States and in Germany—are part of this study. There are research site omissions such as Istanbul or the Central Asian countries of Kazakhstan, Uzbekistan, and Kyrgyzstan that have sizable Uyghur populations. The reason is that I turned to countries where I knew the legal, social, and political system well enough to conduct the research. While being difficult companions, distrust, self-censorship, and fear were important practical guides for me during my research. The East German system taught me well. These guides were theoretical signposts that eventually made me write about the most universal human symbol system—language—and humans' capacity to use it in transgressive and actionable ways. Within these logics, I have not included the term *Uyghur* in the title of the book as the book is not an ethnographic area studies account of a bounded group. The book is about the universal ability of humans to be defiant against dominating cultural and political powers.

What makes the Uyghurs a particularly important case in our global political climate celebrating cultural diversity and human rights, on the one hand, and fear of difference, on the other, is the Uyghurs' embodiment of this diversity, their struggle for socioeconomic and cultural rights, and their instrumentalization as a group to be feared. The book takes the angle of unruly communication, referring to transgressive practices and their sociopolitical and technological moorings. Speech, or more broadly, communication, is understood here as action and as the various types of expressive modes and practices, including oral and written, embodied and digital. By carving out the conditions for these modes and practices, the book also points to the systemic and moral challenges China and what is commonly called "the West" are facing today. These challenges include the negotiation of political and economic difference, increasing nationalisms and protectionism, and the question of fundamental personal and collective rights. Even more, this book is about the potential of alliances and transcending constructed categories of the ethnic, national, and religious bond.

Most of my gratitude goes to the many people who generously shared their time and experiences with me. Those whom I thank in particular include the men and women who invited me to their homes for food and tea, showed me their orchards, shared sweet grapes, and laughed about my bread-making skills. The same gratitude goes to the men and women in Germany and the United States who talked over pulled long noodles, lamb, and vegetables (laghman) and took the time to share their stories. A heartfelt thank you to the Uyghur scholars for sharing their impressive research, including Ildikó Bellér-Hann, Sean Roberts, James Millward, and Dru Gladney who answered my questions in personal interviews or via email.

I am indebted to Fengshi Wu, who journeyed with me to northwestern China for a project on nongovernmental organizations and the environment and whose research and social engagement I admire. The long conversations will stay with me as will the hotpot meals with friends in the TianShan and Kunlun mountains. I also extend my thanks to my colleagues in the Netherlands who gave me a platform for a keynote and for presenting this book. I am particularly grateful to my talented research assistant who contributed to the book through his computational analysis and the creation of the figures. The study benefited immensely from the dedicated readings and suggestions of the anonymous reviewers, for which I am deeply grateful. I wish to acknowledge the excellent editorial assistance provided by Marcela Cristina Maxfield and Sunna Juhn from Stanford University Press and by Charlie Clark and Anita Hueftle from Newgen. I also thank Michael Duckworth, who reviewed some earlier chapter versions.

I would like to express my great appreciation to my PhD supervisor Gerry Philipsen for teaching me how to listen, and listen again, to understand cultural logics at work. I am also deeply grateful to John Stewart, one of my best teachers, who introduced me to the philosophy of communication and to the theory and practice of dialoguing with people with very different points of view. I thank Tamar Katriel; meeting Tamar has been an intellectual and personal gift. Tamar's intellectual companionship and dedicated writings on Palestinian-Israeli relations and peace activism have been a moral compass for me. Thank you for reading a draft of the book and for giving me valuable feedback. Moreover, the intellectual generosity, hospitality, and friendship of my Hong Kong colleagues, the school's staff, and friends have nurtured me during my writing journey. There are too many to mention here but a heartfelt thank you to all for the warm welcome in Hong Kong, the intellectual stimulation, the many Thermos bottles of hot water in my office, my first taste of durian and soju, and the fun Cantonese, Shanghainese, and Taiwanese-themed cookouts over the years.

Without the support of my family who let me leave for the US and then Hong Kong, I would never have written this book. My most profound gratitude goes to my parents who have supported me in all my adventures and who provide a loving home whenever we return to Germany, to my wonderful brother who has shouldered many responsibilities due to my absence, and to my in-laws who have always been there for me. I was lucky to be raised by parents and grandparents who sensitized me and my brother to the art of contextual translation between public and private communication and who taught us to be inquisitive. Geopolitical constellations and peaceful disobedience resulted in the fall of the Berlin Wall and reunification of the Germanys. The reunification enabled me to study in various parts of the world and travel but, more importantly, to meet my husband Tim. His unwavering love and support, intellectual ingenuity, and fantastically cooked meals have been the main pillars of strength for me while writing this book. We were lucky but walls still exist. As of 2022, Uyghurs in China are enclosed by physical and digital walls and are punished for speaking out, as are many other people worldwide who refuse to remain silent in face of ongoing social injustices. This book is dedicated to them.

UNRULY SPEECH

INTRODUCTION

Uyghurs and the Space of the Limit

I HAD CONDUCTED FIELD research in southern Xinjiang[1] for one week when I met an English-speaking Uyghur young man in a carpet store while looking at the woven products. He sat cross-legged on the floor next to a friend. After some negotiations and buying a piece, I asked him about the history of the province, and its linguistic diversity. I had become curious as the hotel staff had given me three maps in three scripts: one in Chinese characters, one in Cyrillic, and a third in the Uyghur script (Arabic). Neither the young man nor his friend said much, but when I inquired whether they knew tour guides for the city and its surroundings, the young man asked for my phone number. The next day I received a call, summoning me to "to talk about the tour" right away. When I arrived, the man gestured for me to enter a room in the back of the store and spoke to me in an urgent voice:

> It is dangerous to ask about history. Very dangerous. Please stop. I have many stories of men who talked to tourists and were asked by undercover police to report to the police station. I sold a very nice carpet once to a tourist and then was questioned by the police. Sometimes they follow you, especially if you are with foreigners. They want to see whether you tell them something dangerous, like politics.

The speaker hesitated but went on to tell me that if I really wanted to know, the area was called a different name but neither he nor anybody else could talk about it. "People stay quiet, they don't want to get in trouble." Only when I got up to leave did the young man say under his breath, "We call it East Turkistan. Don't mention that name." He was immediately reprimanded by the friend who put his index finger briefly to his lips while saying: "Stop the talk. The walls have ears. You know that. We cannot say it. It should be Xinjiang."

The verbal sanctioning of the name *East Turkistan* was an indicator that unruly speech had occurred. The speaker decided, if only for a brief moment, to break into a performative mode by using a repressed set of verbal resources. The urgency with which he spoke, the low voice, and the interruption by his friend were all indicators that the young man had transgressed a limit. The gesture of a hand to lead the listener into a safe space, the finger put before one's mouth, and a smile indicating not knowing an answer were nonverbal cues that I learned to read as announcements of unruly speech and a transgression.

In contrast, *East Turkistan* was the name of choice of Uyghur migrants in Germany and in the United States. In 2008, I observed Uyghurs in Munich, Germany, holding signs during protests and shouting in English, *"Free the Uyghurs, Stop massacres in East Turkistan, Stop the assimilation politics in East Turkistan, Human rights for East Turkistan,"* repeating the messages in German, using the name *Osttürkistan*. For bystanders, Osttürkistan or East Turkistan was a faraway place, and the people holding the flags an unfamiliar group protesting injustice. The boisterous group of Uyghur rights protestors looked like a tiny island in a sea of shoppers, ice cream–eating tourists, and busy, well-dressed Munich residents. In contrast to the case of Tibetans, very few of the passersby had heard of Uyghurs. An older man asked me, "Who are they and what are they talking about? Yogurt?" The man's instinctive phonetic mistranslation demonstrated the large social distance between him and the protestors who had left China for Germany. Phrases like *Free the Uyghurs* or *Human rights for East Turkistan* gained traction when Uyghurs were joined on other days by Tibetan groups, Amnesty International, and UNPO, the Unrepresented Nations and Peoples Organization, which helped raise general awareness about Uyghurs. Nevertheless, in contrast to Tibetans, Uyghurs have been little known in Europe or North America in the past. There are two main reasons, according to Uyghur interviewees in Germany and the United States. First, Uyghurs are Muslims. While Tibetans have gained support from Western governments and people, moral support for Muslims can be scarce as a result of suspicion and distrust after the September 11 attacks in the US, the violent deaths of critics of Islam in Europe such as in the Netherlands and France, and the one-sided and heavily mediated linkages between violence and Islam. Second, unlike the Dalai Lama, Rebiya Kadeer, the former long-time leader of Uyghurs in exile, has gained only marginal global attention and support.

East Turkistan is an example of unruly speech practice. Unruly speech refers to the oral, written, embodied, and digital modes of expression that exceed the limit of what is permitted to be said, written, or shown. Unruly speech calls the limit into question by illuminating its social and political mooring (Foucault 1977) and by pointing to the actors and mechanisms that allow for expression to happen. Unruly speech is transgressive precisely as it questions boundaries between set categories, exposes the limits of the sayable and doable, and reveals the conditions for what can be articulated, heard, and seen (Jervis, 1999) in a communicative space, as in the example in the carpet store. Merleau-Ponty describes this space as "the means whereby the position of things becomes possible" (1962, 167), including an imagination of alternative relations between self and other. The space announced by unruly speech has potential because taken-for-granted communicative roles are rearranged, providing the base for social change. The space can have the qualities of a safe environment in which the unspeakable can be told and trust can be created through productive debate about diverging ideas, as Conley (1997, 180) maintains:

> In these moments pregnant with the fantasy of imminent communi-
> cation, something is about to make manifest the "taking of place" in
> which, suddenly, among a collectivity of participants, a "space" becomes
> invented. In it circulated the affirmative interrogative, "you, too?!" that
> gives cause to solidarity.

Denis Hollier writes that traditional institutions are "able to tolerate any message, including the most subversive ones, so long as they remain messages and do not call its code into question" (1989, 1040). Speech is action, as discussed at length by speech act theorists (Austin 1962; Searle 1969) and

communication scholars (Carbaugh 2017; Philipsen 1992). Culturally situated speakers draw from communicative norms, values, and codes and act upon them in daily life (Katriel 2021; Philipsen 1992, 1997; Philipsen and Coutu 2005). Unruly, transgressive communication engages the codes governing a social and political structure, including the codes to speak, be heard, and be (in)visible. Uyghurs who are represented in this book have called the political and social codes into question. They engaged not only the political code in China but social codes in Uyghur culture as well.

Transgressions also act as catalysts, as Stefan Horlacher maintains (2010, 15). The young man described in the encounter in the carpet store had a scared facial expression when making his transgressive move as he was not sure whether he could trust me as an outsider. At the same time, he seemed to release a pent-up energy through the urge to make known a collective perspective. This urge was expressed in the diaspora in Germany and the United States where Uyghurs advocated for human rights and belonging. In contrast, in Xinjiang, speaking about history became inextricably linked to the question about place and was eventually subject to speech censorship. Fear and distrust by local Uyghurs became even more tangible when I walked through the streets of Kashgar, an old oasis city on the fringes of the Taklamakan desert and a trading hub for centuries, close to the borders with Kyrgyzstan, Pakistan, and Afghanistan. In the old town, Uyghurs hustled out of my way and closed their doors while avoiding my gaze. They were right to be wary of me, as I was shadowed throughout my stay. For example, after visiting the main mosque and standing outside the gate, I was photographed by a young man who exited the premises after prayer. The man also sat in the lobby of the hotel where I stayed the same evening, reading a newspaper. He observed me when I went online in the internet cafe of the hotel and when I went out.

Having grown up in East Germany, I was accustomed to the practice of being followed, along with my family members, physically and symbolically. Low-level surveillance, so it seemed, was a routine way of making the other internalize self-censorship and dissuading people from speaking in unruly ways. Moments of self-censorship represent a productive breach, however. These moments expose the repressed and unspeakable as a rich field for exploring transgression as part of the social process. Uyghurs' self-censorship and discrepancies in naming place oriented me to the names *Xinjiang* and *East Turkistan* as practices that exemplify the crossing of limits.

Practices are understood here as spatially and temporally dispersed ways of acting (Shove, Pantzar, and Watson 2012). Practices are co-constituted by premises and symbols, with a symbol being a "vehicle for a conception" (Philipsen 1992, 8). "Premises express beliefs of existence (what is) and of value (what is good and bad)" (8). In this study, place names are conceived of as vehicles for imagined physical and social place, backed by beliefs of "what is" and their valuation. As such, premises encapsulate the implicit or explicit beliefs that interactants have about each other, the interaction, and the physical and social place in which they find themselves (Carbaugh 2017).

Like place names, testimonios were an unruly speaking practice. They were typically told in unelicited ways in personal interviews. Here is an example. Roshan, a Uyghur woman in her early thirties, was among those who had migrated to Germany. I met her in Munich in 2010 and interviewed her several times. Early on, in a personal interview, she witnessed to experiences of flight and persecution that transcended a personal experience and gestured to a collective narrative. During a business trip to Kazakhstan, she was informed that her mother had taken ill and that she had to return immediately. Roshan knew that her mother had no illness and that she was targeted for her activism and distribution of leaflets addressing forced abortions and discrimination against Uyghurs in the labor market. Roshan never returned to Xinjiang but used her friends' networks to hide in Central Asian countries before starting the journey to Germany, reaching Munich in the early morning hours on a cold winter day and applying for asylum, which was granted. Roshan tried to participate in as many of the Uyghur protests as she could to raise awareness. Roshan's story of flight and ongoing advocacy is typical for Uyghurs in the diaspora who mobilized politically and engaged in defiant ways of speaking and acting. Her testimonio is told in detail in chapter 4.

Even more, testimonios on websites and social media were practices that pushed the human rights discourse. The affordances of digital technologies, such as intertextual linkages and visibility, helped amplify the reach of the testimonios and are also explored in chapter 4. Witness accounts are conceptualized here as *testimonio* in reference to the Latin American political genre of seeking justice by linking individual to collective experience and narrating it to the world (e.g., Beverley 2005; Deeb-Sossa 2019; Figueroa 2015; Marquez 2019; The Latina Feminist Group 2001; Villenas 2019). *Testimonio* grew out of the persecutions, civil wars, and violence experienced by different populations in Latin and South America since the 1960s. I employ *testimonio* instead of the legalistic term *testimony* in this book to position the witness account as a political act. I use the term to highlight an ontology of violence that transcends geopolitical locales and is traceable through the marks it leaves on bodies, minds, words, and human-object relations.

In digital contexts, transgressive practices like naming place and testimonio cannot be discussed without the notion of visibility, as visibility is one main affordance of these contexts (Treem and Leonardi 2013). Media-type visibility is linked to what Brighenti (2007) calls social-type visibility, which means social recognition. Social recognition through mediated visibility is often controlled by political and social actors, including governments, legal bodies, and social groups with the power to influence public and political discourse. Control-type visibility "transform(s) visibility into a strategic resource for regulation," writes Brighenti (2007, 339). Powerful are those who become visible on their own terms. Examples are governments and transnational organizations that create the parameters for what is visible in digital spaces and what remains hidden. Digital testimonios posted on activist, media, and advocacy organization websites, as discussed in chapter 4, are a showcase for open source data and mediated visibility, giving Uyghurs international exposure.

For example, a video witness account was posted on WeChat by a young Uyghur man named Merdan Ghappar. The account was published in an article by the BBC in August of 2020 (Sudworth 2020). Merdan sits handcuffed on the metal frame of his bed in a small room with bare walls. The windows are open and through the metal bars, one can hear public information announcements about Xinjiang politics and history. "Xinjiang has never been 'East Turkistan'" echoes through the loudspeaker, "and neither has a state ever existed by that name." Two years back, Merdan had been the shining example of Uyghur integration, one learns from the BBC article. He had worked as a model for the online retailer Taobao in the southern Chinese city of Foshan and was an eloquent young man with very good Chinese language skills. He was sent to prison for sixteen months for the alleged sale of cannabis. Two months after his jail sentence was served, in January of 2020, he was flown back to Xinjiang and accompanied by two officers to his home town of Kuqa. Merdan then sent a video to his parents, followed by text messages on WeChat. The messages narrated in Chinese what had happened to him after arriving in Kuqa. He was kept in a police jail, wearing a black head sack and leg shackles and handcuffs, connected by an iron chain, according to the WeChat texts displayed in the BBC article (Sudworth 2020). Merdan's whereabouts were still unknown by January of 2022.

Open source information has become important for researching, reporting on, and documenting human rights violations (Dubberley, Koenig, and Murray 2020). Nevertheless, there are challenges. Like Dubberley, Koenig, and Murray (2020), Guay and Rudnick (2020) discuss incidental threats when working with digitized materials and the potential harms for already vulnerable populations resulting from data experiments and unintended data disclosure. The digital testimonios analyzed in chapter 4 are publicly available witness accounts that were posted with the intention of raising awareness and to gather and archive evidence of rights violations. In addition to the empowering aspects of digital technologies, the discussion of digital surveillance of Uyghurs in chapters 2 and 3 illustrates control-type visibility and the power of technology for regulating Uyghurs' speech.

To recapitulate, my research was guided by the questions of how transgressive communication practices challenge and dislocate established social and political limits, how they travel across geographical space, and how they create opportunities for sociopolitical change. Language is inherently dislocating (Cooren 2010) as it evokes principles, rules, persons, and things in whose name people speak. Those principles and things gain agency through the communicative process (Cooren 2010). Naming practices like *East Turkistan* and premises like belonging, human rights, and suffering are assigned agency as people make them "say or do things," thereby acting in their name (Cooren 2010, 9). Communication can move local premises across borders and into a global discourse and vice versa. Migrants are part of this process, which is why displacement, here, refers to the physical dislocation of people as well as the dislocation of meaning.

After having identified place-naming and testimonio as two main practices, I further asked about their key premises and how they motivated transgression. I was also led by the question of the conditions that enable and restrict unruly speech and the reasons why. Eventually, the discussion highlights the competing facets of the Uyghur story, from the perspective of Uyghurs living in Xinjiang, the perspective of Uyghurs in Germany and the United States, and organizations supporting Uyghurs, some of whom have instrumentalized the Uyghur story for their purposes. As indicated before, I use the terms communication and speech synonymously to refer to expressive modes of human relating, including verbal and written, embodied, visual, and digital. I also use the terms *testimonio, witnessing,* and *bearing witness* synonymously. The terms *witnessing* and *bearing witness* allow me to discuss the process character of testimonio and to conceptualize testimonio as a communicative practice.

OVERVIEW OF UYGHURS IN CHINA AND UYGHUR DIASPORAS IN GERMANY AND THE UNITED STATES

Naming place and testimonio oriented me to the displacement of Uyghurs and the production of migrants and diasporas. Diasporas are composed of dislocated people who share the experience of dispossession and transnational imaginaries (e.g., Alonso and Oiarzabal 2010; Arora 2020; Brah 1996; Bernal 2014). Likewise, I use the term *migrant* as a construct that comes into being through mobility across space and the legal and bureaucratic categorization of this mobility, such as labor migrant, skilled migrant, educational migrant, asylum seeker, or refugee (e.g., Witteborn 2011a; Mezzadra and Neilson 2013; Tazzioli 2020; Zetter 2007). For example, an *asylum seeker* is a person who is in the claims-process of seeking protection (IOM 2019, 14). A refugee is formally declared a *refugee* once she or he meets the criteria set out by the Geneva Refugee Convention from 1951 (IOM 2019, 171). This "formal declaration" points to the bureaucratic and legal legitimization of a displaced status and its construction (Zetter 2007). The majority of Uyghurs in Germany were in the process of seeking asylum or were already legitimated refugees. Uyghurs sought asylum in the United States as well but also entered the country as students and labor migrants.

Uyghurs have been embedded in an opaque information environment for at least two decades, and little information has trickled out of China. This has changed since at least 2019. On February 4, 2019, the World Uyghur Association, Human Rights Watch, Amnesty International, and the International Service for Human Rights addressed the UN Human Rights Council to gather facts about alleged internment camps for Uyghurs and other minorities in Xinjiang Uyghur Autonomous Region in China. This request was not new to the council. In September 2018, the United Nations high commissioner for human rights, Michelle Bachelet, had expressed concerns about reeducation camps for Uyghurs and other minorities in China. Evidence of internment and prison facilities has been circulating since 2018 when the BBC reported on satellite images from April 18, 2018, showing large compound structures outside the small town of Dabancheng, a one-hour drive from Urumqi. Architectural forensics identified those as new prison structures (Sudworth 2018).

Since 2018, the topic of human rights violations against the Uyghurs has gathered political steam. In early 2021, there were daily news and government reports on Xinjiang. A tug of war had started through which governments in North America, Europe, and Australia tried to control the narrative about the Uyghurs and their justification of actions against China. These actions included a declaration by the United States on the last day of the Trump administration in January of 2021 that the Chinese government is committing genocide against the Uyghurs, followed by a declaration by the Canadian Parliament in February. Canada's Parliament voted 266–0 for declaring China's Uyghur treatment "genocide." Prime Minister Justin Trudeau and cabinet members abstained (*BBC News* 2021a). Multinationals backed out of using Xinjiang-produced cotton by early 2021 (Zengerle 2021) and were banned on e-commerce platforms in China, with brand ambassadors in China distancing themselves from companies like Nike, Adidas, and H&M. In March of 2021, the US and the EU sanctioned Chinese officials who were alleged to be involved in Uyghur human rights abuses, with China retaliating and sanctioning selected EU and US officials in return. On December 23, 2021, US President Joe Biden signed the Uyghur Forced Labor Prevention Act into law (Blinken 2021).

In the past decade, if information on Uyghurs became public, it was usually about dramatic events that positioned Uyghurs in the tension between freedom fighter and threat to the state. The reports included violent events like the riots in 2009 in Urumqi, the capital of Xinjiang; the attack on October 28, 2013, in Beijing when a car ran over pedestrians in Tiananmen Square; and knife attacks on March 1, 2014, at Kunming Railway Station where thirty-one Han Chinese died and many more were severely injured. The riots in Urumqi in 2009 started after an incident in a factory in Shaoguan, Guangdong province, in the south of China during which two Uyghurs were killed after a dispute between Han and Uyghur migrant workers over the alleged sexual assault of a Han female. During the resulting riots in Urumqi almost two hundred people, most of them Han Chinese, were killed (Wong

2009). The Uyghur death toll, also following detention and imprisonment, remains unclear. The People's Republic of China (PRC) government blamed exile Uyghurs for instigating and fueling the violence, something which the World Uyghur Congress (WUC) as the main diasporic organization of Uyghurs refuted. In China, Uyghurs were shamed into a discourse of national secession and instability as well as international terrorism linked to politicized Islam (Roberts 2020).

The majority of Uyghurs live in China in Xinjiang province, also officially referred to as Xinjiang Uyghur Autonomous Region (XUAR). The province is located in the most northwestern corner of China, bordering Mongolia, Russia, Kazakhstan, Kyrgyzstan, Tajikistan, Afghanistan, and Pakistan. Xinjiang Uyghur Autonomous Region is the northern neighbor of Tibet Autonomous Region. The province's topography is impressive. The Pamir and Karakoram mountain ranges, some of the highest in the world, stretch to the southwest on the borders with Pakistan, Afghanistan, and Tajikistan. The Kunlun mountain ranges are to the south, on the border with Tibet, and the TianShan ranges to the north. The Taklamakan desert extends across Xinjiang Uyghur Autonomous Region, with oasis towns like Kuqa, Aksu, Kashgar, Yarkand, and Khotan dotted along its edges. The region is ethnically diverse with Kazakhs, Tajiks, Kyrgyz, Hui (Chinese Muslims), Russians, Han Chinese, and Uyghurs.

According to China's latest 2020 population census, there are 25,852,345 inhabitants in Xinjiang province, which is an 18.3 percent increase compared to 2010 (Consulate-General of the People's Republic of China in Toronto 2021). Han Chinese counted for 42.24 percent and Uyghurs for 44.96 percent of the province's total population. Compared to the last census in 2010, the Han Chinese population increased by more than two million people, which is higher than the increase of the Uyghur population by 1.6 million. There could be at least two reasons: in-migration of Han Chinese and population control of the Uyghurs. Among the 2.174 million Han Chinese, 1.948 million are migrants from other provinces (Consulate-General of the People's Republic of China in Toronto 2021). Between 2016 and 2019 alone, the population in the province grew by 1.25 million, a third of which was employed by the Xinjiang Production and Construction Corps. This corps is a type of military organization that oversees the economy in the province and is regarded as a main contributor to population growth (Leng and Zhou 2021). Furthermore, for minorities in the province, birth and growth rates have been slowing since 2018. Li Xiaoxia from the Xinjiang Development Research Center attributes this change to strict family planning policies (Leng and Zhou 2021).

The largest cities in the province are the capital, Urumqi, with more than three million people; Shihezi (600,000+); Korla (500,000+); Ghulja, Aksu, and Kashgar (each with more than 450,000); and Qumul (more than 400,000). Uyghurs live mostly in rural southern Xinjiang, which is also the poorest part of the province, as well as in Kashgar, Khotan, Aksu, Turpan, and Ghulja. For Han Chinese, this trend is reversed, with population density highest in the affluent north and along main roads and railroads (Toops 2016).

In contrast to today's largely sedentary reality, Uyghurs had been nomadic steppe peoples before the eighth century, settling in oasis towns from the seventh to ninth centuries in response to the strengthening of a centralized Chinese empire (Barfield 1989; Gladney 2004). Throughout history, Uyghurs have established their own states and khanates (Millward 2007, 377) and gradually converted from Manichaean, Buddhist, and Nestorian Christian beliefs to Islam from the tenth to the sixteenth century. Xinjiang was conquered by the Qing in 1754, and the oasis towns were incorporated into the Chinese empire in 1821 (Gladney 2004). As Millward (2007, xiv) notes, "The history of Xinjiang is the history of many interacting peoples, cultures, and polities, not of a single nation." This diversity explains why the term *Uyghur* only came into being in the early twentieth century (Fletcher 1968, 364, note 96; cited in Newby 2007, 16). At the same time, Uyghur scholars maintain that despite the life in separate oasis towns and vibrant interactions between Turkic Muslims, Armenians, Mongols, Jewish people, Manchus, and Han Chinese, there has been a sense of shared identity between people called *Uyghur* from early times (Millward 2007, xiv; Newby 2007; Rudelson 1997). The province became Xinjiang Uyghur Autonomous Region in 1955, with *Xinjiang* meaning *New Frontier*. The term contradicts the historical inhabitation of the land by Uyghurs, Kazakhs, Tajiks, and many others who dwelled in oasis towns (Rudelson 1997). The young Uyghur man's declaration from the beginning of this introduction, "It should be Xinjiang," is insightful here as it emphasizes the dictum of honoring the definition of the region as a space to be discovered and settled.

Several violent and nonviolent uprisings occurred in northern and southern Xinjiang in the 1990s as a result of dissatisfaction with the social, political, and economic conditions for Uyghurs, the dominance of Han Chinese in politics and business, and the banning of Meshrep clubs in Ghulja in 1995, which provided space for socializing during harvesting times (Millward 2007). In particular, tensions started to mount after the 1990 Baren uprising during which Uyghurs attempted to gain control over a township near Kashgar. Roberts (2020) argues that the September 11, 2001, attacks on the World Trade Center in New York marked the beginning of a rhetorical and political shift in China, with the US-led discourse and War on Terror being conveniently extended to the Uyghurs by the Chinese state. Roberts's research shows how the Chinese government employed the War on Terror discourse as a tool to convince the public of the imminent threat of religious extremism and separatism in China. The riots in Urumqi in 2009 and attacks by Uyghurs on Han civilians in 2013 and 2014 served as legitimations to further control and weaken the identity of Uyghurs and other majority Muslim populations in the country. Two months after the attacks in New York, the Chinese government released the document "Terrorist Activities Perpetrated by 'Eastern Turkestan' Organizations and Their Ties with Osama bin Laden and the Taliban" (Roberts 2018, 232). The document provided the rhetorical ground for actively going against diasporic Uyghur organizations as they were alleged to be financed by radical Islamists like Osama bin Laden and Al-Qaeda. According to Roberts, the document was surprising to scholars of the region as they had not seen any evidence of networked militant support for Uyghurs outside China. In other words, Uyghurs' Muslim identity became the figure (Cooren 2010) to evoke the principle of security and to justify the actions by the Chinese state against the Uyghurs.

From a Uyghur perspective, a sense of inequality with Han Chinese can be traced back more than a century and linked to the tumultuous history of the region and several political and military powers trying to gain control, including Uyghurs themselves. The areas on both sides of the border between the Soviet Union and the Ily region in northern Xinjiang have deep economic, educational, cultural, and political links, and rebels gained the support of the Soviets in 1943 to start an uprising against the Kuomintang (Forbes 1986). The Soviets militarily and economically supported the attempted establishment of a second East Turkistan Republic in the three northern districts—Altai, Ili, and Tarbaghatai—to regain control over the region (Forbes 1986).

The discourse on terrorism also served to secure internal economic development in Xinjiang. During the 1990s and well into the 2010s, the province was a key provider of natural gas to build the national economy, which meant integrating Xinjiang and its ethnic minorities firmly into China from an infrastructural perspective. The pressure for the integration of the Uyghurs has increased even more with the Belt and Road Initiative (BRI). The BRI, initiated by the Chinese government in 2013, aims at developing overland and maritime material and digital infrastructures for enhanced economic growth of the region. Xinjiang is a crucial node here, connecting China to Central and South Asia.

The Chinese government has changed its security strategy in Xinjiang for several years now, with face-to-face control of minorities turning into digital surveillance. "In addition to existing policies of securitization and surveillance, authorities escalated the use of mass detention, ideological reeducation, and pressure on Uyghur diaspora networks," write Chestnut Greitens, Lee, and Yazici (2020). According to the authors, these steps were due to a strengthening perception in China that Uyghurs were about to radicalize and participate in Islamic militant actions in Southeast Asia and the Middle East. Chen Quanguo, who had worked in Tibet before, became the new party secretary in Xinjiang and was a key figure for implementing the new paradigm of preemptive control through algorithmic surveillance and detention for reeducation (Chestnut Greitens, Lee, and Yazici 2020). The internment facilities were created in early 2017 as "Counter-Extremism Training Schools" and were then renamed as "Education and Transformation Training Centers" (Roberts 2018, 250). Numbers of detainees were estimated to be between 100,000 and 500,000 in 2017–18 (Roberts 2018, 251).[2] In an Asia Society podcast, Buzzfeed News correspondent Megha Rajagopalan and investigative journalist Bethany Allen-Ebrahimian (2020), who covers China for the American news platform Axios, stated that 15,683 Xinjiang residents were put into detention camps in one week in June of 2017 alone.

Most of the Uyghurs outside of China live in the neighboring Central Asian countries of Kazakhstan, Uzbekistan, and Kyrgyzstan. In the past, Uyghurs moved to Turkey, Saudi Arabia, Pakistan, or Central Asian countries as traders, work migrants, or for higher education. Since the 1990s, they also have emigrated to claim asylum. In Turkey, there are approximately

50,000 Uyghurs, in Australia 2,000, and in the US more than 1,000 (Chen 2014). Since 2009, the emigration routes via Central Asia have become more difficult, and Uyghurs left China and moved to Southeast Asia to seek asylum (e.g., Thailand, Cambodia, Indonesia, Malaysia) (Soliev 2017).

At the time of the research, the 500 to 700 Uyghurs in Germany lived in and around Munich, partly because it is the seat of the World Uyghur Congress (WUC) but also because other Uyghurs had already settled there. The international board of the WUC is composed of Uyghurs from the United States, Germany, Canada, Sweden, Turkey, the Netherlands, Kyrgyzstan, Kazakhstan, and Norway. The organization, with an elected board and president, serves as the switchboard for all Uyghur organizations worldwide. People came to Germany from China in the 1990s in search of political asylum. Many of them originated from the rural parts of Xinjiang, places of natural beauty and cultural conservatism. The majority of people I interviewed came to seek asylum and had either been recognized as refugees already or lived in asylum shelters. Some had white-collar jobs and very few had higher degrees of education.

In the United States, Uyghur demographics were slightly different. Uyghurs had come to the United States in the 1980s and 1990s, several from Turkey. As in Germany, they are a rather young migrant community of around 800–1,000 people, according to estimates by the interviewees in the US. The Uyghurs I interviewed, starting in the spring of 2009, were generally better educated than their counterparts in Germany. The majority were college graduates. Some interviewees came to the US to study on a scholarship; around one-third came as refugees. Many of them resided in Virginia, in close proximity to Washington, D.C., and lived a middle-class life with high aspirations for their children. As the political center of the United States and an important place for lobby work, Washington was a suitable place for Uyghur settlement. The seat of several Uyghur diasporic associations is there, including the Uyghur American Association (UAA) and the Uyghur Human Rights Project (UHRP), the research advocacy arm of the Uyghur diaspora. As mentioned before, Uyghurs did not only move their bodies, language, families, and hopes. They also moved their communication practices. A formerly transgressive act of naming, like *East Turkistan*, became normalized in the Uyghur diaspora, in its political advocacy on social media, and during direct political action in public spaces.

CONTRIBUTIONS OF THIS BOOK

Unruly speech is similar in principle across the ideological and political spectrum as it questions dominant ways of being and acting. It differs, however, according to its aims and purposes. Scarred populations around the world demand recognition of their civic and political rights and participation in processes of deliberation and institution-building. Far-right-inspired groups like *QAnon* in the United States or *Querdenker* in Germany employ unruly speech to question the foundation of the democratic process and its institutions, while taking advantage of its values like free speech and the right of assembly to make themselves heard. This book situates itself on the side of transgressive speech that affirms the democratic process and opens up spaces of encounter, instead of spaces of hatred and closure.

The book contributes to the migration literature more generally by exploring what happens when unruly communication becomes mobile and gains discursive and material force across geographical and social space. This question is important in the face of economic and cultural globalization, a surge in nationalism and populism, and continuing migratory movements around the world (Mavroudi and Nagel 2016). Transgressive practices point to the myth of the homogeneous cultural group through the discursive and material struggles that its members engage in (Amin 2012; Brah 1996; Hegde 2016). Most importantly, unruly speech and the alliances arising from it are a productive starting point to challenge understandings of transnational migration as a reactive phenomenon (Bojadžijev and Karakayali 2007; Bojadžijev 2012) and to make a case for "the migrant" as a sociopolitical and legal construct. Transnational migration is proactive and best explored in the intersections between those who move and those who remain (e.g., Ahmed [2004] 2014; Sheller and Urry 2006). There are possibilities for social action arising from the intersections. Acknowledging these practices means going beyond traditional push-pull factors to accentuate the mechanisms co-producing migrancy in all its iterations, including the reproduction of gender roles during and after migration. Diasporic advocacy itself can co-constitute the migrant through strategic essentialism (Spivak 1984/85, 2008) and a new orthodoxy in behavioral roles. The resurrection of gendered scripts in Uyghur political work in Germany and the US will illustrate this claim, a development that is at odds with the quest of young Uyghurs in Xinjiang to challenge gender roles. Signifiers like *East Turkistan* follow the logics of strategic essentialism in the name of social justice. Nevertheless, strategic essentialism received cracks in the diaspora, allowing for different forms of belonging to emerge, from women campaigning for gender equality to creative and artistic expression. In other words, looking at communication processes and practices enables a more nuanced understanding of social bonding mechanisms in contexts of migration, from privileged knowledge migration to politically forced displacement. Moreover, looking at process and practice allows for identifying the moments in which breaches occur and the conditions for the breaches to happen. Eventually, exploring unruly speech shifts attention to discursive communities, held together by shared notions of rights.

A related contribution of the book is to the language and social interaction literature. As argued before, the nature of language is inherently dislocating, enabling people to speak in the name of nations, rules, and groups (Cooren 2010). This process is amplified when people move through space and take their practices with them (Blommaert 2001, 2005), thereby leaving historical traces, which need to be identified. Studies in the social interaction and communication tradition have provided evidence of ways of speaking of mostly sedentary groups, including gendered talk, hate speech, organizational discourse, cultural communication, or defiant political discourse (e.g., Boromisza-Habashi 2013; Coutu 2008; Covarrubias 2002; Katriel 1991, 2021; Philipsen 1992, 1997). Those studies have persuasively argued that the local is created and changed through deeply contextualized ways of relating, acting, and (re)membering. The studies have also illustrated how diverging discursive practices represent and constitute social tensions linked to contentious issues (Boromisza-Habashi 2013; Coutu 2008). Defiant discourse has been associated with activism as a cultural formation. For example, Katriel (2021) illustrated how defiant speech by peace activists in Israel merges global components of activism repertoires with local, cultural ways of speaking. Defiant speech is unruly speech as it tackles the limits of the socially and politically acceptable. This type of speech is a signpost of discontent and has the potential for social change, as the chapter on naming and *Xinjiang* shows.

In sum, the book emphasizes the spatial character of language and communication and what happens when not only people but their historically traceable practices are on the move. Hence, in addition to space, the book adds a time component to language and interaction research in general and forced migration research in particular. Given the time span of data collection, this project can be regarded as a historical documentation of transgressive speech before Uyghurs' grievances became known to a larger international audience in the wake of digital surveillance and detention and the trade war between China and the United States. The arguments situate research on technological surveillance and the Uyghurs into a historical context by illustrating embodied surveillance in Xinjiang as a precursor to digital surveillance (Byler 2021b, 2022;[3] Roberts 2020). The account of unruly communication presented in this book highlights that restrictions in religious, linguistic, and cultural practice have been part of the Uyghur experience for a long time but have also crossed borders. Institutional and grassroots digital advocacy work are the responses to these restrictions and represent transgressive political acts. As such, the research is in dialogue with the current literature on the digitization and datafication of mobilities, how those construct populations as datafied entities, and the degrees of freedom left for those caught in digital webs of control (e.g., Fog Olwig et al. 2020; Ruppert and Scheel 2021, Shah 2020; Tazzioli 2020).

Last but not least, the book provides insights into the complex social, cultural, and political life in China from the perspective of those who remain and those who leave. Uyghurs are in a position like the characters in a famous scene from Charlie Chaplin's *The Gold Rush* (1925). Chaplin as the Lone Prospector and Big Jim have to balance themselves in a hut that sits on a cliff. If they move to one side, the hut falls off the cliff. If they move to the other and leave through the door, they will freeze to death. The film highlights the conditions that create unsolvable dilemmas, as Tom Conley points out in his afterword to Michel de Certeau's (1997) edited text *The Capture of Speech and Other Political Writings*. The person has to act to survive, and unruly speech in the forms of coded language and witness accounts is one way of doing so. This type of speech has consequences, however. Even after leaving China, a regular life is difficult for Uyghurs, as for other politicized groups, because moral obligations, fear for family, and survivor's guilt shape life in exile (Witteborn 2007a).

There are several important historical, anthropological, linguistic, and political studies on the Uyghurs (e.g., Bellér-Hann and Hann 2020; Byler 2021b, 2022; Brophy 2016; Chen 2014; Chen 2019; Clarke 2022; Dautcher 2009; Gladney 2004; Grose 2019; Leibold and Grose 2019; Leibold 2020; Millward

2007, 2021; Roberts 2020; Smith Finley 2019; Thum 2014b; Yuan and Zhu 2021, to name just a few). This book shifts the discussion to communication practices and their potential to create spaces for change. The book connects to previous arguments about intersectional networks of cultures and religions in China that have taken on their own meanings over time. In line with the extant literature, it argues that "'China' is a construction, a notion best expressed in Haun Saussy's description of China as an 'artwork whose medium is history'" (Saussy 1993, 151; cited in Thum 2014a, 136). The communication angle offers an understanding of the tensions, alignments, and ruptures created by unruly practices beyond an essentialized China perspective. The long-term perspective of this book, from 2006 to 2021, is important for gaining a more contextualized understanding of a subsection of the people living in the country and migrating from there.

RESEARCH PROCESS
Notes on Reflexivity
The following discussion on participants, privacy, and objectivity is detailed because of the politically strained situation in Xinjiang Uyghur Autonomous Region, the danger that Uyghurs in this study exposed themselves to when being interviewed, and the fact that even empirically grounded studies on the region can be rather contentious. As a researcher interested in the physical and symbolic performance of transgressive speech, I had to understand cultural logics at work. I therefore borrow from the principles of the ethnography of communication (EC), in particular the concepts of grounded ways of communicating and their premises (Philipsen and Coutu 2005). EC studies the cultural organization of everyday life through communicative performance. EC also explores the conditions for communication in a particular place and how they create hierarchies of communicative repertoires (Hymes 1972, 1996). In the tradition of ethnomethodology and Goffman's work (1959, 1967), EC also looks for moments of rupture and breakdown to see how actors orient to each other. The approach taken here builds on these assumptions and the mechanisms that create mutually intelligible practices that link individual and group through shared premises.

The ethnography of communication is based, in principle, on ethnographic methodology (Leeds-Hurwitz 2005). Karen O'Reilly maintains that ethnography refers to "iterative-inductive research (that evolves in design through the study) [. . .] that acknowledges the role of theory as well as the researcher's own role" (2005, 3). Research encounters, the experiences and methodological training of the researcher, and the process of writing are co-constitutive ways of knowledge creation related to others people's lives (Newman 2012). The researcher engages with all of her senses in the research process. The self-reflexive nature of ethnography is not necessarily part of the ethnography of communication tradition (EC). While open to notions of power, the approach does not take the emancipatory agenda of critical epistemologies as its starting point. EC has been closely aligned with an interpretive epistemology in the objectivist social science tradition. This means that the researcher is the analytically distanced observer.

I combined EC concepts, such as communication practices and premises, with critical reflexivity. Reflexivity is especially important in view of critiques of the ethnographic method as being implicated in orders of discourse used for political, social, and cultural domination in the name of knowledge (Ahluwalia 2006). During the research process, I was sometimes asked why a woman from Germany would be interested in researching Uyghurs' communication practices. Here is an example. During a communication and media conference in Prague in May of 2018, I attended a roundtable on the China-Pakistan Economic Corridor, organized by the Centre of Global Studies at the Czech Academy of Sciences. The woman who invited me was a speaker and commented on the Gwadar deep-sea port and transport infrastructure across Pakistan and into Xinjiang province. The panel was attended by the ambassadors of Pakistan and China in the Czech Republic. I asked a question about how this project would shape life for people in Xinjiang. I raised this question as the focus had been on Pakistan and the opportunities of the economic corridor for wealth growth and peace in the country. I had neither mentioned Uyghurs nor human rights as I was interested in the economic and social benefits for the Chinese border region. The same speaker who had invited me approached me afterwards, questioning why I as a "European woman" would raise human rights. I had not mentioned human rights, but my body was automatically implicated in orders of political and historical discourses that it could not escape. Reflexivity was thus not only an academic exercise but a demand imposed by actors in and commentators on this project.

Personally, I have expanded my research agenda on migrant cultures of communication with this book, which began in the United States and continued after I moved to Hong Kong. Politically transgressive speech was a means that I recognized immediately as a result of my upbringing in East Germany. It has been familiar to me since my earliest childhood. I was bilingual early on in terms of proficiency in private and public types of communication. "You can never tell your friends about the things we discuss here," was a phrase used by my grandparents, who lived in the border zone with West Germany, ten kilometers away from the Bavarian border. Only the closest family members could enter this restricted zone with special permits; they had to register with the police and stay within the town limits. On one occasion, our family almost had to return home as our pet budgerigar did not have an entry permit. From the hillside, one could see the next village in West Germany. Sometimes, people in this West German village let balloons fly toward the East German side of the fence with messages like "We are thinking of you" or "We will be together again." In this zone of fenced-in lives and in the wider context of East Germany, speaking rules separating private from public spaces were important. Each individual's personal life depended on this arrangement because defaming East Germany or the government, talking openly about West German TV news, or desiring to leave the German Democratic Republic could result in not going to university at best and a prison sentence at worst. Talking we did in our family. I became aware early on that speaking freely in public was not a given, that self-censorship was part of daily life, and that distrust was a government technology to take control of even the most intimate part of people's lives. During my stay in Xinjiang I recognized distrust and self-censorship like old, unpleasant acquaintances. At the same time, I became acutely aware of sociopolitical breaches and the moments when people shifted into the performance of resistance.

Interviews and Participant Observations

The book has been a long-term project. I collected data materials through personal interviews, participant and nonparticipant observations, organizational and media documents, as well as social media analysis. In particular, I gathered ethnographic materials in Xinjiang, China, in 2006[4] and in Munich, Germany, and Washington, D.C., United States, from 2007 to 2013.[5] From 2007 onwards, I collected digital documents made available by Uyghur organizations in the US and in Germany, including press releases, speeches by Uyghur activists, and digital discussion fora content. In addition, the data corpus includes Twitter data on place names from 2009 to 2021 and data on the circulation of testimonios on Twitter and YouTube.

My research approach for this project is based on theoretical sampling (Strauss and Corbin 1998), which means sampling for theoretically dense concepts instead of people. The goal is "to maximize opportunities to compare events, incidents, or happenings" to refine concepts (Strauss and Corbin 1998, 202). As I heard the name *Xinjiang* as a commonly used identity and place name in China and as I observed early on the occasional use of *East Turkistan*, I traced the names in Xinjiang, Germany, and the United States to understand their premises and how those changed after moving across international borders. I traced as many speech situations as possible in which the names were used.

I started with interviews in the summer of 2006 in the cities of Urumqi and Kashgar and in smaller towns like Aksu and Korla. The research was carried out in tandem with a parallel-funded study on the work of non-governmental organizations (NGOs) in China, which I conducted with a Chinese colleague. During the study with NGOs in Xinjiang, approved by Chinese officials, I also interviewed Han Chinese and Uyghur staff in NGOs on the meaning of *Xinjiang* as a place identity. Several of the interviews were repeat interviews. I was able to get in touch with the friends, family members, and colleagues of the initial interviewees and conducted interviews in organizations, restaurants, shops, and parks or while walking in the city and visiting tourist sites. The men and women I talked with in English and through translators (Uyghur to English or Chinese to English) ranged in age from twenty-five to fifty-five years and were white-collar workers, students, carpet weavers, farmers, homemakers, and tourist guides. In the countryside, people invited me to their homes to sample Uyghur cuisine or to show me their orchards. Some older farmers also invited me to teahouses, which was unusual in the countryside as those were mostly frequented by men. At times, the interviews took an unexpected turn. For example, a Uyghur woman in a small town invited me and my colleague to her orchard after a visit to the organization she worked for. We ate water melons, grapes, and peaches. At one point, the woman asked me how she could gain a visa to Germany for her family. My colleague who had been translating fell silent. After a reluctant translation, I had to tell the woman that I could not help, which left us all standing in silence. Because of the danger of repercussions against interviewees, I have anonymized their names, consent forms, and other identity data, including age or place of residence in Xinjiang.

Long-term research was conducted in the United States and in Germany because the countries are two main centers of Uyghur settlement in the West. In particular, I did field research from 2007 to 2013, supported by a research grant from Hong Kong Special Administrative Region (SAR) from 2008 to 2010. As I did in China, I traced naming practices for place in Germany and in the United States through participant observations and personal interviews. I observed how Uyghurs socialized and celebrated and how they demonstrated, engaged in public speaking, and took part in advocacy conferences. I collected instances of the names *Xinjiang* and *East Turkistan* by interviewing people in their homes or in shops, cafes, restaurants, asylum shelters, and the offices of Uyghur organizations in Munich and Washington, D.C. I soon noticed another practice used in combination with naming place, which was testimonio and speaking as a witness. It is important to note that the testimonios told in personal interviews were unelicited. This means that they were motivated neither by interviewer expectations about narrative style nor by interviewee expectations that testifying would have benefits for them.

Interviewees in Germany ranged from twenty to sixty and the education from sixth grade to high school, with few Uyghurs having a university education. Often the people I interviewed worked in kitchens in Turkish restaurants or were manual laborers or office clerks. Ten of the participants still lived in asylum shelters. Some interviewees worked in white-collar jobs as activists, in the computer industry, or in the governmental and art sectors. Interviewees in the US ranged from nineteen to sixty-five years of age and were professionals, students, PhD holders, and diasporic activists. In Germany and the United States, interviews were conducted in English, Uyghur, and German. A paid research assistant helped with translation from Uyghur to German. Organizational or family members in the US translated from Uyghur to English. The majority of interviewees in the US spoke English.

I also interviewed the leadership of Uyghur advocacy organizations, including Rebiya Kadeer and Alim Seytoff. Kadeer was the second president of the World Uyghur Congress. Her tenure lasted from 2006 to 2017. Alim Seytoff was president of the Uyghur American Association based in Washington, D.C., at the time of the research, and director of the Uyghur Human

Rights Project (UHRP). I further interviewed staff of Human Rights Watch and Amnesty International in Washington, members of the Green Party who supported Uyghur advocacy in Germany, and financial supporters like the National Endowment for Democracy in Washington, D.C. Interviewees in the US and in Germany pointed out that only a small percentage of Uyghurs was involved in advocacy. Interviewees in this study represent both types, those who are active in diasporic politics and those who are not. They also represent a range of degrees of involvement, from being part of the leadership to occasional lobbying.

Continuing up to 2021, I collected digital content made available by Uyghur organizations and their supporters in the United States and in Germany, including press releases, speeches by prominent Uyghurs, and updates on the situation in Xinjiang. As the coordination of political advocacy by Uyghurs has increasingly gained traction through digital platforms, I extended my tracing of naming and testimonio to Twitter and YouTube as two prominent platforms for Uyghur digital advocacy. While I researched open Facebook groups for updates on Uyghur advocacy, I did not do an analysis of the platform because of its privacy terms and closed groups. Moreover, I collected documents about digital surveillance in China and reports by cybersecurity experts. The latter include reports by the University of Toronto's Citizen Lab at the Munk School of Global Affairs and Public Policy and the Xinjiang Documentation Project, co-hosted by the University of British Columbia and Simon Fraser University in Canada (University of British Columbia and Simon Fraser University, n.d.).

Privacy of Participants

Deductive disclosure is possible (Kaiser 2009) when people or groups become identifiable through their age, gender, and professions. Like other ethnographic research, which depends on rich contextual descriptions, this study also faced the tension between precise field accounts and identity protection of interviewees. This was especially true for Xinjiang province where close surveillance of Uyghurs was already a daily practice in 2007. Hence, protection of the identity of the people I interacted with was of the utmost importance. This is also true for Germany and the United States as people had family in China who could become the target of security and police action.

Therefore, I use pseudonyms throughout this book and sometimes leave out city or village names to protect the interviewees' identity.

Kaiser (2009) suggests providing participants in a study with a concrete idea of the audiences and goals of the research in order to make an informed decision on which details can be published and where. I followed this approach when I told participants during the informed consent process that studies coming out of the research would be published in academic journals, edited collections, and a monograph in English, something that participants found exciting as they wanted an international audience to be better informed about the Uyghurs in China. The embodied testimonios are presented as they were told to me. I adjusted the grammar in order not to distract the reader.

As Koch (2013a) and Mitchell (2002) have maintained in contexts of political volatility and autocracy, silence can be more meaningful than words. In this study, silences and other nonverbal cues proved to be strategic after they occurred repeatedly in response to the same question (e.g., "What was this area named before it became Xinjiang?"). Raised shoulders and responses like "I don't know much about the history of the place" became meaningful markers of self-protection. One can also assume that respondents used the name *Xinjiang* instead of other names to protect themselves. Like the culture of fear that Koch (2013b) encountered in Kazakhstan, I encountered a culture of fear and self-censorship in Xinjiang. Self-censorship was not an unreflective move by a conformist individual. Instead, it was a coping strategy by a reflective individual who saw herself in relation to a larger group of people and who wanted to protect herself and the social network she was part of.

Communicative repertoires are presented in this study as Uyghurs have presented them to me. The re-presentation of those repertoires means questioning a "hierarchy of credibility" (Becker 1967, 242), which government and media discourses in and outside China have created about the Uyghurs. This mediated hierarchy includes shifting associations of Uyghurs as religious victims of an unrelenting state and ethno-nationalist freedom fighters (see Witteborn 2011c). Presenting the voices of Uyghurs themselves—from within and outside of China—is a move toward questioning those hierarchies.

CHAPTER OUTLINE

Chapter 1 discusses foundational concepts of this book and their intersections, including unruly speech, transgression, displacement, and the role of technologies in (forced) migration. Chapters 2, 3, and 4 analyze specific communication practices. Chapter 2 focuses on the naming practice *Xinjiang*. Naming has a generative force, and the chapter illustrates how the name is driven by premises like unity, inequality, and participation that Uyghurs desire. While the name is a marker of deficit, it is also a marker of collective aspiration and a cosmopolitan outlook on culture, mobility, and religion. Chapter 3 shows how naming creates the nation, including its digital version. The name *East Turkistan* enacts the premises of belonging and human rights. It performs the nation without a state in digital space. The premises are key resources for creating alliances between Uyghurs and political stakeholders through a strategic discourse on rights. Freedom of expression and cultural belonging move Uyghur grievances and political demands onto the international stage, linking them with global discourses on social injustice and rights violations. Like chapter 2, this chapter highlights how technologies increasingly act as means of surveillance. At the same time, this chapter also illustrates the importance of technology for diasporic mobilization and advocacy work.

Chapter 4 engages with witness accounts by Uyghurs and how those are structured around the premise of suffering. The chapter shows how the shift from embodied to digital testimonios is a shift toward multimodal advocacy work and data evidence. Digital testimonios included various types of evidence posted on websites and social media platforms, such as eyewitness accounts, geolocation data, visuals of people, and court documents to curate dense testimonial datasets to be used for future legal action. This shift to multimodal advocacy is related to a shift toward structured information and data collection, aligning testimonio with a legalistic tradition and evidence-based accounts. Despite their different form from testimonios narrated in interpersonal settings, the digitized version is still testimonio in the activist tradition of speaking to power and exposing collectively experienced injustices. In addition, the chapter shows how testimonios are an example for transgression as they give Uyghur suffering a face and go beyond the mediated stereotype of the premodern rural citizen who needs to be rescued. The final chapter draws conclusions about unruly speech and the role of technology in shaping disobedience through the language of rationality and visibility. It sums up the opportunities that strategic essentialism presents for advocacy work as well as its dangers due to a retreat into myths of cultural purity and sacred territory (Sennett [1977] 2002). The chapter also draws conclusions about the future of Uyghur advocacy and Uyghur life in Xinjiang province, which is key to China's economic and political development.

1 | CONCEPTUAL REFLECTIONS ON TRANSGRESSION, COMMUNICATIVE PRACTICE, AND DISPLACEMENT

TRANSGRESSION HAS BEEN CRUCIAL to cross-disciplinary thought, from Durkheim to Goffman and Foucault. Foucault (1977) discusses it as a process that continuously explicates the limits of what cannot be crossed; a process that binds limit and transgression in infinite cycles:

> The limit and transgression depend on each other for whatever density of being they possess: a limit could not exist if it were absolutely uncrossable and, reciprocally, transgression would be pointless if it merely crossed a limit composed of illusions and shadows. (Foucault 1977, 34)

Foucault compares transgression to a flash of lighting at night that loses itself in space and vanishes after making obscurity visible (1977, 35). Like lightning, transgressive, unruly speech marks a space of existence, but can only do so as it owes this space the illumination of its own appearance. In other words, crossing a limit is not about opposition and "resistance against" existing circumstances, and neither is it violence or "victory over" (Foucault 1977, 35). Instead, transgression reveals that which had always been there but obscured. The limit can only be known through transgression (Bebergal 1998).

Transgression is not "victory over" (Foucault 1977, 35) because a system, structure, or relationship requires transgression to affirm itself, even by

creating spaces in which transgression can be performed. Examples are designated urban spaces for graffiti or the yearly performance of the carnival as a
carefully contained time-space zone of social and moral breaches. Transgressing is a sanctioned process and practice that allows for multiplicity as long
as it performs itself within the assigned time-space parameters of the social
order that allows for it to happen. Foucault understood that "the twentieth
century will undoubtedly have discovered the related categories of exhaustion,
excess, the limit, and transgression—the strange and unyielding form of these
irrevocable movements that consume and consummate us" (Foucault 1998,
84). This analysis was prophetic of the early twenty-first century. Examples
are excess of information and consumption, collective exhaustion through
exponential opportunities for networking, and humanity meeting its limits
of growth and mobility through climate change and the Covid-19 pandemic.
Global climate activism and the Black Lives Matter and Me Too movements
have started challenging received language and social realities. Nevertheless, categories like *community* and *culture* remain strong, maybe precisely
because of a threat to their unraveling. Transgressing is part of maintaining
the status quo, conclude Gournelos and Gunkel (2012) in their introduction
to *Transgression 2.0: Media, Culture, and the Politics of a Digital Age*. Jenks
puts it in these words: "Transgression [. . .] opens up chaos and reminds us
of the necessity of order" (2003, 7). The tackling of social limits becomes a
mediated act and moral reminder of social order, safety, and security.

The limit, in Foucault's work, refers to the limit of philosophical language
and the unity of the speaking subject who is constituted through language
and becomes aware of itself through consciousness, eventually being caught
in its own anthropological finitude. Foucault questions the notion of dialectics that has defined philosophical language since Hegel, Kant, and all
the way back to Greek thought. Removing dialectics means introducing the
limits of language:

> In a language stripped of dialectics, the philosopher learns that even he
> or she does not inhabit the whole of his language. Next to himself or
> herself, he or she discovers the existence of another language that also
> speaks and of which he or she is not the master or the mistress, one that
> strives, fails, and falls silent, one that he or she cannot manipulate. (Nigro
> 2005, 656)

The limits of dialectical language are made apparent in tears, ecstasy, laughter, and the premonition of finitude. Tears and desperate looks were often present when Uyghurs testified about their experiences and when the people stared into the abyss of violence, life in exile, and loneliness. Ecstasy, on the other hand, manifested itself when people protested and chanted "East Turkistan" as the imagined home and nation of Uyghurs and other minorities.

In addition to Foucault, the work by social interaction scholars such as Erving Goffman is valuable for understanding transgression on the micro-level of daily practice. Both Goffman and Foucault theorized transgression in relation to coercion (Hacking 2004). "The normative order is sustained or undermined, abided by or transgressed through social interaction" write Hancock and Garner in their review of Goffman's writings (2011, 320). Eventually, Goffman and Foucault are both concerned with revealing the forces that govern social interaction and produce social order through the logics of domination, which is not only negative but can be a productive force. Foucault draws parallels between his and Goffman's work in relation to the techniques of power used to normalize social interactions:

> My problem is to show and analyze the way in which a set of power techniques is related to forms, political forms like states, or social forms. Goffman's problem is the institution itself. My problem is the rationalization of the management of the individual. My own work is not a history of institutions or a history of ideas, but the history of rationality as it works in institutions and in the behavior of people. (Dillon and Foucault 1980, 4)

Despite the differences, one common denominator of Foucault's and Goffman's work is the attempt to understand social order as normative and framed through control of the transgressive. Emile Durkheim (1982) needs mention here in relation to Goffman's writings. Durkheim introduced the notion of the social fact as the texture of social life (1982, 53–56). The social fact exists externally, preceding the individual and governing human action through coercion. Social facts remain hidden until they are breached and eventually corrected and integrated into the moral order. Breaches, in turn, are the theoretical starting points and methodological entryways into understanding social interaction norms in ethnomethodology (Garfinkel 1967), the micro-practices constituting everyday life (Goffman 1959, 1963, 1967), and social dramas in the tradition of Victor Turner (1980). The social breach is also of major interest in this study. It is exemplified in the vignette from the carpet store in the Introduction as a breach of code. For a keen observer, the breach and resulting correction make social and political conventions available to the empirical eye.

The Durkheimian approach is represented in the work of Jenks (2003) and Jervis (1999). Both Jenks and Jervis theorized the conditions of the limit (Foucault 1977).[1] Jenks writes that to "transgress is to go beyond the bounds or limits set by a commandment or law or convention, it is to violate or infringe. But to transgress is also more than this, it is to announce and even laudate the commandment, the law or the convention" (Jenks 2003, 2). Jervis stresses that transgression is not just resistance but part of the social order and the forces, individual and collective, that attempt to recreate alignment and cohesion in the name of social, political, and moral stability:

> It is not, in itself, subversion; it is not an overt and deliberate challenge to the status quo. What it does do, though, is implicitly interrogate the law, pointing not just to the specific, and frequently arbitrary, mechanisms of power on which it rests—despite its universalizing pretensions—but also to its complicity, its involvement in what it prohibits. (Jervis 1999, 4)

Writers like Jenks see transgression as "a deeply reflexive act of denial and affirmation" (2003, 2). Foucault (1977), Bataille (1986), and Blanchot (Hart and Hartman 2004) do quite the opposite as they do not see transgression as positive or negative. Foucault, like Blanchot, tries to free transgression from association with ethical value, dialectics, and the ahistorical subject. Foucault, Bataille, and Goffman discussed the limit in pre-digital times. The question becomes how the limit is crossed in and through the digital network and who controls the process.

Critical technology scholarship has demonstrated how transgression is woven into the relationship between digital network and sovereign power and how sovereign power preempts and steers modes of connectivity. Bratich maintains that "[s]overeignty, in order to dissuade via the punishment of transgressors, needs continually to draw and redraw the demarcation among hybrids, to incessantly select among mutations in order to preempt certain mutations from emerging as dominant" (2012, 233). Bratich argues that the convergence between digital network and sovereign power gestures to new forms of control as well as new conditions for resistance, returning to the valuation of transgression as a positive or negative process.

The idea that the limit is spatial and temporal has long been acknowledged in sociology, philosophy, and literature. The limit is built into social relationships and structures to guarantee stability over time. In a networked culture, however, the spatial and temporal dimensions become more intertwined as data harvesting and digital surveillance are dependent on time-space constellations for their predictive valuation. Prediction and preemption subsume the limit and make it part of networked logics (see Amoore 2013). In the case of the Uyghurs in China, digital networks are enabled, regulated, and sanctioned by the government and its political codes. While the private sector and military research drive technological invention and digital network applications, as chapters 2 and 3 argue, the Chinese government heavily regulates the content and connectivity of the network. Diasporic Uyghurs make use of the opportunities for digital speech in Germany and the United States, access a multiplicity of social media platforms, and communicate in English as the lingua franca for advocacy. The Twitter analysis in chapters 3 and 4 illustrates this point and examines Uyghurs' unruly digital speech and its control.

In digital contexts, transgressions are heard *and* seen. In other words, visibility is woven into digital social interactions. Brighenti argues that "[v]isibility is precisely the complex field where the visible and the articulable coexist, rather than excluding each other" (2007, 329). Seeing and perceiving are governed by asymmetries, making visibility "a site of strategy" (326). Surveillance engineers visibilities (336). Digital technologies with their tensions between user-generated content, corporate-designed infrastructure, and state and supra-state regulation play a fundamental role in deciding the terms for what can be seen and what remains invisible.

In the case of the Uyghurs in China, the terms for becoming visible are set by the government and technology companies, as chapters 2 and 3 show. Surveillance in China is not new. It is an extension of traditional methods, including the historical *Baojia* system and the moral and legal principle of *guilt by association* common in ancient Imperial China (McNeill and Sedlar 1970). The Baojia system (*baojiazhi)* goes back to the Song dynasty (960–1279 A.D.). It was a system of neighborhood organizations where ten families were organized into a collective to maintain a self-regulating system of legal and social control and to act as a link as well as a buffer between the government and the people (Li 2005; Mote 2003). Some of the early tasks were supplying the government with men for the military or to collect taxes during the Ming dynasty. Over time, the system morphed into a moral control system all across China, especially under the Qing (1644–1912) (Mote 2003). The chief of the collective cluster was responsible for public order and informing the central government of any problems. *Guilt by association* implicates members of the family and the collective in the alleged wrongdoings of a person and can result in anything from harassment to legal persecution. In other words, control of the moral, social, and political behaviors of populations in China is part of the history of this large country and not just a recent invention (Miracola 2019).

Nevertheless, despite technological and social surveillance, people keep building communicative spaces to counterbalance transgressions by the state. Uyghurs create visibility on their own terms by engaging in advocacy in embodied public spaces or on social media. The digital testimony by Merdan, reported in the Introduction, is an example. It opens up an interaction space for witnessing injustice and makes the situation of Uyghurs visible for an international audience. Young Merdan not only turns back the gaze at the perpetrators by looking out of his prison but relocates the visibility of his imprisoned position across space and time through his video message. He mediates the technique of "re"-education used for Uyghurs and invites a national and international audience to witness the conditions upon which this technique is built, including fear and physical violence. The destabilizing effect lies in the fact that the international community witnesses social engineering at work. The video is powerful as it deflects attention from the individual to a larger infrastructure of violence, evidenced by the prison cell, the shackles, and constant exposure to a soundscape of renunciation ("Xinjiang has never been 'East Turkistan'").

The video testimony announces the space of the limit: the limit of who is allowed to talk and what is permissible to show. In the video, the transgressive move entails the shift from telling to showing. The move delineates the limit not as a line to be crossed but as a space in which the possible, permissible, and prohibited are illuminated. Communicative space comes into being through the unruly act. The relational nature of communicative space is the manifestation of self and world encountering each other (Merleau-Ponty 1962). This phenomenological take on space fits the theoretical underpinnings of the social interaction approach used in this book in terms of the linkage between cultural knowledge, communicative practice, and sensemaking. Showing the silent person imprisoned in a soundscape points to the conditions for speech for Uyghurs: Uyghurs are not in control of language and meaning. They are spoken for by political and other social actors (e.g., the national and international media). The digital device becomes the main actor to record and arrange meaning temporarily. Technology is the tool to challenge the limits of silence and to create a space for political and moral engagement.

Unruliness allows for the capture of speech, to use de Certeau's words (1997), and provides a means for people to create spaces of potentiality. People can shift out of binary categories (e.g., Uyghur versus Han Chinese, or Xinjiang versus East Turkistan) into silence or other forms of nonverbal cues. These can be moments when the subject stops speaking in the conventional way as language cannot express the inarticulable (Nigro 2005). The void starts talking but not in the corset of received language. Crying, sobbing, and chants for social justice become part of the quest for change and the creation of new interaction spaces. In these spaces, there is freedom to imagine belonging through political recognition, alliances, and mutual respect, a freedom that is restricted at the same time by technology, moral codes, and the law. Digital surveillance affirms the political order in the name of security. Human rights codes affirm the moral order in the name of individual and group protection. In order to focus on communicative practice and the regulatory codes for its performance, I turn now to the ethnography of communication (EC) and the practices of naming place and testimonio.

COMMUNICATION PRACTICES: NAMING PLACE AND TESTIMONIO
The ethnography of communication (EC) focuses on exploring the role of situated communication repertoires in social grouping processes (e.g., Carbaugh 1996; Covarrubias 2002; Fitch 1998, 2003; Hymes 1964; Katriel and Philipsen 1981; Philipsen 1992, 2002; Philipsen and Coutu 2005). The EC is an inherently grounded way of understanding situated everyday practice. Communicative repertoires should be studied in their own right, referring to how interactants engage with them, why, and to what end. The approach

allows for an interpretive as well as a critical epistemology, with the question of the mechanisms that marginalize particular practices built into the methodology (Blommaert 2009; Hymes 1985).

The EC approach enabled me to account for the transgressive communication practices of spatially dispersed people and the shared premises constituting their speech. The analytical focus shifts from an a priori defined entity, such as *Uyghur culture,* to the practices constituting group life in a locale and across space. *Culture,* and this is an important point, relates to the premises of interactional conduct and *not* to entities like ethnicity, nationality, religion, or territory. The principles of EC provided me with an analytical frame to orient to the situated practices through which Uyghurs relate with each other and with political and historical discourses. Naming place and testimonio were two of those practices, which I identified through theoretical sampling.

The EC project has not lost its political appeal since the 1970s when scholars like Dell Hymes linked the study of almost eradicated languages and cultural knowledges to social justice: "The transformation of society to a juster, more equal way of life requires transformation of genuine equalities in verbal resource" (Hymes 1996, 46). Ironically, Dell Hymes turned out to be violating the principles of justice and equality in grave ways when former students disclosed his sexual harassment practices at the University of Pennsylvania (Elegant 2018).

Other researchers developing the EC have worked in more ethical ways and produced an impressive body of literature about locally grounded knowledge and interaction practices. Communication scholars like Gerry Philipsen (1992, 1997) and many others in the tradition of the ethnography of communication have treated the local as a resource of distinct knowledge and practice as well as experiential introspection and distinction. EC allows the identification of competing local discourses by looking at communicative settings, events, and acts across embodied and digital communication (Coutu 2008; Philipsen and Coutu 2005). By analyzing grounded practice, the researcher can learn about the cultural logics at work and what it means to live in a physical and imagined place. People speak and act from places in the geographical, sociocultural, linguistic, and political sense (Blommaert 2005, 2014; Philipsen 1992).

Scholars have used the principles of the ethnography of communication to study the role of silence in Native American or Finnish-speaking cultures (Basso 1970; Carbaugh 1999; Carbaugh, Berry, and Nurmikari-Berry 2006), forms of personal address in organizations in Mexico (Covarrubias 2002), interpersonal relating in Colombia (Fitch 1998), grouping processes in public deliberations (Witteborn and Sprain 2009), secret-sharing in Israel (Katriel 1991), defiant discourses and the link between talk and action (Katriel 2021), aspirational digital performance by forced migrants (Witteborn 2021), or the role of white, middle-class speech codes in the US (Philipsen 1992). In all of those studies the authors illustrate how the recurrent use of particular communicative means creates and breaks social fabric through interaction rituals.

EC can expose contested premises about personhood, group relations, and social change. As such, EC is more than an analytical instrument. EC is a theoretical lens to understand situated cultural logics. EC is also a practical theory in that it can assist in the design of locally meaningful solutions to situated problems. In this function, EC has been employed for social programming design by UN organizations (Miller and Rudnick 2008) and in other applied design, organizational, and digital contexts (Hart 2015; Kalou and Sadler-Smith 2015; Leighter, Rudnick, and Edmonds 2013; Milburn 2015; Sprain and Boromisza-Habashi 2013). EC has also been concerned with the spatial aspects of communicative conduct (Katriel 2015). However, communicative conduct has mostly been studied in settings that are already "emplaced" (Katriel 2015, 455). Although a comparative logic is encouraged, the majority of studies have focused on one practice and place. This study moves beyond a comparative logic and turns to tracing transgressive communication practices of spatially dispersed people by the examples of naming place and testimonio.

There is a body of literature on how place names dislocate meaning and co-create national topographies and identities. Contributions in the edited collection *Critical Toponymies* (Vuolteenaho and Berg 2016), for example, highlight contested geographical naming practices that erase indigenous identities or inscribe nationalism into urban spaces. Likewise, Saparov (2017) explores the use of place names for political legitimization and national identity creation by the example of post-Soviet Azerbaijan and the violent conflict between Armenians and Azerbaijani in Nagorno-Karabakh. Saparov shows the intersection between strategic renaming to legitimize political leadership and erasure of "'enemy' toponyms" (2017, 536). Moreover, Saparov points to the fact that the emergent nationalisms in the region and symbolic strategies for legitimation can only be understood through a historical lens, such as the Soviet legacy.

In another piece on migration and naming, Cohen and Yefet (2021) discuss the Iranian diaspora and how people constitute an identity narrative that references pre-Islamic Persia and cosmopolitanism, while moving away from national politics and a one-dimensional definition of imposed belonging. *Persia* becomes an identifier of a place, high culture, and historical grandeur and as such a positive identity reference for some diasporic members, especially those who do not support the politics of the Islamic Republic of Iran. In sum, place names are vehicles for "longings" and "beliefs" (Geertz 1973, 91) and as such become agents in social interactions. When used across space and time, they can gain discursive power as people speak in their name with actionable consequences. In other words, names indicating physical and social place can become a practice with disruptive value (Witteborn 2007b). Disruption happens when names have the agency to engage in social and political breaches by crossing a limit. When transgressing this limit, names can reveal a hierarchy of premises linked to desirable and undesirable identity repertoires. Chapters 2 and 3 highlight how *Xinjiang* and *East Turkistan* are constituted by different premises that still have similarities. The premises structure the usage of these names and eventually the sociopolitical spaces those names create.

The second communication practice discussed in this book—testimonio— is a witness account that shifts difficult collective histories from the margins to the center. Testimonio is an important genre in the process of decolonizing epistemologies and knowledge (Mignolo 2007). It emphasizes personal experience as an epistemological point of departure for reclaiming collective rights (Delgado Bernal, Burciaga, and Flores Carmona 2012). A growing body of literature discusses testimonio as a variant of pragmatic storytelling with a social justice intention. The purposes of testimonio are to expose violence against particular groups and to build alliances for political and legal action (Delgado Bernal et al. 2012).

Testimonio is a methodology for knowledge creation and an emancipatory pedagogy in that it creates a space for deliberation. This space can be productive as it enables voices to come together in their declaration of indignation and to gesture to larger structures that are defined by lack (de Certeau 1997): the lack of communication about injustices and, even more importantly, the lack of political and legal action to correct moral and physical wrongs. The Latina Feminist Group (2001), for example, engaged *testimonialistas* as researcher/participants who bore witness to collective silence due to trauma as well as to situated resistant practices (Delgado Bernal et al. 2012). Testimonio produces theory about interactional processes, as chapter 4 shows. It also opens up spaces for working with this knowledge, as in the case of testimonial theater of Filipina migrant domestic workers (Pratt and Johnston 2017) or as in the case of the "birth" of testimonio by Rigoberta Menchú, the indigenous human rights activist from Guatemala who narrated the brutality against her family and people to the Venezuelan anthropologist Elizabeth Burgos and to an international audience (Menchú 1984). Pratt and Johnston (2017) address the practical potential of witnessing with a gesture to performance theorist Jill Dolan (2005). Dolan highlights the act of bearing witness as a productive moment for affective alignment and an articulation of "the possible, rather than the insurmountable obstacles to human potential" (Dolan 2005, 2). Imagining the possible through affective dialogue can lead to different points of departure: retreat into nostalgia or continuing the mobilization for social justice. Uyghurs' testimonios in this study do both, as chapter 4 shows.

There is ample research about testimony in the context of geopolitical Asia although few studies use the genre of *testimonio*. Ala (2021), Pham (2007), and Gupta (2022) are examples for studies that do. As an exile, Mamtimin Ala (2021) provides a deeply personal testimonio about the recent situation of the Uyghurs in Xinjiang and their detention in the name of reeducation. Allie Pham analyzes testimonios of Vietnamese refugees and migrants in the US through the lens of Asian critical race theory to argue for the incorporation of Asian American memory and experience into the grammar of race struggle in the country. Sonya Surabhi Gupta (2022) discusses testimonio in the context of Latin America and India and shows how autobiographical writings by Dalits are political statements about collective memory and marginalization. Blackburn (2009) focuses on the oral testimony of the survivors of the

Japanese occupation during the Asia-Pacific War in Malaysia and Singapore and argues that collective traumatic experiences can help in coming to terms with personal ones. In the context of East Asia, the sexual enslavement of Korean women in Japan's Asia-Pacific War has been widely explored through the witness accounts of survivors (Howard 1995; Nozaki 2005; Yang 2008). Several of them became spokeswomen for transnational peace movements (Kim and Lee 2017).

Moreover, the broader witness literature in geopolitical Asia has put the spotlight on gender. Das (2017) highlights the importance of testimonial writing to understand the gendered nature of war in the context of the 1971 war of liberation of Bangladesh. Sankey (2016) shifts attention to testimony and the gendered experiences of forced movement, starvation, and family separation during the Khmer Rouge reign in Cambodia. The legal perspective highlights that gendered experiences have often remained unaddressed in international criminal law. Likewise, Roy (2013) explores testimonies about political violence by members of the Naxalbari movement in eastern India. Like other authors (e.g., Höglund 2019), Roy argues that female testimony tends to focus on the plight of others instead of personal abuse, thereby further silencing personal pain that might be collective but remains unrecognized. Höglund (2019) turns attention to the constructed nature of public testimony in transitional justice and reconciliation efforts in Sri Lanka. The author illustrates that testimonies are shaped by existing conditions, such as a militarized society and the conduct of truth commissions. The argument supports one strand of reasoning in testimony research: women's testimonies suppress experienced violence in the name of uncertainty and future safety.

Other research has focused on the Western-centric take on speech genres, including witness accounts. Cecile Jackson (2012), for example, uses a cultural approach to discuss gender performance, emphasizing the overtly Western attention to speech opportunities, public access to speech, and assumptions about silence. Jackson shows how muted groups, who have neither the social capital nor the structural advantages to speak out, revert to myth and poetry to express themselves. Jackson cites Anna Tsing's (1993) research on the creative reconfiguration of public speech genres. In Tsing's research with women shamans on Kalimantan in Indonesia, one woman, Uma Adang, had collected "fake-Koran readings, pompous 'government' speeches full of unintelligible patriotic verbiage, and eerie pronouncements about the political intersections of the past and future" (Tsing 1993, 11). The study shows the gendered invention of new speech forms that expose the limits of language and meaning-making. Spiritually and politically acknowledged genres are made unrecognizable and ungovernable in the moment of their performance. Verbal and affective contestation expose the limits of rationality, bureaucracy, and institutionalized spirituality.

In sum, testimonio is a refusal to remain silent and participate in historical narratives of harmony. Testimonio dislocates received meanings and creates safe spaces for acknowledging trauma, and for legal intervention and societal healing. Testimonio can thus be the first step for claiming rights: the right to expression and the right to say no. Chapter 4 shows how testimonio creates safe spaces for displaced Uyghurs in embodied and digital settings and how those spaces are used for legal action and diasporic activism. The chapter further explicates the social and technological conditions supporting the practice of witnessing, including a language of rationality and verifiable information, visibility, and intertextuality.

DISPLACEMENT, TRANSNATIONAL MIGRANTS, AND UNRULY SPEECH

In this section, I focus on physical displacement and communicative practice. There is a thriving body of literature on the mediated construction of the displaced and how the people resist incriminating discourses in their daily lives. Since September 2001, many migrants have lived in the shadow of the asserted link between Islam, terrorism, and migration. Cultural minorities and transnational migrants have to continuously prove themselves as loyal citizens. Jilly Boyce Kay (2020) makes this point in her exploration of gendered speech in *Gender, Media and Voice: Communicative Injustice and Public Speech*. Through case studies, the book discusses the tension between the promise of voice and the structures that keep women's voices in place by assigning to them stereotypical commonplaces, such as the nagging or traumatized woman. In white-majority societies, the expression of anger is only permissible for some female groups, which means mostly white, middle-class women. Kay explored women's unruly speech through the case of Katie Hopkins, an alt-right white, middle-class public figure, whose public speech is often found "racist, homophobic, transphobic, Islamophobic and anti-feminist" (Kay 2020, 83). Hopkins benefited from the reductive histories of women's speech, advocating her position as a brave woman who aims to tell the "truth" and refuses to be silenced.

In contrast, Yassmin Abdel-Magied, a public figure whose parents had moved to Australia as skilled knowledge migrants, had to position herself rather differently when speaking out in public. She was criticized and threatened on account of her outspoken support of the feminist orientations in Islam. The boundaries in which she could position herself were more limited than Hopkins's, and the punishment for transgression more severe (she left Australia). The backlash highlights the limitation of the promise of voice for women. A transgressive voice is only acceptable within certain political, historical, and ideological parameters. While women have historically been punished for too much speech or for engaging in deviant speech, they were also encouraged to speak out to demonstrate that they are deserving humans and citizens. In contrast to Hopkins, Abdel-Magied had to withdraw, as her body, appearance, and thoughts did not fit the requirements of the majority ideology in Australia (Kay 2020). At the core, Jilly Boyce Kay (2020) argues for engagement with the political and social structure in the struggle for communicative and distributive justice instead of scratching at the surface with interventions, claiming voice.

Rebiya Kadeer, for example, the leader until 2017 of Uyghurs in exile whose advocacy is addressed in chapters 3 and 4, was allowed to speak in the name of human rights with her ethnic body. Kadeer spoke in public with braided hair and traditional Uyghur clothes, an appearance that makes her nonthreatening for a Western audience and yet potent enough to accuse China of rights violations. Unlike Abdel-Magied, who was punished for transgressing as a politicized Other, Rebiya Kadeer was encouraged to speak, as her Muslim identity was overlaid by her cultural appearance, which made her a symbol in her struggle for the rights of small, marginalized groups. Kadeer's advocacy stayed firmly within the bounds of demarcated gender speak and the trope of the suffering ethnic mother, caring for her Uyghur family. While Abdel-Magied questioned a gendered, racial, and geopolitical hierarchy, Kadeer had to confirm it as the price for bringing the Uyghurs to international attention. Overall, Kadeer's mediated image advances the quest of the West for moral leadership on issues like human rights.

Many scholars have illustrated how the discourse on threat and the Other has been constructed in and through the media. Media shape not only public opinion but also place for migrants in Europe through the binary tropes of victimhood and threat (e.g., Chouliaraki and Zaborowski 2017; Eberl et al. 2018; Leudar et al. 2008). The tropes are powerful discursive ways to exclude migrants from participating in the political and economic processes at the core of a European imagination (Chouliaraki and Zaborowski 2017). The trope of threat has been static over time, as Eberl and coauthors (2018) show. The authors argue that *immigration and integration* was the third most negatively connoted topic in political news coverage in European print media in more than a decade. Migrants were generally underrepresented. If they were represented, media frames related to criminalization of migrants and delegitimization of refugees prevailed—especially in the UK. Speaking to power in this climate is particularly challenging. The migrant-as-threat-topic is prevalent on other continents as well, including North America. Das Gupta (2006) demonstrates in her book *Unruly Migrants* how South Asians creatively challenge their assigned places through rights claims. Those rights are not based on citizenship and the received narrative of South Asians as model minorities. Instead, migrants claim gendered and economic justice and anti-violence in the name of migrant rights instead of citizenship rights. Das Gupta shows that migrants illuminate the limits of the rights of Others and how South Asian queer communities are doubly marginalized in the United States by South Asian diasporas as well as queer communities.

Tamar Katriel's *Defiant Discourse: Speech and Action in Grassroots Activism* also needs mention here. Although not a book on migrants per se, the research theorizes transgressive communication in the context of occupation and displacement. In particular, the book asks how activists localize a global genre by grounding it in situated cultural discourse. Katriel defines "defiant discourse" as a "composite speech activity that poses a challenge to mainstream society by giving voice to oppositional positions and attitudes through the efforts of organized groups" (2021, 1). Defiant speech, thus defined, is resistant speech with the goal of challenging the status quo. As in the Uyghur case, Katriel identifies witnessing as a speech activity that challenges hegemonic norms. She illustrates how witnessing is a global format of speaking to power, which grassroots activists in Israel use to identify the problems linked to the occupation of the Palestinian territories by the Israeli state.

Play on speech is an important component for transgressing received language and social norms, especially in the borderlands. In the context of students in the US-Mexico borderlands, O'Connor (2017) explores un-expected language use by high school students in southern Arizona. The study shows how the young people scanned their own and others' speech for transgressive traces, including stylized speech and gaffes to enact a Mexican sense of belonging. By doing so, the young people playfully highlighted the limits of what is permissible for a brown body in the United States. Similar claims about identity are made by Charalambous (2012) in her research on silly talk in a Greek-Cypriot classroom. In Cypriote-Turkish language class-rooms, students became defiant by engaging in whispered conversations and backstage talk. Their communicative acts need to be understood within the historical and political context of Cyprus. Students performed themselves as Cypriots, with the dominant Greek-centered ideology remaining intact.

DISPLACEMENT, TRANSNATIONAL MIGRANTS, AND DIGITAL PRACTICE

Migrants are related across space through a digitally networked ontology that enables transgressive communication. Diminescu (2008) coined the term *connected migrant*, illustrating this claim through the e-Diasporas Atlas, a project that visualizes the networked interactions between diasporic individuals and organizations as well as locally and globally relevant actors (Diminescu 2012). The networks highlight how migrants relate across space and insert themselves into the social fabric of the receiving societies. They use linguistic knowledge, create cultural and political organizations to represent themselves, and establish media presence through traditional as well as social media. Like other groups, Uyghurs have become digitally connected migrants, as chapters 3 and 4 illustrate.

Technologies enable new connectivities, and the internet has been used as a tool for nation-building and human rights for decades (Brinkerhoff 2009; Alonso and Oiarzabal 2010; Retis and Tsagarousianou 2019). Technologies create spatial linkages that shape transnational diasporic spheres (Diminescu 2012, 2020). An expansive body of literature has illustrated diasporic cultural production (Afolabi 2009; Gajjala and Oh 2013; Hegde 2016), the mediation of urban cosmopolitanism and difference (Georgiou 2013), and thriving digital youth cultures (Leurs 2015, 2016, 2017). Digital technologies create place for Venezuelan refugees in Brazil (Alencar 2020), Kurds in Turkey, and rural migrants in China (Costa and Wang 2020). Young migrants also use digital platforms like YouTube to advocate against racism (Yu 2020). Moreover, digital diasporic networks challenge or strengthen narratives about the nation (Hegde 2016; Gajjala 2019). Radha Hedge (2016), for example, illustrates the contested figure of the migrant who is caught in mediated political, moral, and legal discourses while contributing to nation-building from afar through digital participation. Digital engagement is not just personal or collective but structured by the forces of global migration policies and neoliberalism. The research addresses important questions such as belonging and citizenship and debates about who can claim authenticity as a cultural member. Using an innovative format, including ethnography and conversations, Radhika Gajjala (2019) presents gendered diasporic networking practices with a focus on India, including digital place-making as well as feminist positioning and debate on social media platforms. The research documents the formation of digital diasporas through transnational imaginaries and political mobilization.

The internet has always been important for diasporic transnational mobilization and advocacy, as the studies from several continents have shown. In one of the early studies, Bernal (2006) illustrates how Eritreans used the internet to influence politics and economic development in Eritrea by recording history, identity, and democratic ideas. Van den Bos and Nell (2006) demonstrate that Turkish Kurds employed the web to connect with Kurds in third countries and in Turkey, creating a strong base for transnational identity and counter-narratives against the dominant Turkish state and nation. Network-analysis studies on Somalis have made a case for the importance of imagined communities as this imagination holds de-territorialized activities together (Kok and Rogers 2017). Kok and Rogers highlight that diasporic Somalis focus on local community practices and social integration efforts in their host country but have limited political influence on Somalia. Local, national, and transnational networks thus coexist but in different action spheres. In other contexts, transnational connections were built through the digital mediation of peaceful rights claims (e.g., Arora 2020; Bernal 2014) and civic deliberation (Parham 2004) but also through militant advocacy (Vergani and Zuev 2015). More recently, Dwonch (2019) highlights in her study of Palestinian grassroots youth movements the use of digital technologies to mobilize politically across generations. Dwonch observes the importance of decentralized offline mobilization and the affordances of digital connectivity for actions beyond traditional institutional advocacy. Grassroots embodied and digital advocacy spaces were also central to the political work of diasporic Uyghurs, as the discussion in chapters 3 and 4 shows. In all of the political advocacy efforts, language is the social glue. Some diasporas use digital creolization and nonstandard English in their advocacy and strategically counter supposedly global values in relation to gender, race, and platform communication through creative performance of the English language and artifacts (Enteen 2010). For Uyghurs, at least in the sample for this study, the main language of advocacy in the US and Germany is standard English, as the Twitter analysis in chapters 3 and 4 shows.

As for diasporas, digital communication is key for the nation-state to connect with transnational communities and sway them to represent the homeland in a positive light. The Chinese government, for example, has made efforts over time to construct a favorable international image with the help of a transnationally connected Chinese diaspora (Ding 2007). Diasporic Uyghurs, however, have not fully cooperated in these efforts. Shichor (2010), for example, provides a useful historical overview of digital outlets for Uyghur advocacy from the late 1990s to 2010, including websites, newsletters (e.g., the *Turkistan Newsletter* noted in Shichor 2010, 300), mailing lists, and discussion fora. All of those were created outside of China and hosted by Uyghur and international advocacy and media organizations as well as academic institutes. Shichor points to early hacking attacks by China to compromise these digital outlets. He concludes that digital media helped Uyghur identity to proliferate and contrast itself against related collective identities, including Pan-Turkic and Turkic ones. In contrast to early predictions of the internet and globalization helping to weaken ethno-nationalism, the opposite happened. Historic nationalist sentiments gained traction through the discursive resurrection of nationalistic ideas and the transnational diffusion of political agendas through activism as a "full-time (if not lifetime) commitment" (Shichor 2010, 306). At the same time, Shichor maintains that early Uyghur online activism had limited effect and required embodied action.

As of 2022, Uyghur digital activism has gained in importance for collecting and presenting data evidence for alleged injustices to international bodies (e.g., the Uyghur Tribunal in the UK). Digital actions by Uyghur individuals are impactful mostly as part of a collective effort. The video testimony by Kewser Wayit posted on Facebook is an example (Wayit, 2020). The video

appeared at a time of international attention to the situation of the Uyghurs
in China and can thus be regarded as an individual's contribution to a larger
collective effort to raise awareness. The video shows a young Uyghur college
student in the United States with tape over his mouth, storytelling the fate
of his interned father through flip cards. The response of merely 205 likes, 6
comments, and 329 shares implies that individual mobilization for human
rights for Uyghurs is an intervention that needs the collective as it does not
have much effect by itself, similar to what Shichor argues. All of the comments
appear to be from Uyghurs, as are the majority of the likes, judging from the
Uyghur names. Grassroots activists, discussed in chapter 4, have used digital
technologies to some effect by creating testimonial infrastructures with a
global reach to amplify the Uyghurs' human rights discourse.

In addition to transnational diasporas, there is a large body of literature
on the role of technology in the lives of the forcibly displaced, asylum seekers
and refugees in particular. Technology has been part of displaced lives for
more than a decade now, including for Uyghurs (Leung 2007, 2010; Witteborn
2011b, 2011c, 2012a). The literature has demonstrated in detail how asylum
seekers and refugees use technologies to manage everyday life, thereby opposing the mediated threat-or-victim binary. An almost celebratory discourse
on the digital agency of refugees has emerged and has been critiqued as
utilitarian (Awad and Tossell 2019). Nevertheless, mobile technologies have
become essential for navigating border management and to organize flight
routes (e.g., Gillespie et al. 2016), to create information landscapes and identify disinformation (Borkert, Fisher, and Yafi 2018; Maitland 2018), to cope
with information precarity (e.g., Wall, Otis Campbell, and Janbek 2017), to
gain agency in social integration processes (Alencar 2018; Kaufmann 2018),
and engage as political subjects (Marlowe 2019). Many of those practices can
be conceived of as unruly as they provide migrants with resources in the face
of sociopolitical and legal obstacles and require competence in digital literacy,
which has often been denied to refugees. Emotional digital labor is another
resistance strategy that forced migrants use to manage uncertainty. Twigt
(2018), for example, theorizes everyday digital practice and how Iraqi refugees
in Jordan mediate waiting, uncertainty, and hope. Smets (2019) underlines
how digital sensory practice can foster a sense of immobility by the example
of refugees in Turkey and Belgium. People disconnect from technologies
to avoid distress linked to memories of family and instead use artifacts to

resurrect positive memories. Memory and digital technologies are linked as digital technologies are key to archiving collective memory. Horsti (2017, 2019) and Horsti and Neumann (2019) accentuate the role of social media space for refugees to testify about collective trauma, an argument that is bolstered by the role of digital testimonio in Uyghur diasporic advocacy.

Digital agency cannot be discussed without digital control. The latter is particularly important for restricting the digital reach of Uyghur diasporic mobilization, as chapters 3 and 4 illustrate. Research on digital control has convincingly demonstrated that knowledge about migration is produced through data processes, including biometric data collection at borders, digitalization of migration management, and migrant datafication (e.g., Ajana 2013; Amoore 2011; Broeders and Dijstelbloem 2016; Leurs and Witteborn 2021; Madianou 2019; Pollozek and Passoth 2019; Roth and Luczak-Roesch 2020; Scheel, Ruppert, and Ustek-Spilda 2019). Practices of knowledge production sort mobile populations and legitimize them as subjects with particular rights or as objects of knowledge and control, as Tazzioli argues in *The Making of Migration: The Biopolitics of Mobility at Europe's Borders* (2020). Biometric technologies and sorting mechanisms promise risk management in the name of neutrality and security (Fog Olwig et al. 2020). Digital identification is replacing embodied identity, as Nishant Shah (2020) illustrates by the example of Aadhaar in India. The notions of the replacement of embodied identity by digital identity, the datafication of the diasporic body, and digital control of populations are applicable to Uyghurs as well and are explored in the following chapters.

CONCLUSION

This chapter deepens the conceptual reflection from the Introduction on transgression, communicative practice, and displacement. It argues for understanding displacement in at least two ways: as the dislocation of meaning through communicative practice and as the forced movement of people. Transgressive speech, identified through the methodological principles of the ethnography of communication, challenges the codes of the sociopolitical structure and exposes the limits of what can be said, heard, and seen. Transgressive speech also outlines the potentiality of the spaces created through this speech. Young Uyghurs in Xinjiang dislocate cultural and political codes and create new spaces for social relating. Diasporic Uyghurs publicly shift the limits of communicative codes after migration and announce the space of the possible through the name *East Turkistan*. Sometimes, the premises for unruly speech align for those who stay and for those who leave, as chapters 2 to 4 illustrate.

In contexts of migration, the *displaced* is a figure with agency. Those who are labeled *displaced* (from privileged knowledge migrants to refugees), the actors in the management of migration (e.g., the state and the media), and diasporic support organizations compete to gain definitional power over the figure through material and symbolic processes. The following chapters focus on communication practices by Uyghurs in China and in the diaspora. Naming practices like *Xinjiang* (chapter 2) or *East Turkistan* (chapter 3) and testimonio (chapter 4) open up communicative spaces for deliberation but also present challenges due to their transgressive nature. Uyghurs in and outside China, governments, and diasporic advocacy donors support and oppose those transgressions, thereby becoming actors in defining the space of the limit through received value hierarchies, symbolic human rights gestures, and technological surveillance. The next chapter illuminates how Uyghurs in China become resistant as they call for collective unity and social participation while struggling against social inequalities and received sociocultural norms.

2 | *XINJIANG*

Unity in Inequality

PLACE AND IDENTITY NAMES position people in a physical and social location and hierarchy (Philipsen 1992). For naming to become a practice, communication patterns, verbal and nonverbal, need to be iterable and taken up by interlocutors (Cooren 2010). *Xinjiang* was such a practice. The name was uttered in various settings, including in conversations between staff in NGOs, by college teachers, by tour guides during trips, in private homes over lunch, and during the harvest of water melons and grapes I participated in. Carbaugh and Rudnick (2006), gesturing to Philipsen, emphasize the importance of place names in understanding the various meanings ascribed to a physical and identity location: "[S]o do all people, in all places, come to know the meanings of at least some places through names, with the stories about them capturing their deeper significance, from the sacred to the mundane" (167).

I identified the premises of unity, inequality, and participation when analyzing the settings, participants, and meanings arising from the usage of the name *Xinjiang*. Through these premises, Uyghur respondents positioned themselves as a united group in a historical place and challenged the political narrative of prosperity for all but also questioned received Uyghur tradition. Even more, the premises opened up a space for discussing ethnic relations in China, the advantages of social participation, and the threat of sociocultural and economic inequalities. At the time of the research, *Xinjiang* was an unruly speaking practice as it created a political opportunity for dialogue and social debate that now may have passed.

Using the name *Xinjiang* was transgressive in two ways. First, self-interruption and self-correction were cues that a communicative and social breach had occurred. Smiles, shrugging shoulders, and "not knowing about history" signaled to me that speakers had reached a linguistic and political limit. Second, the name *Xinjiang* evoked premises like ethno-religious unity, participation in public life, and inequality that were transgressions as they pointed to political problems in China, which could not be openly addressed in public. Premises like participation also pointed to problems within Uyghur society and young people challenging received values as well as gender and age hierarchies.

Historically, place names were a political resource to question the narrative of a unified China and the idea of Uyghurs being a homogeneous group. Before being incorporated into the Chinese empire in 1884, the oasis towns south of the TianShan mountain range lacked a political and administrative structure weaving them together (Bellér-Hann et al. 2007; Thum 2014a, 2014b). The diversity of oasis identities and the politics of naming place are reflected in the fact that interviewees always referred to their cities, towns, and villages in Uyghur and immediately corrected me when I used the Chinese names. Examples are Kashgar (Uyghur) versus Kashi (Chinese) and Ghulja (Uyghur) versus Yining (Chinese). There is more to the linguistic nature of the names, however. The following discussion of the main premises linked to the name *Xinjiang*—unity, inequality, and participation—speaks to this claim and shows how diverse Uyghurs are in terms of generational values and lived cultural and religious identity.

UNITY: SPEAKING IN ONE VOICE

I walked down a busy shopping street with Ali, a tourist guide in his early thirties, who showed me the small stores of the bazaar area that offered carved wooden goods, artfully ornamented knives, and carpets. Ali used the name *Xinjiang* regularly in conversations. When asked what *Xinjiang* meant to him, he answered:

> It is like a new territory in the Chinese language, a place where you move to. You build the place with your ideas and tell the people who were there before you that they need to learn and be like you to be better people.

Ali mentioned how cities and towns were transformed through Chinese-style architecture, Chinese character landscapes, and torn-down mosques replaced by shopping centers. After a short pause, Ali took a deep breath, telling me that this was one version of how to think about *Xinjiang*. Another, related version was the notion of the Uyghur community: "We should always use 'we' when we speak as Uyghurs, as our way of life is under threat. We are a community in Xinjiang like Kazakhs or Uzbeks." In interactions in private homes or during walks in Atush, Kashgar, and Urumqi, Uyghurs emphasized unity as a main principle when talking about a perceived group identity. Terms and phrases such as *united, come together, don't separate,* and *community* were brought up consistently.

Unity outlined the tension between being self- and other-defined. Ali pointed to the problem of the majority society perceiving Uyghurs as a rather homogeneous and religious group, thereby obfuscating the diversity of Uyghur communities. Like Ali, other interviewees emphasized that "Uyghur" was promoted by tourist agencies through cultural essentialism, which morphed the idea of Uyghur identity into a valuable tourist resource, with Uyghurs becoming a proxy for the cultural diversity of China. Indeed, the "dancing and kebab-eating Uyghur" was promoted on tourist websites and on posters in the old town of Kashgar where buses stopped in a stylized "Uyghur street" to get a pleasant taste of Uyghur life, which was cleansed of politics and religion. Gladney (2004) had illustrated almost two decades ago how Han Chinese society normalizes itself through culturalizing the Other, creating firm lines between the modern Han subject and ethnic minorities in China. In sum, the premise of unity was indexical of social relations—imagined and real—and an important part of creating a narrative of cultural continuity and togetherness for Uyghurs in Xinjiang.

The aspirational call for unity is historical. As suggested by Newby (2007), in the eighteenth and nineteenth centuries there were already strong group boundaries between the sedentary Turkic Muslims and non-Turkic groups like Armenians, Mongols, or Han Chinese. There were also strong social boundaries between settled Turkic Muslims and nomadic groups like Kazakhs or Kyrgyz. At the time, the region was composed of the main areas of Altishahr (referring to six cities along the Tarim Basin rim, with Kashgar being one of them) and Uyghuristan (named for the Qumul-Turpan area from the ninth to the fifteenth century; Newby 2007, 16). Rudelson (1997) supports the claim of a highly localized sense of identity through his review of naming practices like *Kashgarlik* (dwellers of the oasis of Kashgar).

Uyghur scholarship has produced a wealth of studies on Uyghur identity, history, art, and the role of Uyghurs within the Chinese nation-state. Scholars have worked on dissecting a homogeneous notion of Uyghurs as an ethnic group and shown how local culture has always been fused with practices and beliefs from elsewhere (Smith Finley 2007, 2013; Smith Finley and Zang 2015; Schluessel 2007, 2009; Thum 2014a, 2014b). Uyghurs have had vibrant trade connections for centuries through the Silk Road and have learned to interact with people who were culturally and religiously different, including Muslims, Buddhists, Christians, Armenians, Mongols, Manchus, and Han Chinese (Millward 2007, 2021; Newby 2007; Rudelson 1997). Thus, scholarship has challenged the claim that a Uyghur identity was largely constructed in response to the Chinese empire and state (Bellér-Hann 2008; Newby 2007; Smith Finley 2013; Thum 2014b). Cultural and religious influences from western Asia, Central Asia, and North Africa have shaped Uyghur communities as intensely hybrid.

Thum (2014a) maintains that Islam and Sufism in the region have always been cosmopolitan in outlook. Likewise, the collection by Bellér-Hann and coauthors (2007) addresses the topic of hybrid Uyghur practices, with the contribution by Harris (2007; also 2016) on the genre of the Twelve Muqam (set of fixed musical suites) as a case in point. Harris illustrates how this form has to be understood within a wider tradition of sociocultural and spiritual practice and overlapping music traditions from Central Asia to Kashmir and northwestern China. The traditions, in turn, cannot be understood apart from Islamic art and Sufism. Chinese music, in contrast, has not influenced Uyghur music and arts that much, which is again an argument against positioning Uyghur culture only in relation to China.

A growing cosmopolitanism among Uyghur youth has been discussed for a while, including the urbanization of Uyghur life (Byler 2021a; Grose 2019; Smith Finley 2007) and interactions in border zones (Roberts 2007). Uyghur internal migration has also played a role in the exposure to difference. Tursun (2017), for example, illustrates the intersections between gender, social mobility, migration, and globalization and how educated Uyghur women working in east coast cities like Shanghai have to straddle traditional values with careers and loneliness. Females have always been key to the moral and economic reproduction of the Uyghur family and nation (Bellér-Hann 2008; Brophy 2005; Smith Finley 2013). At the same time, Uyghur women have to negotiate the newly won freedoms as they struggle with stereotypes exoticizing or vilifying them (Gladney 2004). In sum, Uyghur local cultural practices have been influenced by linguistic and political forces from elsewhere, from traders to pilgrims, art, music, the internet, and transnational NGOs, as the following chapters highlight. The aspirational call for unity is a response to this diversity. More specifically, the call for unity was related to changing cultural values.

Changing Cultural Values

The aspirational dimension of unity is linked to a changing Uyghur society, characterized by urbanization and shifting gender and consumption values, as well as the pressures on cultural identity. "One of my students made good money through trade with Central Asia and he wants to give up studying. We should stand together and protect the young generation from chasing after money. This is Xinjiang today, with young Uyghurs forgetting about their history, literature, and language," was the statement by a college teacher from Urumqi in 2006. He clarified that *we* meant not only educators but a whole generation of Uyghur men and women who understood the desire for material well-being but also the value of education and being willing to care for others beyond material considerations. The teacher felt that the communal *we* was in danger of getting dissolved through an increasing individualism, the migration of young people to cities, and internet consumerism.

The premise of unity is aspirational as it aims at transcending age, regional identity, and class, which was a big challenge, according to the interviewees. Urbanites in the capital Urumqi raised the topic of unity when discussing *Xinjiang* and when we ate together in local restaurants. Young people could be seen chatting in mixed groups of males and females, or glued to their mobile phones. In Urumqi, young people enjoyed a freer life than in the more rural and culturally conservative parts of the province. Men and women watched movies together, talked on park benches, or worked in mixed-gender teams in universities and professional work settings. Young Uyghurs looked toward Central Asia, Turkey, Russia, Europe, and the United States and consumed popular culture online (Smith Finley and Zang 2015).

Even in towns in the southern parts of the province like Yarkand, two hundred kilometers from Kashgar, young men and women could be seen in internet cafes at three o'clock in the afternoon, playing video games. When I entered one of those cafes and started chatting with a young woman who wanted to practice her English, she asked me whether I liked Xinjiang. She wore a dress and a headscarf with a colorful floral print. The woman said she was eighteen and liked playing fast video games, such as ones with car races. The young man next to her smiled. She was very good at the game she played and could not spend much time with me as she had paid for the hour and wanted to finish the game. After she was finished, she joined me outside and said: "I want to learn how to work with computers and go to the big city." But she also said that her parents needed her to help with the animals and the harvest, so her hopes were not high to be able to leave. When parting, she said: "The women sell animals and I drive cars," laughing and pointing to two older women sitting under an umbrella in the afternoon heat, selling goat heads. When they saw me, the women pulled their brown knitted scarves over their faces. The young woman had pointed to an important gender shift in traditional customs. Adventurous young women eyed the big cities as places of learning beyond traditional farming tasks; technology was especially interesting to them. Technology meant mediated entertainment, which was limited in rural regions and reduced at the time of the research to internet cafes and older TV sets. In the evenings, people of all ages gathered in the night markets to watch soap operas.

Other types of popular culture had gained a strong following at the time. Arken Abdullah is a Uyghur singer who had become popular in the year 2000 through his first album, *The Dolan Who Walked Out of the Desert*. He was one of the first singers who called for looking beyond the boundaries of one's known environment, socially and geographically speaking (Baranovitch 2007; Smith Finley and Zang 2015). The Six City Rap Collective from Urumqi is another example of how young people started questioning traditional ways of life. The young men were part of a growing rap scene that evolved around the time I was in the province in 2006, and young Uyghurs mentioned rap to me. The group raps in Uyghur but also in Putonghua (Standard Chinese) in order to reach a larger Chinese fan base, streaming its videos on You-Tube. Dressed in rapper fashion and coming from the poor neighborhoods in Urumqi, members do not address interethnic politics directly. At the same time, their texts about poverty, being caught between traditional Uyghur culture and a desire to break out, and drug abuse point to challenging social issues. Those issues were addressed by interviewees repeatedly and are explored in the sections on inequality and social participation. The rap collective is an early example of Uyghur youth orienting themselves in an urbanizing China where everything seemed possible, social roles were shifting, and making money had become an important life goal. In addition to a growing music scene, Turkish soap operas were of interest to the young people, and music and food from Turkey and Central Asia continue to be magnets (Smith Finley and Zang 2015).

The young people interviewed for this book who felt caught in the tension between a traditional Uyghur way of life and changing social roles predominantly came from the more affluent parts of Urumqi. They tended to have an education beyond high school. Hamid is an example. He was a man in his early thirties and lived in Urumqi. He enjoyed the big city life with its relaxed social norms and compared it to Kashgar, the city situated in the western, culturally more traditional part of Xinjiang, close to the border with Kyrgyzstan and Pakistan. He summarized his view in a nutshell:

> In Urumqi I can drink. In Kashgar I can't. In this place I can smoke. It is hard to find female friends in Kashgar. In Urumqi it is easy. Kashgar is a very old place and people's minds are more closed. Young people in Urumqi are like in America. [. . .] I change my behavior when I go back to Kashgar. In Kashgar they notice your manners. They are very polite in Kashgar. The old way, you know? You say "Assalamu Aleikum" instead of saying "Good day" or "Hello." In Kashgar, the people work hard. The young people in Urumqi are lazy. But in Kashgar I will be the slave of our Uyghur system. When I go to visit my grandmother's home, I must be very careful about dressing. Don't talk too much. She asks. I answer. If she doesn't say anything, I have no right to say something. Traditional, you know?

Ritualized speech acts and structured turn-taking are the base for clearly defined social roles. Having "no right to say something" is a clear indication of the formalized distribution of communication rights. Hamid questioned this unequal distribution, as did other young people I met. By doing so, he challenged received norms and values and in turn the communicative base on which the unity among Uyghurs could be based.

Chinese government education initiatives target the desire of younger Uyghurs to break out of received traditions and a rural lifestyle. The *Xinjiang Class* (*Xinjiang ban*) is an example. The *Xinjiang Class* is part of a program of "interior ethnic boarding classes" (*neidi minzu ban*), also known as "interior classes" (*neidiban*) by the Chinese government. The goal is to bring ethnic minority students, from Tibetans to Uyghurs, Kazakh, Hui, and even a minority of Han students living in Xinjiang, to central and eastern China for state education in Putonghua (Chen 2019; Grose 2015a, 2015b, 2019; Leibold 2019; Yuan and Zhu 2021). Introduced in 2000 by the Chinese Communist Party, the classes have steadily increased enrollment. While the assimilationist goal of the program is clear, the application numbers are high and the program is very competitive (Leibold 2019). The boarding schools are so popular because they are subsidized, academically prestigious, and promise social mobility, especially for poor children from farmers' families (Yuan and Zhu 2021). In the year 2000, one thousand students studied in what were then twelve schools for Xinjiang students to complete their senior-secondary education (Chen 2008; Grose 2013; cited in Leibold 2019, 6). The initiative has expanded fast. In 2017, 36,400 Xinjiang students attended classes in forty-five cities in fourteen provinces in China (Liu and Wang 2017; cited in Leibold 2019, 6). More than 100,000 students have been recruited over time from Xinjiang, especially from the rural, poor south (Leibold 2019, 6). Since 2004, "feeder schools" exist in Xinjiang that prepare students for high schools and their *neidiban* schooling career outside Xinjiang, provided they pass the exam (Leibold 2019, 6).

The articles in the special issue of *Asian Studies Review* edited by Leibold (2019) illustrate how the education program presents young Uyghurs with the challenge of a transaction: cultural assimilation in return for upward social mobility. The goals of the program are clear: to raise loyal citizens who can fill key positions in various levels of the Chinese bureaucracy and act as role models for interethnic integration. As such, the programs can be regarded as highly transactional trajectories of shaping the modern citizen. In his special issue, Leibold (2019) states that graduates enter the top universities in China, study abroad, or go back to Xinjiang to work as teachers and government officials. However, the cost of the programs in terms of individual well-being and cultural identity can be heavy. Grose (2015b) illustrates how Uyghur students struggled with the rigorous curriculum in Chinese and long study days, which started at eight o'clock in the morning and ended at ten o'clock in the evening when the lights in the dormitories had to be turned off. This schedule is similar to other boarding schools for Chinese students, but political indoctrination is more pronounced with a focus on love for the motherland, Chinese culture, and socialism with Chinese characteristics. Uyghur written and spoken language and cultural skills fade over the years and students can feel alienated from the communities they grew up in (Leibold 2019). At the time of Grose's study in 2015, for example, students got one day off for major Muslim celebrations like Eid al-Fitr or Eid al-Adha, but the days were spent with cultural activities and not religious observance. Nevertheless, the Uyghur students showed a renewed interest in practicing Islam. Several students had small prayer corners in their rooms, prayed before eating, and eventually strengthened the practice of praying and reading the Qur'an after graduation. Grose also illustrates the transnational diplomatic support of religious practice. This support included the Saudi Arabian embassy distributing Uyghur-language Qur'ans and the Sudanese embassy maintaining a mosque in Beijing. At the time of the study, travel to Egypt had not been that restricted and transnational marriage was important to revive religious practice. Grose observes how several of the young women started wearing hijab again as they had when they arrived in the boarding schools from their predominantly southern Xinjiang birth places. Grose's discussion is careful not to fall into the trope of young people retreating into religious fundamentalisms. Instead, he points to the productive functions of gendered practices such as female sociality and solidarity as well as charity. He concludes that despite and because of the study environment in the *Xinjiang Class*, which promoted cultural assimilation, the students felt inclined to look deeper into their own ways of seeing the world, with a distinct Uyghur and Muslim identity emerging. This strengthened identity might also be due to the fact that the majority of students came from southern Xinjiang, an area composed of small towns and rural communities with strong religious identification. There is a chance that the students had already been socialized into a religious identity, which became salient again during their studies in a secular environment.

Nevertheless, graduates struggled with their multiple cultural identities (Smith Finley and Zang 2015) and their expected tasks of being role models for other minorities while living with the stigma of the in-between, as Leibold and Grose argue (2019). The authors conclude: "Over time, the neidiban system accomplishes an important strategic goal for the CCP: the creation of an ethno-comprador elite who are willing to do the Party's bidding even if it comes at a deep psychological and cultural cost" (19). Research also shows the unexpected outcomes of the education programs due to unmet socio-economic expectations in terms of employment, social status, and salaries. Yangbin Chen (2019), for example, argues that Uyghur students rediscover their Uyghur identity ("re-ethnicisation," 81) after entering the job market with an excellent education and a learned elitist self-image but become disappointed by discrimination, competition, and lack of opportunity. This argument is similar to Grose's (2015b) about young Uyghurs' strengthened religious identity during and after attending the *Xinjiang Class*. Findings on gender are also interesting. Chen (2019), for example, argued that female students were more likely to go back to Xinjiang to be with family and to look after aging family members, which meant lower salaries and less prestigious jobs. The move replicated expected gender roles. Uyghur women in the diaspora, as shown later, are still under the spell of these gendered roles, even when moving abroad.

Diverse Religious Practices

Uyghurs called for unity in face of diverse religious practice and challenged the Chinese government's attempts to weaken Uyghur religious identity. With the call for unity, people also challenged religious diversity in Uyghur communities, with institutionalized religion being seen as superior to folk religion. Religious practice in Uyghur communities tends to be essentialized through the label *Muslim* by the media, in public, and through the international security discourse (e.g., Fuller and Lipman 2004; Gunaratna, Acharya, and Pengxin 2010; Roberts 2020). There is the narrative of religion as being a, if not the, separatist force in Xinjiang province (Holdstock 2015). In the first years of the 2000s, some authors argued that orthodox Islam and Wahhabism were on the rise in the south of Xinjiang (Fuller and Lipman 2004). Other scholars have tried to explain the rise of an orthodox Islam in China with the instrumentalization of suppressed religious identity by extremist organizations like Al-Qaeda or ISIL (Gutnaratna et al. 2010). According to these scholars, extremists have trained Uyghurs in Pakistan and master-minded attacks in China, with new technologies playing a key role in the dissemination of religious propaganda. While providing detailed examples for alleged leaders trained by Al-Qaeda, there is the danger that writings like these contribute to the creation of *the* Uyghur Muslim as a fixed category and engrave violence on an Islamized body (see Ahmed [2004] 2014). The trope of the violent Muslim feeds into the syncretized idea of the Muslim Uyghur who needs to be controlled, a step that the Chinese government seems to have taken in the summer of 2017 by rounding up Uyghur students at Al-Azhar University in Egypt and forcefully returning them to China (Radio Free Asia 2017a).

The decade-long pressure on Muslim identity in Xinjiang, restriction of religious practice, limited exposure to religious debate, and a renewed interest by young Muslims in Islam can be seen as contributing elements to a homogenizing religious discourse and a perceived sense of unity among Muslims in Xinjiang. Uyghurs of different ages talked about the importance of the family and how they were socialized into Islam. "Not the violent type of Islam but an Islam that is good." As a man in his forties put it: "Islam is important for us. It's good. The tradition is good. It teaches you how to act in life."

The facets of religiosity and spirituality are highly complex as they draw from deeply situated local meanings of a mix of orthodox Islam, Sufism, Buddhism, Zoroastrianism, and shamanism (Holdstock 2015). Islam has never been a monolithic way of life for the Uyghurs. It hails from different geopolitical regions and traditions, resulting in localized histories, which are connected to other places and times, such as Central Asian Sufi networks or Indo-Persian narrative traditions, and yet have developed their own deeply situated meanings over time (Thum 2014a, 2014b). This orientation to Islamic practice from elsewhere has been interpreted in several ways. Some scholars see in those developments a dangerous strengthening of an ethno-nationalist identity based on fundamentalist Islamic ideology in the new millennium (Gunaratna et al. 2010). Other scholars have interpreted increasing religiosity as a response to the assimilation politics in China, the protection of a local identity (Gladney 2004), and a quest for an ethical way of life in face of the challenges Uyghurs face.

Tobin's (2020) analysis of educational texts used in China shows how the *Turk* category is used in tandem with an East Turkistan narrative to situate an outside security threat within the borders of territorial and cultural China. Uyghur religion and language are constructed as security issues in these texts. *East Turkistan* serves as a concept used by official discourses to establish terrorism, separatism, and extremism as transnational phenomena that threaten the stability of China. Tobin also illustrates how the discourse of East Turkistan being a threat is appropriated by Uyghurs and configurated into alternative identity narratives.

The following example illustrates the latter point. I bought a carpet in a small shop in a town in southwest Xinjiang run by a young carpet weaver family consisting of a twenty-eight-year-old man, his twenty-four-year-old second wife, and his seven-year-old daughter, who went to school. The first wife had died but the second wife and daughter got on well together. After I bought the carpet, the wife invited me to have lunch on the small terrace of the adobe house. While sitting at the table with them, I mentioned the noticeable number of adobe houses that had been partly or fully demolished to make place for new brick houses. After lunch, I accompanied the daughter down the stairs into the living area where she brought out a Qur'an and started reading. The father told me that he had asked his daughter to read the Qur'an on a daily basis. He hailed from a southern town along the Tarim Basin, where religion was practiced by many families. Studying the Qur'an at home was not a preferred practice from the viewpoint of the Chinese government, even back in 2006.

However, the daughter was not the only one studying the holy scriptures at home. The father told me that he knew many neighbors and friends of the daughter who did the same. Reading the Qu'ran confronted the fear of government repression and transformed the fear into a collective gesture of defiance. The space of religious learning was a space of cultural rejuvenation as well as of ethical and moral education. For the father, it was important for the girl to learn values that emphasized a sense of belonging and community. The latter included helping others, being respectful, and having a moral compass in life.

Unity among Muslims has to be understood within the political and historical context of religious practice in Xinjiang. Waite (2006) argues in his study of Kashgari religious practice that socialist rule and suppression of free circulation of media did not allow for reformist movements in local Muslim communities, so that people had to rely on the orally transmitted knowledge of religious leaders. One consequence was that religious ideology has not been challenged much since 1949 as a result of the regulation of religion by the Chinese Communist Party, the shift of religious practice to the domestic space of the family, dependence on religious elders for teachings, and the lack of communicative space for debates about sacred matters. Waite describes in detail how sharia courts and religious judges were abolished in 1950 and how the China Islamic Association was created in 1953 in line with other organizations. The goals were to show the party's goodwill in relation to Muslims but also to control the education of religious leaders and the production and circulation of religious materials. During the Great Leap Forward, from 1958 to 1962, the association was abolished and the grip on religious practice severely tightened, with mosques closing. Muslims in Xinjiang became even further isolated in their practice as cross-border interactions with Central Asian Muslims were severely restricted until the mid-1980s because of deteriorating relationships between China and the Soviet Union.

While the reform era of the 1980s saw the reopening of mosques and the reestablishment of the China Islamic Association, the "Strike Hard" campaign of 1996 caused a tightening of religious activities. The practice of tightening has continued. The amendment to the Regulations of Xinjiang Uyghur Autonomous Region on Religious Affairs from 1994 was adopted by the 11th meeting of the Standing Committee of the 12th People's Congress of the Xinjiang Uyghur Autonomous Region on November 28, 2014 (Lavička 2021). The regulations ensure freedom of religion as long as it does not interfere with the promotion of patriotism, harmony, and development. Nevertheless, under these amendments (Articles 12–14), religious homeschooling is banned, as is scripture reading in unauthorized places, including the home. Article 37 prohibits religious practice by minors (below the age of eighteen). Article 29 outlines the political training of clergy, including religious interpretation and knowledge. Article 38 stipulates the prohibition of "abnormal" and "imported" styles of clothing and religious symbols (Lavička 2021, 69), including the burqa, veil, long beard, and any symbol referring to *East Turkistan* or pan-Turkic inclinations. In the amendment, the media get a special spotlight. Articles 40–41 prohibit the use of digital media to promote separatism, religious extremism and terrorism, and the consumption of religious content on satellite TV and radio programs.

I would concur with Lavička that these regulations are a threat to religious identity as young Uyghurs cannot participate in religious practice in their most formative years. At the same time, the regulations could potentially lead to more conservative religious practices as debates and critiques of religious dogma are banished from collective conversations. Although some young urban Uyghurs argued for secularism and relegating religious life to the family home, as I show later, a strict prohibition of religious practice was not on their mind. Therefore, unity and speaking in one voice as Uyghur and Muslim has to be understood in the intersection between the restrictions in religious practices and a surge in religious identification.

I turn now to another dimension of the call for unity, which is the diversity in spiritual and religious practice in Uyghur communities. I use a trip to Yarkand, an ancient place of learning, as an example to illustrate how and why unity and speaking in one voice was important to Uyghurs. Yarkand is around 190 kilometers away from Kashgar. It is part of the Altishahr region, referring to the aforementioned *Six Cities* and the oasis towns and cities south of the TianShan mountains such as Kashgar, Yarkand, Khotan, Aksu, Kuqa, and Turpan (see Bellér-Hann 2008). I went with two men, a driver and a tourist guide from Kashgar. Both had nine years of education although they told me that in the villages, children often went to school for only three to four years. We visited the two-thousand-year-old town, which was once a great place of learning, similar to Bukhara in Uzbekistan. We walked by houses with wooden carved balconies and women selling slaughtered goats before arriving at the Altunluq shrine complex. The latter is a cemetery including the shrines of the Seven Muhammads (see Thum 2014b), the tombs of the khans of the Yarkand Moghul Khanate, and the tombs of the leaders of the Black Mountain Naqshbandi Sufi order. Both the Moghul khans and the Black Mountain khojas, political and religious leaders in the region, were implicated in complex political struggles in the Altishahr region, including confrontations with the Chinese Qing dynasty armies. These complexities might explain why the Black Mountain leader graves were unmarked and the khans' tombs put in the shadows of the mausoleum of Queen Amannisakhan, who was revered as a promoter of Uyghur music and art (see Thum 2014b for related observations).

We arrived at the tombs of the Seven Muhammads after passing by people praying and a man with a donkey and a cart sprinkling water on the ground. When the Kashgari guide asked the man what he was doing, the people who were with him said he was doing something "against spirits." The idea of spirits is in line with the observation by Thum (2014b) during his visits to the cemetery and people telling him they could feel the spirits' presence. My guide and driver chuckled at the idea of spirits and then asked the locals whether this was in the spirit of Islam. From the expressions on the faces of the Yarkandis, I could see that this question had offended them. "Of course, we are Muslim," my guide translated but one could see from his face that he regarded neither the practice nor the people as following Islam.

On the way back to Kashgar the guide explained that he and the driver found the Yarkandis a rather funny people. They spoke with a strong dialect and seemed to be suspicious of outsiders, including the Kashgari men whom they recognized immediately by their dialect. To the Kashgaris, the people in the cemetery practiced folk religion and were superstitious, which made them inferior in their view. "They are mostly farmers there" was a phrase that the two men used, linking rural life and class to a spirituality that was not institutionalized and hence not credible. While the Yarkandi man in the cemetery claimed a shared identity—that of Muslim—the Kashgari men did not accept this identity. "If you are Muslim, act like a Muslim" was a sentence that the Kashgari guide uttered and the driver confirmed. Acting and speaking like a Muslim, a Sunni Muslim in particular as the majority branch of Islam in Xinjiang, was announced as a normative way of life. Superstitious beliefs were relegated to the rural margins and the past.

Religious practice in Xinjiang needs to be seen in relation to the geospatial influences of Sufism and Islam brought to the area by traders and pilgrims (Thum 2014b). History was taught in sacred spaces like shrines. However, historical manuscripts and the oral tradition of teaching history in sacred spaces have almost disappeared (Thum 2014b). The local is a palimpsest, which makes it difficult for Uyghur Muslims to claim history and speak in one voice when historical documents are lacking, oral traditions are replaced by secular schooling, and religious teachings are supervised by the government or driven underground. The layered character of religious identity becomes explicit in Thum's example of the Afaq Khoja shrine near Kashgar. Afaq Khoja was a religious and political figure who founded a line of rebellious Sufi leaders. I had visited the shrine and saw the name of Afaq Khoja associated with it. The name was also pointed out by the Uyghur tour guide who led me there. However, the story of Afaq Khoja is overwritten by the story of Xiang Fei, the fragrant concubine, who had to serve the emperor after capture by the Qing. The narrative is a gesture toward the historical unity between Uyghurs, Manchu, and Han Chinese and an example of the feminization of interethnic memory. This feminization can also be seen in the figure of Queen Amannisakhan, whose mausoleum and accompanying narrative is emasculating the memory of the male Islamic figures of the khans and khojas buried in the Altunluq complex (Thum 2014b).

The observations support extant research like Thum's (2014b) in that the resurrection of female historical figures was an ideological move by the government to rewrite the history of Uyghur-Han relations by giving it a feminine and thereby unthreatening touch. This feminization depoliticizes the local and minimizes the importance of Sufism and other lived variants of Islam for local resistance against outside domination. The feminized historical narrative sidelines the complex power struggles in the region and the historical and cultural networks with Central Asia, thus making Chinese influence a centerpiece of Uyghur history (Bellér-Hann 2008; Newby 2007; Smith Finley 2013; and see Thum 2014b for a critique of the China-centric view of Uyghur history and culture). Uyghur exiles also used gendered strategies in their advocacy for unity and social justice, as I show in the following chapters. They feminized the political struggle through the trope of the caring mother who is a culturally powerful figure. Unlike the sexual playmate or the supporter of the arts who depoliticizes sacred space, *the mother* is an asexual figure and linked to independence movements worldwide. This figure makes the struggle for freedom less threatening by shifting it from the physical to the affective realm (McClintock 1997). Next, I turn to another premise evoked through the name Xinjiang, which is inequality.

INEQUALITY: MOBILITY AND LANGUAGE

Talking about inequality was unruly as this talk investigated the complicit structures that caused inequality (Jervis 1999). Mobility inequality was one theme. "Traveling is expensive for Uyghurs. We need to pay a lot of money to get a passport," a young tourist guide in the old city of Yarkand told me. I asked why and he said with a smile, "because I am Uyghur and I live in Xinjiang." The young man's dream was to see the world and how other Uyghurs lived abroad in places like Montreal, New York, Sweden, and Germany. He wanted to go abroad, study, and get rich, he said. He was aware of the challenges he would meet along the way but he was determined to try as others had tried before him. There was not much for him to do "in Xinjiang," he added, no jobs. He liked his birthplace and the people, the food, the familiar environment, and his family and friends. But he wanted to leave and see different places like the "president of the region who went to Germany in the 1920s before it became Xinjiang."

In the 1920s and early 1930s, Uyghurs enjoyed international mobility. Intellectuals studied in Russia and Central Asia in the tumultuous times of the Bolshevik Revolution and national demarcation in Central Asia, during which Uyghurs were regarded by the Soviet government as a nation with its own standardized language (Brophy 2016). This was a time of rising Uyghur nationalism with plans for statehood. Russia and the Soviet Union have always had close ties with Xinjiang due to changing political alliances between Russian or Soviet military forces and the changing powers governing Xinjiang, from Chinese administrators during the Republican era to the Kuomintang.[1] There were also strong economic interests in the resource-rich region and a pan-Turkic and pan-Islamic ideology by Muslim Uyghurs on either side of the border, nurtured by trade, education of Uyghurs in the Soviet republics of Central Asia, and exchange of clergy (Forbes 1986).

Like all the other interviewees, the young tourist guide used the name *Xinjiang*. When I took him up on the name and asked what the place was called "before it became Xinjiang," he smiled and said, "I don't know." Smiling and pretending ignorance are tactics of disobedience, which illuminate the possible act of transgression and self-censorship. Employing the official speech code is a type of mimicry used by those without much economic, political, and sociocultural power (Bhabha 1994). Mimicry introduces instability into the social contract as those in power see the mirror images of the social codes they maintain. Using the name *Xinjiang* with a smirk or shrugged shoulder is an example of mimicry that gestures to a problem without naming it. It is unruly behavior that is "contagious, and dangerous because it touches this obscure zone that every system takes for granted" (de Certeau 1997, 8). This zone or space demarcates the limit that cannot be crossed.

In addition to mobility, linguistic inequality was the most consistent theme in the interviews. A Uyghur man in his early twenties said:

> Xinjiang makes you speak Chinese [laughs]. Until several years ago all students got their education in our own language. Now we get education in Chinese. Even some of them [Han Chinese] have lived here for ten to twenty years, they don't know much about the Uyghur language. Simple words they know. They hope we know about Chinese language and culture. They want us to understand them more but they don't want to understand us. They think it's useless, a waste of time. It does not feel good. We live together in Xinjiang. They should know something about us. They should understand our feelings. They think it's useless.

"Xinjiang makes you speak Chinese" is an example of how a name becomes an agent shaping communicative conduct and a sense of place in the world. The name structures group interactions through hierarchies of languages and creates valuations of identities and human life. The man gestures to the fact that Chinese has become the language of public life in the province, which prompts me to explain the intersection between language and politics from a historical perspective.

The Chinese language, referring here to Standard Chinese and the official language of the People's Republic of China,[2] was introduced in higher education in 2002, and from 2004 onwards in secondary schools and kindergartens (Schluessel 2007, 2009). Schluessel noted in 2007 that Chinese as the universal language of instruction "seems to have led to more resentment than acceptance, primarily among Uyghurs living in Xinjiang's cities, and this trend is likely to continue" (3). The quality of education for Uyghur students has declined as a result of this policy, so Schluessel argues, partially because students do not feel inclined to think, speak, and learn in an imposed language, an attitude that impacts learning.

Umit seemed to confirm this claim. He was a student in his twenties whom I met in Munich where he studied engineering. I met him in an outside cafe in the center of the city. He was one of the very few Uyghurs I encountered who had not come to Germany as a refugee. He had been in

Germany since 2006. His grandmother was the manager of a hospital and his grandfather a judge in what Umit called *Xinjiang*. His reasoning for this label was that official and administrative posts like *judge* demanded the use of a legally sanctioned place name. He described himself as "neither religious nor communist but as a reflective thinker who did not argue with emotions but rational arguments." He told me that his major concern was the situation at home in terms of work opportunities, social order, and increasing youth unemployment. He had studied economy but because of a lack of industry in the mainly rural province and government policies favoring Han Chinese in the job market, employment was difficult. Uyghur was his language of instruction until 2002 when the language of higher education became Putonghua (Schluessel 2007, 2009). For Uyghur students, this became a problem, according to Umit:

> Me and my study colleagues did not like it. We had great difficulties following the lectures in Chinese as the teachers, who were Uyghur native speakers, were trained badly. They did not have the language competence. They read the books to us in Chinese, as they could not verbalize it in their own words. Our teacher wanted to tell us something in our own language but the officials of the university walked through the hallways and classes and checked whether the teachers really taught in Chinese. It impacted our understanding of the subject matter. Therefore, although we studied for five years at our university in Xinjiang, many students did not have a clue what they were studying. Getting a job proved even more difficult as the Chinese owners of companies now even had a reason not to employ us in their company. Bad Chinese language skills. Except for the restaurant business there were no important Uyghur companies in Xinjiang.

For Umit, *Xinjiang* meant unequal resource distribution, with language education being a major obstacle to social and economic well-being. Language skills are directly tied to success in the job market (Schluessel 2007), thus structuring a person's position in a social and economic hierarchy. The introduction of Putonghua as the language of higher education in 2002 did not happen by chance and reflects the belief of the central and local governments that Chinese is the language of modernity. Wang Lequan, regional party secretary of Xinjiang Uyghur Autonomous Region at the time, was a strong supporter of Chinese language education (Smith Finley 2013, 43, as cited by Bequelin 2004, 376):

> The languages of the minority nationalities [. . .] do not contain many of the expressions in modern science and technology, which makes education in these concepts impossible. [. . .] This is why the Chinese language is now used. [. . .] This way, the quality of the Uyghur youth will not be poorer than that of their Han peers when they grow up.

Chinese became the language of collective optimization. Uyghur middle-class parents encouraged their children to learn Chinese to enter the job market and for better chances to attend one of the prestigious Chinese or overseas universities (Smith Finley 2013). Under-resourced education in an imposed language with low public acceptance is challenging, as Umit indicated. The college teachers I talked with in Urumqi backed Umit's view and pointed to another problem: language script. They explained how the rates of literacy in Uyghur varied, depending on which script a person had been taught in the past, making access to sources about Uyghur literature and history difficult. To explain the importance of the link between writing systems, knowledge, and education, I will briefly outline the script changes of the Uyghur language.

The Uyghur script has been changed several times, from the Perso-Arabic script to Latin in the 1920s, Cyrillic in the 1930s, the Latin script again between the 1960s to the 1980s, and back to Perso-Arabic and a newly revised Latin script (Bellér-Hann 1991; Dwyer 2005; Smith Finley 2013). The linguistic changes mirror geopolitical ties between China and its neighbors. For example, the Cyrillic alphabet had its heyday from 1955 to 1958 (Dwyer 2005), reflecting the friendly relationship between the Chinese Communist Party and the Soviet Union. The political and linguistic ties were dissolved in the late 1950s and 1960s in favor of a Latin alphabet. In the 1980s, the Perso-Arabic script was reintroduced in China (Dwyer 2005). This script was used in the media and in literature and was received favorably by the Uyghur population as it was interpreted as a way to protect a Uyghur as well as a Muslim identity (Bellér-Hann 1991). However, as Benson (2004) suggests, the frequent changes had an impact on the development and maintenance of Uyghur identity beyond the borders of China and were a political tactic to fracture pan-ethnic relations between Turkic-speaking groups across China and Central Asia.

The changes also disrupted intergenerational communication and the maintenance of a coherent intellectual tradition in Uyghur societies.

Even more, Uyghurs I spoke to suspected that frequent changes in the Uyghur script disrupted collective identification by rendering different Uyghur generations illiterate. Uyghurs were prevented from identifying with Arabic-speaking and -writing Muslims or Uyghurs living in Central Asia, some of whom still used Cyrillic, as in Kazakhstan. These observations have been confirmed by several scholars (Dwyer 2005; McMurray 2017; Schluessel 2007, 2009; Smith Finley 2013). In her insightful ethnography, Smith Finley observes that she rarely found Uyghur-language publications on Uyghur cultural traditions in the bookstores in the capital of Xinjiang in 1995. Her observation backs the complaints by Uyghurs in this study that Uyghur-language publications were limited while publications in Putonghua on Uyghur culture and customs were abundant.

Language policy has been addressed repeatedly by scholars over the years as it is fundamental to a person's sense of place in the world (e.g., Bellér-Hann 1991; Dwyer 2005; Smith Finley 2013). In June 2015, the first International Uyghur Language Day was celebrated and a report on bilingual education published by the Uyghur Human Rights Project in Washington, D.C. (UHRP 2015). In this report, scholars and activists highlighted the challenges of a bilingual language policy in Xinjiang such as the loss of a Uyghur identity, lack of funding for Uyghur schools, and the lack of employment for young Uyghur graduates even after attaining fluency in Chinese. The placement rate for Uyghur university graduates was less than 15 percent (UHRP 2015, 6). Parents faced a difficult choice. They could either decide on a Chinese-language education to improve the academic and employment prospects for their children. Or they could choose a Uyghur school to maintain a sense of identity but risk further economic and social marginalization (UHRP 2015).

Class and geographical region played a role in how Uyghurs perceived the importance of learning and communicating in Uyghur. *Minkaohan* education (referring to "nationalities" tested in the Han Chinese language) tends to be favored by members of the educational elite who want their children to be bilingual and have a promising future in China (Smith Finley 2013; Smith Finley and Zang 2015). The prestigious schools and *neidiban*-education have been discussed in the literature, as have the problems that come with identity politics and Uyghur students feeling caught between cultural identities and loyalties (Chen 2019; Grose 2015b, 2019; Leibold 2019; Yuan and Zhu 2021). Although the government has provided opportunities for Uyghurs to go to universities since the 1980s through affirmative action boni, which means Uyghur students get extra points for university entrance, this policy cemented Chinese language education. Even back in the 1990s, Chinese-educated students received more credit for entrance than those who had attended minority-language schools (Sautman 1998).

In addition to class, choices about schooling varied along oasis identities in the past (Rudelson 1997). Parents from the south of Xinjiang like Kashgar and Khotan preferred Uyghur schools. Those from the northern regions like Ghulja, Qumul, and Turpan preferred Han schools. The arguments for Han school education ranged from not isolating oneself as a group to access to better-funded Chinese-speaking schools. Rudelson's (1997) research is illustrative. Two men were arguing over Chinese-language education. The opponent claimed that Uyghur schools were in a better position to preserve Uyghur language and history. The supporter of the Chinese-speaking school asked the other man to name some works of classic Uyghur literature. The man educated in the Uyghur school could only name a few. The man educated in the Chinese school gave a long list. The moral of the story is that Chinese-speaking schools are better funded, which interviewees kept mentioning more than a decade after Rudelson's research.

Teachers were acutely aware of the educational inequalities in what they named *Xinjiang*. I met a university teacher in his thirties to talk over tea about education. He had been teaching for several years at the university and liked his job. Nonetheless he had reservations about how the school and university systems functioned in Xinjiang. Like many other people I met, he mentioned unequal resource distribution in careful ways:

> I think this is a main problem in what I call here Xinjiang. This area is Uyghur, this is Chinese. They [the schools] are very different, they have different amounts of money. You can see the difference in Urumqi too or any part where Uyghurs live. I hope we will be respected, we hope to get money and be equal to that people [Chinese].

The phrase "what I call here Xinjiang" startled me. I asked what "here" meant in this context. The teacher replied that "Xinjiang" was the official name of the province in Chinese. "There are some other names but I would prefer not to talk about it," he added. Self-censorship meant staying within the safe space of assigned speech codes. This space still enabled the discussion of contentious topics like economic inequality.

Local resource exploitation, overrepresentation of Han Chinese in highly skilled sectors, and accumulation of wealth by Han Chinese have resulted in rising income gaps. Those factors have also resulted in slower social mobility and overrepresentation of Uyghurs from the rural south in the low-skilled and low-paid service sectors of the more affluent north (Howell and Fan 2011). Hasmath (2019) makes a similar argument about Han Chinese wealth accumulation in Xinjiang eight years later. He connects the strengthening of Uyghur identity to increasing discontent. The discontent, according to the author, is fueled by Han overrepresentation in wealthier urban areas and high-paying jobs in the private sector, with 80 percent of Uyghurs still working in agriculture. Tight social networks enabled Han Chinese to dominate the private sector, leaving Uyghurs with low-paying jobs. This argument is similar to Howell and Fan's (2011) despite the time span between the studies. One result, according to Hasmath, is further Uyghur socioeconomic isolation and dissatisfaction.

The idea of development on the terms of the Han majority is steeped in history. Han migration to Xinjiang after 1945 has been abundantly documented and used to develop the western part of China through strategic settlement. State-owned production corps, which had partially evolved out of People's Liberation Army (PLA) troops, ensured ethnic and sociocultural protectionism for arriving Han Chinese, military resources and manpower to develop the region, and the integration of Uyghurs and other minorities into the Chinese nation (Bequelin 2000, 2004). "If you think the Uyghur is like you, treat him equally," was a motto among urban and rural, younger and older Uyghurs I interviewed. This motto can be understood in the context of assimilation, which other ethnic groups in China have experienced throughout history, such as the Yi peoples of Southwest China (Harrell 2001). In the Ming and Qing dynasties, troops and expeditions were sent to the remote and mountainous minority areas in Southwest China. Local authorities were replaced with appointed ones and ethnic groups pressured into assimilation policies, which favored Han styles of centralized political authority, according to Harrell (2001).

As migration to Xinjiang has been engineered by the state since 1949, the perceived and material inequality remains real for many Uyghurs, as Zang argues (2016, 2017). Zang's studies illustrate that ethnic identity was a main predictor for class self-identification, with Uyghurs in urban Urumqi avowing themselves a lower-class status than their Han Chinese counterparts. Unemployment among Uyghur youth was a serious problem; the preference of Han Chinese in leading positions in the province another. Both of these problems are related to inequality in terms of resource distribution, education, and political representation (Smith Finley 2013). Especially educators were concerned about the Uyghur youth. Rahman, a college teacher in his thirties, discussed the problem of youth unemployment and that Uyghur students could not get a job after graduation from college. "Many of them drink alcohol to forget the pressure. They don't get jobs in Xinjiang." I heard about the alcohol problem many times, especially in the city of Urumqi. And the answer by young and older people was the same: people wanted jobs but they were hard to find outside the retail and hospitality sector. They pointed out advertisements saying, "Han only" or "We are looking for a good-looking waitress. Han only." "What can we do in Xinjiang, except leave?" asked Rahman, shrugging his shoulders.

In sum, the premise of inequality pointed to systemic problems of resource distribution in what interviewees called *Xinjiang*. By addressing inequality, a space of interaction opened up in which *Xinjiang* became a symbol of contestation over mobility, language, education, economic resources, group relations, and eventually cultural survival. Research from the Oxford Internet Institute illustrates that many parts of the world are excluded from global knowledge production as a result of the dominance of particular languages and the marginalization of smaller linguistic groups (Graham, Hale, and Stephens 2011). One can deduce that if political actors continue to promote majority languages, collective ways of knowing will further converge and silence groups without a strong local and global lobby.

SOCIAL PARTICIPATION: CHALLENGING HIERARCHIES

Young Uyghurs in particular challenged received ways of social participation. They linked inequality to a lack of participation in society but also to conservative cultural norms, which felt limiting to them. These young people looked beyond the borders of China. They favored self-expression and participatory decision-making in the family and in work life. In other words, they questioned traditional ways of life.

I had been in Urumqi, the capital of Xinjiang province, for only two days when a young man in a shirt with the Brazilian flag approached me in the middle of a big boulevard. He was tall and slim, with fair, curly hair and green eyes. He had an open smile and animated way of speaking. He asked me in fluent English if I was a foreigner. "I am always trying to talk to foreigners," he said, "to practice my English." I guessed his age to be around nineteen as he studied medicine at a university in Urumqi in his first year. During his summer vacations he was working in a cafe in Kashgar, which was eighteen train hours away at the time of the research. He used the Uyghur name *Kashgar* for the city instead of the Chinese term *Kashi*. The young man told me that he spoke Uyghur, Putonghua, and English. He had gone to kindergarten with Han Chinese children and had been fluent in Putonghua since he was five years old. His parents, who were Uyghur, had sent him. He had learned conversational English in the Kashgar cafe, as there were many tourists in Kashgar, from organized tour groups to backpackers. He was curious about countries outside of China and his goal was to walk across the globe.

He asked me where I was from and when I said Germany, he got excited. He loved German soccer. The young man told me that he thought a lot about the world and the different countries and cultures and what it must be like to live somewhere else. He said he thought of himself as Chinese but not Han. He was a strong believer in what he called "development," a term he used several times in our conversation about Xinjiang and Uyghurs. Unlike other Uyghurs who thought about development as exacerbating the economic and social inequalities between Han Chinese and Uyghurs, this young man argued for development as a linear way of social and personal betterment.

"Xinjiang's way is development," he said. He linked development to a cosmopolitan outlook and practice as he wanted to travel internationally, watch media from all over the world, and be part of creating what he called "a prosperous and open society," characterized by social fairness for all. Religion was not part of this open society, according to him. The young man pointed at a mosque that we were passing by. "I don't call myself Muslim. I don't pray, nor do I go to mosque," he explained. Many younger people he knew in the city were not religious. He came back to the idea of development. "It has its price," he said and mentioned how many old houses and mosques had disappeared just the week before in Kashgar. "The city looked different ten years back. Many new buildings are there now and parts of the old city demolished. But the government has learnt and protects it. Otherwise the tourists won't come. Xinjiang is a very interesting place to visit," he said, "and I hope you will come back." I met similar young, urban, middle-class Uyghurs throughout my stay. Not all were Minkaohan and had gone to Chinese kindergartens. Politics and religion were complicated matters that did not speak to them. What spoke to them was participation in the social and economic life of what they called *Xinjiang*. The thirst for knowledge and exposure to different ways of thinking and interacting was strong.

Especially those working for transnational organizations had found a place in which they could learn new ways of interacting, ways that distributed interaction rights more evenly. Belonging, in the sense of cultural and religious identification, shifted for these young people from a cultural to an organizational perspective. Culture was relegated to the private sphere of the family where it could play a special, albeit somewhat old-fashioned, role. This is at least how the young people I interviewed saw it at the time of the research. Traditional culture could be left behind once the person entered the space of modern organizational life with its new ways of productivity and transnational relations. The young people admired individual expressivity and collective decision-making, which in turn showed their desire for social participation and having a voice in matters concerning their education and career. The following case study of Save the Children in the city of Urumqi exemplifies these claims.[3]

Save the Children is an independent relief and advocacy organization for children's rights. Founded in 1919 in the United Kingdom, the Save the Children alliance works in more than seventy countries, including China (Save the Children 2009b). The mission of the organization is to ensure the physical and mental well-being of children, reduce violence against children through education, empower families economically, engage in HIV/AIDS education, and help communities to help themselves (Save the Children 2009a). The ethics of the organization are based on the UN Convention on the Rights of the Child (OHCHR 2007; UNICEF 2010), standards that have been signed by 192 countries as of 2005 and include respecting a child's view; freedom of expression, thought, and association; the rights to privacy and to access to information; among others (Witteborn 2010).

The Urumqi Save the Children office was set up in 2003. At the time of my visit, it was committed to health training, especially in relation to HIV/AIDS awareness. Drug injections among Uyghur males, commercial sex work, and lack of sex and health education were some of the reasons at the time for the increase in HIV/AIDS infections in the province (Hayes 2012). The program manager of the organization was from the US, while the staff were Uyghur and Han Chinese. When I started interviewing in the summer of 2006, a young Uyghur woman, Aynur, who had been a member of the organization for several months, greeted me in a modern office. Aynur was in her mid-twenties. *Xinjiang*, for her, was a name of promise and a place with natural resources like gas, rich cultures, and young people with a thirst for education. She found her work in the NGO meaningful as she learned about topics she deeply cared about like education, nutrition, and health but also about how to communicate those topics to the people in the small towns and villages of Xinjiang. Aynur felt she was participating in social change, which was partially accomplished through the introduction of new management and teaching styles by the organization. She found the participatory management style of the US staff especially exciting. This style challenged received hierarchies and put the individual first:

> I really prefer the American-style individualism. Here in Xinjiang, we base everything on collectivity. We ignore the value of individuality. In every community, there are individuals. Happiness has to be placed on the individual. We want to become westernized. They've developed ways of technologies. We also need to learn from them the tolerance for different cultures. You can live freely and you can preserve your own culture.

Aynur, like other young people I talked with, celebrated individualism and its iterations, such as free thought and speech. Tolerance was another value that spoke to her. The latter was a main concern for Aynur, who was very aware of the multiple ethnic groups in Xinjiang and the importance of their social and economic participation. Transnational organizations, for young people like Aynur, were sites for learning about interaction practices from elsewhere, but they were also sites that challenged local norms and practices. For example, Aynur praised the transparent style of her manager repeatedly:

> There is something special about the management style. Management is very *transparent* and *open*. We encourage *teamwork*. You can do things working in teams and also independently. Manager X was there coaching us. He was always there *chatting, talking, asking questions, exploring.* The most important thing I learnt from X is *talking with people.* [Italics added.]

"Talking" in the English language implies a focus on substantive topics while the relationship between people is explored (Dirven et al. 1982). *Talking* as a communicative practice focuses on task orientation through relationship development, displaying truthful personal views while building the relationship between self and other in a transparent fashion. *Talking with people* is not only a practice but reveals values about communication. Those values are openness in interactions, expressing a standpoint honestly, and being unthreatening. *Chatting* and *exploring,* the terms that Aynur uses, indicate informal styles of communicating. While *chatting* points to lighthearted and phatic communication for the purpose of relationship maintenance, *exploring* is a goal- and action-oriented process. *Asking questions* and *exploring* value the opinion of the other instead of imposing one's own ideas. The communicative terms are reminiscent of Katriel and Philipsen's (1981) landmark study on the cultural meaning of communication in the United States, where close, flexible, and supportive speech was identified as the basis for successful relationship work and social bonding in white, middle-class America. *Chatting, asking questions,* and *exploring* were inextricably linked to the premise of participation for Aynur:

> I feel empowered. I can participate in decision-making and be part of a transparent management style in which no information is hidden by superiors but is circulated amongst the staff, so that everybody can make constructive contributions to solve problems.

Overall, Aynur uses terms for communication that are the scripts of neoliberal organizational change management. This type of communication emphasizes the moral improvement of individuals through communication that is tied to an affective economy, with expression, sharing, and therapeutic talk at its base, turning people into profit centers. Eva Illouz's work is en-lightening here as is the work on *Sharing* by Nicholas John (2017). Illouz (2007, 2008) argues that emotional styles create imaginations of equality and cooperation and have become key tools in managing organizational life in the (post)production-based economy. In hyper-market-driven economies like the United States, emotional styles based on egalitarianism and cooperation have morphed into bonding mechanisms, in which open, flexible, and supportive communication are emotional techniques, circulated by US media and pop-ular culture as well as transnational organizations. Aynur celebrated open, flexible, and participatory communication as the foundation of much larger social changes, including relating in the family, between generations, and genders. "Xinjiang," as Aynur put it, was not the place yet where participation and shared decision-making had become a reality.

"Every innovation begins as a transgression signaled by a few surprising vocables," writes de Certeau (1997, 32). The vocabulary signaling transgression was *participation*, which referred to an aspirational change in social norms and values pertaining to gender and age hierarchies within Uyghur commu-nities. For Aynur, for example, participation was linked to gender roles that were strong, especially in smaller towns and the rural Uyghur communities in Xinjiang. According to her, Uyghur women needed to be given more op-portunities for participation in public life, and girls needed more role models to transcend the domestic sphere. "People like me can be models," she said.

Traditionally, Uyghur children were socialized in families as well as in local neighborhoods (the Mehelle). The Mehelle has always been a religious and organizational entity, with the mosque and the mosque community the social heart of the neighborhood (Waite 2006). Dautcher (2009) studied the performance of masculinity in such a neighborhood in the town of Ghulja. He showed how Uyghur children were socialized through linguistic prac-tices. Male drinking rituals, nicknaming, and teasing were important ways of teaching boys what it meant to be a man, as was inhabiting the public spaces of the street, market, and mosque. Dautcher's study recalls Philipsen's (1992) book about social place and gender in a Chicago neighborhood. There, masculinity was performed through the code of honor, which was tied to a social position in a physical, gendered, and classed place. Byler (2021a) argues that Uyghur definitions of masculinity have shifted in the wake of the migration of males to the cities and the discourse on terror, resulting in

Islamophobia, suspicion, and police surveillance. Previously, young males were socialized into male competition and patrilineal role performances in the villages and small towns, but the new situation required the young men to rely on homosocial support networks in the city. Byler shows how the friendships became protection mechanisms against the discrimination practices of the settler society (154) and anti-terror measures that the men encountered on a daily basis. Storytelling, literature, and poetry became ways to cope with the experiences of anger and trauma and with living in a society that shifted between indifference and hostility. Several of the interviewees in his study disappeared, according to Byler, giving the study the quality of a witness account.

Returning to Aynur, her communicative aspirations illustrate several aspects of unruly speech. *Xinjiang* became the metaphor for socioeconomic opportunity and participation. The premise of participation, in turn, engaged the status quo. De Certeau writes, "[I]t is impossible to take speech and to retain it without a taking of power. To want *to be heard* means being committed to *making* history" (1997, 32). There is no indication of Aynur wanting to make history. However, there is an indication of Aynur being curious about interaction values that encouraged personal responsibility as well as a collective search for solutions to problems. The call for open and expressive communication was a call to assert herself as an organizational member, a woman, and a young person in Xinjiang interested in constructive social change. The call for a change in communicative norms was a call to separate cultural and socioeconomic spaces. The private space of the home was imagined to be the space of cultural reproduction while the space of schools, companies, and transnational organizations became the space of social and economic reproduction. In 2006, the interviewees could not anticipate how the cultural space of the home would be one of the last frontiers to be controlled by state-driven digital surveillance, as discussed later.

Participation connected the individual to a discourse on rights. Organizations like Save the Children based their work on the international human rights discourse. The UN Convention on the Rights of the Child figures especially strongly in Save the Children's mission:

Save the Children provides opportunities for children to develop practical skills which enhance their self-confidence and self-esteem, enable them to communicate, to cooperate, to negotiate, to make decisions which encourage their independence. We support children to express their views and encourage children's participation through children's forums, children's research projects, children managing activity centres and directly presenting recommendations to policy makers. (Save the Children China 2006)

Participation means the right to shape communal life through freedom of expression and thought, privacy, and access to information (UNICEF 2010). The right to participation, as proposed in the NGO's mission, presumes that humans engage through their independent selves. What it means to be a person, in this organizational view, is defined through voicing one's ideas, which are unique. At the same time, the unique self is not an isolated self. The unique self, which strives toward independence in terms of ethical and moral decision-making, is bound into a web of social relationships that the self needs to honor. In order to reconcile the seeming tension between a unique self and the need to relate to other unique selves, truthful expression is encouraged to balance the tension (Carbaugh 2007; Philipsen 1987; Witteborn 2010). The individualized self has the moral obligation to take others seriously and engage in processes of acknowledging self and other through mutual interaction work, which has to be open and transparent.[4] In order to engage mutually, one needs equal positions with regard to the right to ask questions, make comments, disagree, and make decisions.

The call in the Save the Children quote above promotes the self-reflexive person and the critical, reflective citizen. Participatory desires can destabilize as multiple opinions compete for recognition. The manager of Save the Children remarked tongue in cheek that he was looking forward to his transfer to Sudan, which was a single country at the time, as it was easier working there than under the Chinese government's strict control of NGOs. Control of NGOs has further increased after the implementation of new rules for foreign NGOs operating in China (Ministry of Public Security of the People's Republic of China 2016). According to these rules, NGOs have to register with the Ministry of Public Security, and all of their operations need to be monitored by the police. They also need a Chinese partner organization. These measures can be read as a response to the work of NGOs like Save the Children and the ways those organizations contribute to social change in

China. Save the Children applied participatory teaching methods during their awareness workshops, taking local experiences into consideration, including a fear of talking about intimate behaviors and religious moral values. In the words of the manager in charge of the NGO in Urumqi:

> Our workshops on HIV/AIDS are different from the traditional ones. In the traditional model, people line up, somebody lectures, people listen, and then leave. Our workshops emphasize participatory styles. A lot of partners have benefited because they're learning through their own experience. They see how practical it is.

This example illustrates how participation was a new premise insofar as it promoted the notion of a self-directed and yet interrelated self, which improves morally and practically through self-reflection and self-expression. This is not to say that interaction practices imported from the United States or Europe are the only ones changing social interactions in China. Historically, there have been many calls for participation (He 2007). People have pushed for participation in the political, civic, and organizational sectors, based on freedom of speech, the press, and assembly. Those rights have been enshrined in Article 35 of the Constitution of the PRC since 1982. Nevertheless, participation runs counter to many government-regulated practices as well as traditional hierarchies between those in positions to talk and those in positions to listen. At the same time, transnational NGOs have been part of social change in Xinjiang. Teamwork and shared decision-making had created a productive organizational climate in the NGO Save the Children and an organizational culture that rewarded input, curiosity, and creative problem-solving. Flattened social hierarchies encouraged shared decision-making, and the people I interviewed appreciated these new strategies. The findings are in line with studies that highlight the desire of young Uyghurs to work for transnational organizations and to live and work abroad (Grose 2015b).

DIGITAL POLICING OF UNRULY SPEECH

The premises of unity, inequality, and participation were challenged by technological surveillance and control. According to a *Wall Street Journal* report from December 19, 2017, Xinjiang had become a digitally surveilled area, with Uyghurs and Han Chinese residents restricted in their physical

movement and sociality in the name of national security. The measures are
the technological response to the deadly riots between Uyghurs and Han
Chinese in Urumqi in 2009, the explosion of a car in Beijing in 2013, and
the Kunming knife attacks at a train station in March of 2014. Scholars of
the region like David Brophy and Rian Thum have observed a similar trend
(see Vanderklippe 2017).

Presidents of China have had different approaches to maintaining social
peace. President Hu Jintao, the predecessor of current president Xi Jinping,
had emphasized economic development in Xinjiang to ensure interethnic
peace. President Xi followed a different strategy. He was faced with a growing
dissatisfaction and anger among Uyghur communities. The attacks on Han
Chinese civilians in 2009, 2013, and 2014 were the deadly consequences of
this anger. Anti-terrorism laws were introduced in 2014 as President Xi's
government wanted to prevent in Xinjiang what the United States had failed
to prevent in the Middle East. The government wanted to block a spread
of violence from Afghanistan and Syria into China and joined forces with
private industry to create surveillance infrastructure in northwestern China
(Byler 2020, 2021b; Leibold 2020).

Digital infrastructure has become the key to social control in Xinjiang.
When I started my field research in 2006, this infrastructure was just being developed. People used older versions of mobile phones at the time and
bought their SIM cards in small stores. The ubiquitous internet cafe could be
found in small towns in the south, such as in Yarkand, where teenagers spent
the afternoons playing video games, while donkey carts with farmers bumped
past one another. Some scholars argue that the year 2010 marked the shift
from allowing Uyghurs to communicate online, albeit with surveillance, to
fully controlling Uyghur communication (Byler 2019). In 2011, according to
Byler, 3G mobile data networks had been introduced in the capital Urumqi
and only three years later, in 2014, the majority of adults seemed to carry
a smartphone. Approximately 49 percent of people living in Xinjiang had
internet access in 2014, which ranked the province ninth out of thirty-one
listed regions (CNNIC 2014). As almost 75 percent of mobile internet users
lived in cities, one can assume that Uyghurs in rural areas had less mobile
access to the internet, which left them to use either internet cafes where
surveillance was high (UHRP 2014) or home computers.

Since 2013, mobile phone users in China must register with their names and show IDs for the purchase of SIM cards. Uyghurs also have to use their real names for micro-blogging services (UHRP 2014). The authorities cracked down on Uyghur bloggers and netizens, especially after the riots in 2009, with several of them still in jail by 2015 (UHRP 2015). Bamman, O'Connor, and Smith (2012) conclude that more than 50 percent of social media posts were deleted in Xinjiang, Tibet, and Qinghai at the time. Surveillance was still rather embodied at the time of my research in 2006. When I returned to the hotel in the evenings, a man would look over my shoulder when I used the computer in the lobby. The same man would sit on a chair in the lobby when I came down for breakfast, checking in on foreigners in the hotel, which was designated for people like me.

By 2017, scattered media reports emerged that confirmed that President Xi's ubiquitous surveillance vision had become a reality. The Uyghur Service of Radio Free Asia (2017b) reported on house searches for religious paraphernalia and restrictions on religious naming for newborn children. Around the same time, a growing number of media reports, academic journals, and monographs started discussing the mass surveillance of Uyghurs and other minorities in Xinjiang (e.g., Allen-Ebrahimian 2019; Human Rights Watch 2020; Grauer 2021 for the *Intercept*). In a special issue on the securitization of Xinjiang, Joanne Smith Finley (2019) and contributors historicize the internment of Uyghurs in Xinjiang in the name of security and stability. Harris and Isa (2019) explore the revival of Islam in Xinjiang up to 2014 and its manifestations in daily life. This revival, which was enabled through digital technology and linked to a strengthened Uyghur consciousness, would eventually legitimate the state to intervene through reeducation, the militarization of society, and governing by fear.

Byler (2021b) illustrates the material and symbolic structures and consequences of forced compliance. The ethnographic accounts of the survivors of detention make clear that refusal remains the last option of personal autonomy in face of violence. Refusal challenges the limit and can open up communicative spaces in which solidarity can thrive. As in Foucault's allegory of the lightning that illuminates the night sky and announces the limit (Foucault 1977), the introduction of an elaborate surveillance system reveals what has always been there but obscured. Technological surveillance marks the limits of cultural and political expression and controls the space of this expression. Datafication of the body and Uyghur society is not what young people like Aynur anticipated when being enthusiastic about social participation and relegating Uyghur cultural practices to the private space of the family. Private space has come under the digital control of the state. Any object, practice, or language related to cultural identification (e.g., having traditional Uyghur knives in the home without registration) is subject to data analytics and clearance (Grauer 2021).

A sophisticated system of practices and platforms creates dense datasets about Uyghurs' behaviors. The datasets include biometric and movement data, keywords from social media texts, phone records, browsing histories, banking records, passport applications, web subscriptions, and e-commerce consumption. Qualitative data collected by Han Chinese visitors to Uyghur homes add to these datasets (Byler 2020). The Integrated Joint Operations Platform (IJOP) centralizes the gathered data for analytical processing and decision-making, such as detaining a person. Human Rights Watch (2020) explains that the IJOP platform works through aggregate data logics in order to identify people deemed dangerous to the Chinese state. People can be identified as dangerous for reading the Qur'an without permission; preaching the Qur'an without the state's permission; wearing the burqa, veil, or having a long beard; underage marriage; going on Hajj; using a VPN (virtual private network), Skype, or P2P (peer-to-peer) file-sharing platforms; and traveling to countries identified as sensitive, including Turkey, Afghanistan, or Kyrgyzstan. Travel within China is also deemed suspicious without registration with local authorities. Particular practices raise red flags, such as switching off mobile phones or using a SIM card not registered in one's name. Other reasons for flagging people are having "complex social ties," "unstable thoughts," or "improper (sexual) relations" (Human Rights Watch 2020). Experts estimate that platforms like IJOP are machine-learning platforms representative of the most advanced police, military, and intelligence strategies (Allen-Ebrahimian 2019).

Various news and investigative outlets have written about the different data collection tools, including the "Physicals for All" program as described by Yael Grauer (2021) for the *Intercept*: "Under the 'Physicals for All' program, citizens are required to have their faces scanned and voice signatures analyzed, as well as give DNA. Documents describing the program indicate it is part of the policing system." The biometric data can be used at police checkpoints to authenticate a person and verify his or her behavior as acceptable. In Urumqi alone, there were two million checkpoint stops over two years, according to Grauer (2021). Identity data are checked through facial recognition. A color system (yellow, orange, red) indicates whether a person is evaluated as suspicious. The database has other categories, including criminal arrest, time spent abroad, relatives detained, psychiatric records, and participation in the Urumqi protests in July of 2009 (Grauer 2021).

In addition, people have to download apps that check the complete communication ecology of the person, including texts, pictures taken, videos shared, and social networks (Byler 2019; Grauer 2021; Rajagopalan 2018). The phone readings gather phone contacts, times called, location, browsing history, messages, videos, audio, and pictures, as well as words listed as dangerous. The data are sent to the Integrated Joint Operations Platform. Police can force people at checkpoints to read out their phones or to download an app specifically designed for readouts. Rajagopalan (2018) describes how the app *Jīngwǎng* or "clean internet" collects a complete set of data files from a smartphone and sends it to an outside server.

With the support of Red Team Lab, which offers third-party support and finances to conduct security audits of open-source internet freedom software, the Open Technology Fund confirmed that the mentioned app extracts information, which enables detailed tracking of the device and content produced (Lynn 2018). Through an MD5 hash that is a unique file identifier able to detect files on a mobile device, all files on the device are sent to a server and compared to a list of file hashes (Lynn 2018). If a "harmful" file is identified, the user has to delete it. The report also found that all data and files transmitted to the server can easily be intercepted by a third party with minimal technical knowledge, paving the way for content manipulation. The Open Technology Fund made the MD5 hash list available on its website to encourage transparency about which content is flagged as dangerous.

Surveillance using artificial intelligence (AI) in Xinjiang is compounded by embodied surveillance through dense police checkpoints and police checks in cities, towns, and on highways, as well as through home visits. Byler (2018) describes "older brother and sister volunteers" and "relatives" as an approach to surveillance. People, most of whom were Han Chinese, stayed with Uyghur families to assess the loyalty to the Chinese state. Interviews and observations of family life were used as data materials to rank people as "trustworthy," "average," or "untrustworthy" (Byler 2018). Criteria for the ranking were Uyghur ethnicity, military age, underemployment, prayer patterns, unauthorized knowledge of Islam, teaching children about Islam at home, ownership of passports, travel to twenty-six Muslim countries, or having relatives abroad. Those people with the label *untrustworthy* were asked to report names of other *untrustworthy* persons they knew who would then come under close scrutiny with the help of digital tracing. Rajagopalan (2018) notes very similar patterns:

> The state also assigned an additional 1.1 million Han and Uighur "big brothers and sisters" to conduct week-long assessments on Uighur families as uninvited guests in Uighur homes. Over the course of these stays, the relatives tested the "safe" qualities of those Uighurs who remained outside of the camp system by forcing them to participate in activities forbidden by certain forms of Islamic piety, such as drinking, smoking and dancing. They looked for any sign of resentment or any lack of enthusiasm in Chinese patriotic activities.

Automated data surveillance supported by AI also comes in the form of another app, *Baixing Anquan* (Citizen Security). This app enables the digitized version of traditional control. Citizens report suspicious behaviors by posting incriminating evidence on WeChat accounts (Grauer 2021). In other words, massive datasets are created through personal identification (facial scans, voice detection, DNA, camera tracking systems), tracing of mobility (GPS tracking and checkpoints), and surveillance of communication (keyword search on WeChat and QQ email), as well as database entries on banking, medical, study, and employment histories. Byler (2020) concludes:

> The expropriation of Turkic Muslim social networks and biometrics by companies like Tencent and Sensetime in service to a new counter-terrorism surveillance economy, places state contractors and the police in control of the means of social interaction, information and, ultimately, economic productivity and social reproduction.

The US-led War on Terror (Roberts 2018, 2020) legitimizes the development and financial support of sophisticated surveillance technologies (USD 7.2 billion within two years, according to Byler 2019). Uyghurs are part of a massively growing pool of phenotypical and behavioral data, which makes risk modeling possible (Amoore 2011, 2013). As Shah (2020) argues, identification replaces expressed identity, with the machine and algorithm evaluating and calculating lives. Andrejevic (2020) put it in these words: "The black box [. . .] replaces sharing with operationalism: the goal is not to tell or to explain, but to form a link in a process of decision or classification" (2). For Uyghurs, this link means being a potential suspect who needs to be transformed into a suitable citizen. Expressive life becomes automated and resistance ever more difficult. Quoting an interviewee from Khotan in Xinjiang, Megha Rajagopalan (2018) summarized the situation as follows:

> The only kind of Uighur life that can be recognised by the state is the one that the computer sees. This makes Uighurs [. . .] feel as though their lives only matter as data—code on a screen, numbers in camps. They have adapted their behaviour, and slowly even their thoughts, to the system.

Uyghurs' bodies and the tracking of movement and behaviors, as well as digital content, become the instruments for technological innovation. Inequality is amplified through automated modeling and decision-making, using minorities like Uyghurs as testing grounds for automated data collection, the development of AI-driven technologies, and for experimenting with data analytics. Uyghurs are not the only social testing ground, however. A recent MIT study by Beraja, Yang, and Yuchtman (2020) shows that data generated from populations in public settings are far richer in terms of volume than data collected in corporate settings (e.g., offices). In other contexts, refugees have been shown to be a "suitable" population for data experimentation. Biometric fingerprinting and iris recognition have become part of the relief organizations' toolbox for fast resource distribution and population management in refugee camps (Lindskov Jacobsen 2015). Digital identity (Cheesman 2020) and blockchain technology for data sharing are just some examples of the automation of humanitarian management (Witteborn 2022). Digital border and population management in Europe (Ruppert and Scheel 2021; Tazzioli 2020) is another piece of evidence for the techno-control of movement of humans and things.

Therefore, it comes as no surprise that technological surveillance is not just a booming sector in China but of interest to many governments in the world. Government agencies as well as domestic and international companies took part in the China-Eurasia Security Expo in Urumqi in August of 2017, according to Xinhua (2018), including companies from the United States, France, Israel, and the Philippines (Byler 2019). Investment, cooperation, and poverty alleviation are advertised as goals of the expo. Security and facial recognition technology developed by controversial companies like Megvii and SenseTime were part of the event (Ding 2019).

CONCLUSION

Uyghurs have become proficient in mimicry and the "tactical art of adaptation" (de Certeau 1997, 168) while exposing the moorings of the communicative status quo. Mimicry (Bhabha 1994) is a tool for self-protection and an autonomous act that exposes the rules that keep the social infrastructure intact, including self-censorship and historical narratives that are not supposed to be questioned. Mimicry undermines these rules through artful practice that transcends verbal language through smiles, smirks, and shrugs. Capturing speech through transgression is a "form of refusal. It is a protestation," as de Certeau (1997, 12) maintains in another historical context, namely that of the student revolts in Paris in May of 1968. The act of performing *Xinjiang* through shrugs and smiles was an act of autonomy. Imitating the norm that declared speech to be censored was an act of freedom that opened up a space of imagination and expressivity.

Unity was more than a revisionist call for ethno-nationalistic identity. Unity was a call for the preservation and adaptation of a social body under pressure to a changing social landscape as well as a response to socioeconomic inequalities and marginalization of the Uyghur language and culture. The aspirational call for unity through religious identity showed religion to be an important part of the cultural economy and intended to keep Uyghurs together as a social body. Cultural relics have "poetic" power (de Certeau 1997, 172) as they can trigger innovation, including new tactics for how to keep Uyghur history, culture, and language alive. The intricate tactics of a dense cultural economy are hard to destroy, as in the example of the little girl who read the Qur'an in the backroom of a carpet store and who smiled while hiding it artfully under heaps of woolen blankets. These tactics live on obstinately despite censorship, the intellectual ruptures due to changing language scripts, and the impact of Putonghua language policies on Uyghur education. The arguments are backed by Harris and Isa (2019) on the revival of Islam in the region. Through the analysis of WeChat in 2013 and 2014, the authors interpret this revival as a response to the 2009 riots and ensuing state violence against the Uyghurs. Digital participation of Uyghurs in religious debates beyond China was another reason for the revival, until the state started detaining people as punishment for this digital engagement. According to the authors, the religious revival ranged from nation-centered political Islam to pious devotion through prayer and poetry. Harris and Isa conclude that religious revival is tightly linked to the revival of a Uyghur nation and the protection of the social body from dissolution.

The call for unity can also be regarded as a response to changing cultural values among the younger generation. Young, urban Uyghurs wanted more self-expression, decision-making, and overall social participation. They strengthened the pressure for cultural reform and questioned traditional values as traces of a bygone era. Local knowledges are important resources for people to live their lives, Appiah (2006) argues, but the globalized world, in which difference is encountered, is challenging these local knowledges. Difference can motivate cultural change, as could be seen in the example of communication practices introduced by the transnational organization Save the Children. Debate, feedback, and participatory decision-making resonated with young staff members but contradicted received cultural order.

The imagined split between private cultural reproduction and public socioeconomic reproduction was in the spirit of the state, which allows for cultural practice as long as it is conducted within prescribed rules or for purposes of public spectacle. The real and imagined relegation of culture into private space enables stronger surveillance of this space in the name of security. The speech that was starting to be captured by Uyghurs in 2006, in de Certeau's (1997) words, has been taken back by the state.

De Certeau (1997) describes the displacement of tradition as "relics of a lost social body, detached from the whole in which they played a part. [. . .] They are isolated, inert, planted into another body. [. . .] They no longer have a language that symbolizes or unites them" (171). De Certeau predicts that tearing the fabric of cultural practices of the marginalized will result in violence (171). The remnants of a once-intact cultural economy might lie dormant, but they are there and ready to be awakened with unforeseen consequences. Those consequences became apparent during the protests in 2009 in Urumqi that turned violent, injuring and killing many Han Chinese civilians, Uyghurs, and police.

There was an opening in the early 2000s, and a hopeful youth looked toward Central Asia, Turkey, and Arab nations as well as Europe and the United States. The opening was linked to the economic development of China, with Xinjiang as a key region and gateway to Central, western, and South Asia. By 1995, 96 percent of small towns and villages were connected by highways (Smith Finley 2013) and regular flights linked Xinjiang to other countries. Since December 2014, a high-speed railway connects Urumqi to Lanzhou in the province of Gansu, 1,800 kilometers away. Xinjiang Uyghur Autonomous Region is now a major trade link to Pakistan through the China-Pakistan Economic Corridor (CPEC). The deep-sea port in Gwadar, Pakistan, is part of the Belt and Road and the Maritime Silk Road Initiatives. The infrastructure is an extensive supply-chain network that connects China's northwest to South Asia, Africa, and the Middle East and promises regional connectivity and economic integration as well as access to important economic zones (Khursheed et al. 2019). Despite these openings, the pressure to watch one's talk could be felt in the early 2000s and has grown over time into systemic, automated surveillance of everyday life. The private technology and startup sectors in China are drivers of this surveillance vision, supported by the state and military technology (Miracola 2019). Nevertheless, those Uyghurs who have left China use digital technologies for their own purposes and have created extensive digital support networks in their advocacy for human rights and self-determination, as chapters 3 and 4 illustrate.

3 | *EAST TURKISTAN*

Belonging and Human Rights

EAST TURKISTAN **WAS THE LABEL** for political mobilization in the United States and Germany, based on the premises of belonging
and human rights. *East Turkistan* was an unruly naming practice mostly employed by diasporic Uyghur organizations and individuals but only carefully
used by donors, political parties, and transnational NGOs. It questioned a
discursive code that rendered Uyghurs as too recognizable (e.g., the extremist Muslim or premodern subject to be modernized) or too unrecognizable
(the human with a need for safety from violence). This claim gestures to
Athanasiou, who writes in a conversation with Judith Butler (Butler and
Athanasiou, 2013, 69):

> If we make, unmake, and remake ourselves, such makings only occur
> with and through others. [. . .] So it is with others that we assume and, at
> the same time, potentially dismantle the norms that threaten to render us
> either unrecognizable or too recognizable.

When people use names, according to Cooren (2010), they evoke particular values, principles, emotions, or policies that are guidelines for action.
Names become agents. Names can speak for a principle and move people to
engage in particular activities (e.g., protest) through repeated performance.
Cooren (2010, 37) notes: "[I]n order to be performable and recognizable, these

performances must be repeatable, iterable *for another next first time.*" The performance of *East Turkistan* and the orientation of interlocutors to this name is key to understanding unruly speech and its two main premises: belonging and human rights, which are discussed next.

BELONGING

East Turkistan was the vehicle through which a cultural sense of belonging was transported on the aspirational way to political and territorial recognition. Unity, discussed in chapter 2, and belonging are related. Unity was a response to the danger of social disintegration due to political pressures, a varied spiritual and religious heritage, and the diversification of cultural norms along generational lines. Belonging is integral to unity, realized through the proposition of *East Turkistan* as the territorial and cultural nation in which the unity of Uyghurs can be realized. *East Turkistan* (in English), *Sherqi Turkistan* (Uyghur), and *Osttürkistan* (German) are central symbols at the heart of Uyghur diasporic advocacy in the United States and in Germany. I use the term *East Turkistan* for analysis here as the English version represents the most frequently used label in digital and embodied interactions in Germany and the United States. This is because English was a lingua franca when Uyghurs gathered and interacted with NGOs and public officials.

East Turkistan figured prominently during protests, political events, and personal interviews, and in press releases. Through the Uyghur community in Munich, Germany, I had met Yusup, a young man in his thirties. I interviewed him in a cafe where he told me about himself. He was a tailor by training, had been in Germany for several years, and was learning German. When asked what he called his home, he answered *East Turkistan.* He said in a wavering voice: "My home, this is my homeland." The strength of the reply surprised me as I have rarely seen Uyghur men express emotions like this with a stranger in public. He lived in Munich but he knew that he would never be of this place. *Home* was used synonymously with *homeland* and was associated with local language and dialects, smells, sounds, and deep social relations between family members and neighbors. He came as an asylum seeker to Munich and was still living in a shared asylum seeker accommodation. He hoped to find work as a tailor or just do any job to help his wife and young son. He was evasive when talking about what he had experienced in "the homeland," as he continued calling the place he grew up. He said he "had engaged in activities like handing out fliers with political speech" and was caught doing so. The police had only given him a warning but he was on the radar of the officials, which meant observation of his movement in public, harassment of his parents and wife, and living with fear of detainment.

Eventually, he had to leave China. His wife decided to accompany him. She had not been sure how long it would take for the couple to see each other again if she did not come. Yusup was emotional on the day I met him. He told me that his wife was very unhappy. "Don't get me wrong," he said. "I am very glad I am safe at the moment and so is my wife. But I am scared as I don't know whether I will get asylum. It's been two years now. And my wife is tired and angry at me. We live in a small room in a refugee shelter with many other people. People are loud in the place, so it is difficult to sleep, especially for my son. I feel so sorry my wife has to go through this. We had a big house in the countryside and a garden with grapes and watermelon and peaches. [He started smiling.] Here, we have nothing. I don't speak the language well and I can never go back." At this point, Yusup fell silent. I looked down at my cup of coffee, not sure how to console him. I had encountered situations like this many times in interviews when people stopped speaking out of despair. Some were frustrated about having sacrificed the happiness of family members for their political activities. After several minutes in silence, Yusup eventually started speaking again. He wanted to tell me that despite the burden of exile, he felt that what he had done was right. "You can never give up your freedom and live in fear," he said. "If you do, you are already dead." Belonging, for Yusup, meant being part of a collective and place.

Yusup was too scared to partake in Uyghur political activities in Munich, such as regular protests in the Marienplatz, the main plaza by the city hall where Uyghurs tended to gather. He feared that his asylum claim would be endangered if he participated in political activities. He was also not willing to tell his story to local journalists who had heard of Uyghurs and wanted to write a personalized story. Yusup excused himself as he had to see a social worker in the shelter he lived in. Bureaucratic matters, fear, and lingering exhaustion did not leave much energy for protest for several of the asylum seekers I interviewed.

Nevertheless, there were politically active Uyghurs in Munich. Aygul is an example. She had come to Germany via Kazakhstan. She was a nurse and married to a German husband. Her husband was worried and did not want her to protest or blog about her home. He feared for the safety of his in-laws in China. Therefore, Aygul only occasionally attended protests, but she contributed to discussions in digital forums. Sometimes she would stand in the Marienplatz, the central square in Munich, carrying a banner or just silently walking with the protesters. "East Turkistan is my home," she said, and it was the loss of this home that motivated her to overcome her fear. She was reportedly proud of expressing belonging through her banner and the slogans she sang, such as "Freedom for Uyghurs, freedom for East Turkistan." She was proud to act in the name of Uyghurs, she said, through her presence in a public space. Her acting was not just about home and justice. It was also about the personal redemption of having left home. By that, she assuaged some of the guilt of having left China and raising her family in relative affluence and political stability.

Uyghurs have increasingly turned to digital spaces to build a digital nation. Uyghur diasporic organizations, in particular, play an important role in the connective digital infrastructure, creating a visual and textual narrative of the homeland. The name *East Turkistan* was used consistently on diasporic organization websites like that of the World Uyghur Congress, the Uyghur American Association, and the Uyghur Human Rights Project (UHRP). The UHRP website, for example, states: "The Uyghur Human Rights Project promotes the rights of the Uyghurs and other Turkic Muslim peoples in East Turkistan, referred to by the Chinese government as the Xinjiang Uyghur Autonomous Region, through research-based advocacy" (https://uhrp.org/about). Belonging was realized through the idea of a homeland, which is typical for imaginations of diasporas that struggle for political recognition (e.g., Brinkerhoff 2009; Smets et al. 2020). The homeland was represented through textual, visual, and auditory constellations, including maps, photographs, reports, and music. Uyghur advocacy organizations published nostalgic images of nature, history, and Uyghur people as well as reports on human rights violations in Xinjiang province or China. The premise of belonging therefore nurtured exilic imaginations of the East Turkistan nation.

The World Uyghur Congress website is an example of digital nation-building. The website was published in five languages in 2009, since then extended to ten, including Japanese, Russian, Turkish, Arabic, and French. It offers an instantaneous overlap of tradition and technology as it expands its reach through hyperlinked information and visual narratives. Hyperlinks to Uyghur history, geography, language, culture, and society serve as navigational signposts. They also embed a connective logic that reinforces a homogeneous Uyghur culture as a rationale for an identity politics bolstered through up-to-date reports on the situation of Uyghurs as well as other marginalized groups in China, including Han Chinese dissidents and minority groups in Xinjiang.

Overall, digital platforms have been key for dissent and for antagonizing the state. Bernal (2014) shows in her longitudinal and innovative work how the Eritrean diaspora engaged in political advocacy through communication technologies. She illustrates the struggle over information management and representation in digital diasporic politics, thereby questioning the idea of homogeneous imagined communities (Anderson 1991). Uyghurs follow Tibetans (Drissel 2008; Yeh 2007) in challenging the Chinese government through digital nation-building and human rights claims, with *East Turkistan* being a reminder of a politics of resistance playing out in digital space. Reyhan (2012), one of the early digital network researchers of the Uyghur diaspora, confirms the importance of the internet for political activism and diasporic identification when she states: "As a young population sensitive to ICT, Uyghurs are putting together a classical diaspora as well as a digital diaspora."

Reyhan (2012) argues that a connected Uyghur diaspora came into being thanks to technology. She conducted one of the first digital tracing projects of the Uyghur diaspora to understand their social networks, locations, and content produced (see Reyhan and Grin 2014). The project was linked to the e-Diasporas Atlas, initiated by Dana Diminescu (2012). Reyhan found that in 2012 there were 843 Uyghur websites, forums, and blogs, of which 314 were active. Among the websites, 146 were run by Uyghurs outside China, 17 by government organizations in China, and 151 by Uyghurs in China (Reyhan 2012). In the diaspora, politics was the most popular topic (30 percent), followed by religion (12 percent), culture (11 percent), and education (8 percent). The numbers are evidence of the strong political orientation of the Uyghur diaspora. While religion was the second-most prominent topic, it was found mostly on websites in Turkey and Saudi Arabia. In China, politics was digitally absent and religion almost invisible, accounting for only 1 percent of the websites in the country. In the diaspora, all of the websites dedicated to politics were coordinated by the World Uyghur Congress (WUC) and its subcommittees. Radio Free Asia and the WUC were the most extensively linked organizations in the diaspora.

The United States was the country with the highest count of Uyghur diasporic websites (40), followed by Turkey (25), France (16), Japan, (15), Canada (12), and the Netherlands (5). There were only three active Uyghur websites in Germany. This means that the United States hosted almost one-third of the websites of the Uyghur diaspora, with the Uyghur American Association website being a bridge between political topics and other clusters linked to the organization (Reyhan 2012). Yu-Wen Chen (2014) confirmed the latter point in her network analysis of Uyghur advocacy organizations in the United States, Germany, and Japan. Interestingly, Reyhan also shows that France's small Uyghur community had a much larger internet presence than Germany's in 2012, despite the fact that Germany is the center of Uyghur activism in Europe. The research suggests that most of the Uyghurs in France came as students while most of the Uyghurs in Germany came as refugees, a claim confirmed by the research for this book. As refugees, Uyghurs had comparatively less digital literacy and access to technology than the students in France, which meant less digital diasporic activity.

Organizational websites remain important for Uyghur activism and outreach. The Uyghur American Association website, for example, combines symbols of multiple allegiances and global connections. In 2012, the horizontal head bar contained a symbol with the combined Uyghur and US flags. There were pictures of glacial mountains representing purity and timeless strength, the Idkah mosque in Kashgar, capturing a historically continuous identity of the Uyghurs, and the US Capitol, gesturing to political allegiance and alliances. In 2021, the landing page contained large visual images including the term "genocide," referring to the declaration by the United States in January of 2021 that the Chinese government is committing genocide against the Uyghurs.

HUMAN RIGHTS

Uyghurs in Germany and the United States have shifted the premises of unity, inequality, and social participation associated with the name *Xinjiang* in China to political participation, legitimated through the premise of *human rights*. The Universal Declaration of Human Rights was introduced after World War II and adopted in 1948. Historically, states were the entities that had the means to guarantee human rights to citizens. Normative human rights discourse is based on a universal claim of humans to have and declare rights (Schultheis Moore 2016), with the autonomous subject building the core of human rights law. Rights are central to the struggle for recognition as a person and as a member of a group, according to Douzinas: "[T]o be a person you must be in the law, you must have rights" (Douzinas 2007, 39).

In their advocacy, the Uyghur leadership has accepted the idea of a secularized and autonomous self who has the right to participate in society and express opinions freely. There is a strong concern with Article 19 of the Human Rights Declaration and the premises of freedom of expression and political self-determination. These premises, as part of the human rights code, are key for Uyghur diasporic advocacy. Kreide (2013, 88) suggests seeing human rights as judicial in nature and the outcome of political processes. She identifies four characteristics of a political imagination of human rights: injustice experiences, ongoing interpretation and critique, access to resources and institutions, and institutional actors as regulatory mechanisms to claim human rights. These actors include suprastate actors, such as the European Union, as well as states and citizens (Menke and Pollmann 2007, 31; cited in Kreide 2013, 95). For Uyghurs, the United Nations, the federal and state governments of the United States and Germany, funding organizations like the National Endowment for Democracy, and local nongovernmental organizations are important supporting actors. Kreide (2013) maintains that there cannot be human rights demands without public political discourse (97). Organizations like the National Endowment for Democracy keep the Uyghurs in international public discourse while pushing their own democracy mission in China, as I discuss later.

The Uyghurs' call for free thought, free speech, and political self-determination is a transgressive act, which crosses the limits of political and legal codes in China. Freedom of thought, speech, and political participation could be detected in all of the mission statements of Uyghur diasporic associations, including the Uyghur American Association (UAA), the World Uyghur Congress (WUC), and the Uyghur Human Rights Project (UHRP), founded in 2004 and an autonomous organization since 2015. The Uyghur American Association (UAA, since 1998) was an initiator of the UHRP and has a strong focus on human rights, leadership, and community:

By leveraging our collective voice, and upholding democratic values and human rights to the highest value, we aim to create the political will necessary to improve the lives of Uyghurs in their homeland. (UAA, n.d.)

Likewise, the UHRP's mission emphasizes evidence-based human rights reporting and advocacy. As of 2021, the executive director is Omer Kanat, a former journalist. He took part in the founding of the UHRP in 2003 and the WUC in 2004 where he has been vice president since 2006. Louisa Greve, who was vice president for programs and East Asia director at the National Endowment for Democracy, is now the director of global advocacy for the UHRP.

In 2009, Uyghurs gained visibility through a high-profile staging of their political advocacy in the United States Congress, which I could observe for this research. The event was part of the Third Assembly of the World Uyghur Congress in Washington, D.C., from May 21 to 25. Uyghurs reached out to other groups under pressure, including Tibetans and Han Chinese dissidents. Uyghurs from Kazakhstan, Canada, Sweden, Turkey, and Germany as well as activists and government officials joined the event at which Rebiya Kadeer was reelected president of the WUC. The session was supported by the National Endowment for Democracy (NED), the Unrepresented Nations and Peoples Organization (UNPO), and included a panel discussion organized by Human Rights Watch.

On the day of the US Congress event, there was heavy press presence in anticipation of this rather politicized forum, which included several members of Congress who spoke in support of the Uyghurs and condemned restrictions on freedom of speech and religion in China. Other speakers were Bhuchung Tsering, the head of a Tibetan dissident organization; Tienchi Liao-Martin, the director of the Laogai Research Foundation; Louisa Greve, the vice president of NED; Kara Abramson, the advocacy director of the Congressional Executive Commission on China; T. Kumar, Asia director of Amnesty International; Marino Busdachin, the UNPO general secretary; and others. The presence of all these speakers and organizations illustrates that the WUC had secured the attention and support of several important players in the human rights field.

In the event's digital announcement by the Uyghur American Association (UAA), Rebiya Kadeer was introduced as the "democratic leader of the Uyghur people in East Turkistan (aka: Xinjiang Uyghur Autonomous Region of China)." *Xinjiang Uyghur Autonomous Region* was used in official documents to situate *East Turkistan* within a geopolitical context and to make the political demands of the diasporic associations clear. The opening ceremony in the US Capitol on the morning of May 21, 2009, started with the anthems of East Turkistan and the United States. When the East Turkistan anthem started playing, Uyghur attendees smiled, some of them with tears in their eyes. The United States seemed to have recognized their cause. Playing the anthem staged the nation without a state, an act that was illegal in China and carried severe punishment. The audience bore witness to a ritual that conjured up the nation as a collective aspiration, uniting the people who pledged allegiance.

The Uyghur leadership and advocacy organizations' missions have always emphasized freedom of speech as well as cultural and political self-determination. In particular, they have based their advocacy on the International Bill of Human Rights, including the Universal Declaration of Human Rights, the International Covenant on Economic, Social, and Cultural Rights (ICESCR), and the International Covenant on Civil and Political Rights (ICCPR). The ICCPR was adopted by the United Nations General Assembly in 1966 (United Nations 1976) and includes the right to life and freedom of speech, religion, and assembly, as well as voting rights. The Uyghur leadership tended to focus on self-determination but not independence, with the right to self-determination stipulated in Article 1.1 of the ICCPR (United Nations 1976). It states: "All peoples have the right of self-determination. By virtue of that right they freely determine their political status and freely pursue their economic, social and cultural development" (United Nations 1976, 173).

Moreover, the name *East Turkistan* and the notion of self-determination were tied to the free performance of culture, language, and religion, as stated in Article 27 of the ICCPR: "In those States in which ethnic, religious or linguistic minorities exist, persons belonging to such minorities shall not be denied the right, in community with the other members of their group, to enjoy their own culture, to profess and practise their own religion, or to use their own language" (United Nations 1976, 179). The right to self-determination is tied to political status and the free enactment of cultural identity but has slippery legal grounds for minorities within a sovereign state. Even more, the right to self-determination has been linked to *peoples*

(United Nations 1976, 173), and no clear distinction has been made among concepts like *peoples, indigenous* groups, and *minority* groups (Bloch 2001). *East Turkistan,* as used by diasporic Uyghurs, was associated with freedom of thought and religion as stated in the ICCPR (Article 18), freedom of expression and information (Article 19), and the right to democratic governance and participation (Article 25). The latter includes the right to partake in the conduct of public affairs. Article 21(3) of the Universal Declaration of Human Rights highlights the people's will as the legitimate base for a government's authority (United Nations 1948). Uyghurs appealed to this will as the base for political and cultural self-determination.

Donors are key for the political advocacy of underrepresented groups (Bob 2005). Over the years, the National Endowment for Democracy (NED) has been a major donor to Uyghur advocacy. NED was founded in the early 1980s and describes itself as a private, nonprofit foundation dedicated to the growth and strengthening of democratic institutions around the world. Each year, with funding from the US Congress, the NED supports more than 1,600 projects of nongovernmental groups in more than ninety countries (https:// www.ned.org/about/). There is debate about whether an organization can be private and independent if oversight lies with Congress and the Department of State. This debate is fueled by the fact that the organization was founded by members of Congress in the final decade of the Cold War and has supported anti-communist and pro-market forces from Latin America to Southeast Asia (for the origins of the NED, see Søndergaard 2020). Nevertheless, the organization has always had its defenders, such as historian Timothy Garton Ash (2004), who argues that authoritarian governments like those in the Balkans would still be in place had it not been for the intervention of the NED. As one of the biggest financial and political supporters of Uyghur advocacy, the organization is a catalyst in promoting the Uyghur cause across national borders and through panel discussions, conferences, and leadership workshops from Washington, D.C., to Geneva. As a semi-autonomous organization with oversight by the US Congress and the Department of State, the NED cannot support independence struggles. However, it finds other ways to advocate on behalf of the groups it funds, such as using the names *Xinjiang* as well as *East Turkistan* for Uyghur advocacy projects and supporting self-determination of the Uyghurs as a push for Western-style democracy in the region.

During my interviews with NED managing staff in Washington, D.C., they emphasized transparency about project funding and the fact that the NED only supports Uyghur democracy and human rights efforts such as freedom of expression and religion. It does not support independence. All funded projects are listed on its website, including the ones related to Uyghur advocacy. A search for "East Turkistan" on the NED's grants page displays several projects (NED 2021). The text describes the supported project country as "Xinjiang/East Turkistan (China)" and thus acknowledges the Uyghurs' struggle for self-determination while paying diplomatic tribute to a sovereign country (China). The NED-supported projects have a clear focus on research and documentation of human rights violations in Xinjiang, and on advocacy training and capacity building, including Uyghur women and youth. Related projects focus on the digital documentation of rights violations as well as intervention through the arts. The financial support ranges from USD 55,000 to USD 400,000.

There are other contexts in which the NED gestured to the support of self-determination of the Uyghurs in an autonomous "East Turkistan." An example is the speech by Louisa Greve, NED vice president at the time of the quote below. In her opening of a panel on the future of Uyghur-Han relations in China on December 16, 2011, she insisted that the organization does not support secessionism, something that the Chinese government has accused the Uyghur leadership of in the past:

> [N]one of these groups are advocating to split the country. They are not raising the flag of independence. They want to leave open the question of democratic voice, democratic decision-making processes to determine the future of China and for the people living in Xinjiang eh or East Turkistan, another term for the same eh land. (Greve 2011, 5:20)

Louisa Greve navigated the difficult terrain of international diplomacy by contesting any critique against the NED to undermine China's national sovereignty by funding Uyghur advocacy groups. She makes clear that the NED supports a democratic and human rights agenda, also in the case of the Uyghurs. Greve self-corrects after uttering the name *Xinjiang*. She adds the name *East Turkistan* as "another term for the same eh land," possibly as a gesture to the naming practice used by Uyghur advocacy groups. As a policy expert, Putonghua speaker, and vice president, Greve must be aware of the contested nature of the term *East Turkistan*. Nevertheless, in order to show consistent support for the Uyghurs and their projects, the name is inserted into political discourse. In an act of late retaliation, China sanctioned the NED in 2019 in response to the Hong Kong Human Rights and Democracy Act by the US Congress, alongside Human Rights Watch (NED 2019).

The human rights and democracy discourses are part of a metalanguage that is fit to be used along the political spectrum for various purposes, from arguing for freedom of religion to invading Iraq (Douzinas 2007). In lieu of an alternative means for inducing political change, *human rights* is the main premise in the Uyghurs' and their supporters' struggle in the United States and in Germany. Douzinas puts it in these words:

> Every time a poor, oppressed, tortured person uses the language of rights—because no other is currently available—to protest, resist, fight, she draws from and connects with the most honourable [. . .] morality and politics of the Western world. (2007, 33)

The "Western" approach to use and misuse human rights is ripe for critique. The disenfranchised cannot easily push for human rights as a legitimate tool for political mobilization (Dutt 2001). The mobilization must be supported by influential actors, many of whom are embedded in the geopolitical logics of a Western-based legal codex emphasizing the liberal, autonomous, and free-willed subject. In their special issue on dispossession and human rights from a feminist perspective, critics like Hesford and Lewis (2016) argue that human rights cement geopolitical hierarchies in the name of a politicized humanism. This claim seems to apply to the National Endowment for Democracy, whose support of the Uyghurs cannot be understood without its broader ideological mission of democratizing ascending nations like China.

Schultheis Moore (2016) asks about the alternatives to claim rights as a person beyond the rigid individualism and legal personhood that have historically defined human rights discourse. She suggests basing human rights definitions on subjects bound by historical dispossession, as in the case of the descendants of slaves claiming reparations from Europe. Schultheis Moore built on Butler and Athanasiou (2013), who propose a shift in human rights law and discourse from the autonomous self to collectivity in the struggle against dispossession. Dispossession, in their writing, refers to being disposable as a person and group and yet having the potential for political agency growing out of the experience of not being a person before the law (Schultheis Moore 2016, 167). While Uyghurs are persons before the law, in China and abroad, they can be said to have experience of ultimate physical and symbolic dispossession, based on the ongoing marginalization of their language and culture as well as the growing evidence of forced internment in China (Byler 2021b; Clarke 2022; University of British Columbia and Simon Fraser University n.d.).

Scholars have long pointed to the fact that bearing witness to violence is still regarded an act by an autonomous subject. They have highlighted the relationality of humans and social processes and asked to go beyond identitarian discourses of recognition toward "response-ability" for each other (Oliver 2001, 5). The latter includes historical contextualization (Schultheis Moore 2016, 169). For the Chinese government, Xinjiang—like Tibet—has been and will always be an integral part of the Chinese state and territory. For Uyghurs and their supporters, this claim is historically contested. Therefore, historical contextualization will always be subject to heated political, legal, and academic debates.

As a further critique, Ignatieff (2002, 74) describes the discursive misuse of human rights as a "sekuläre Religion" ("secular religion"). Human rights are a popular term in Western discourse with strong moral undertones. They are part of the rhetorical toolbox of politicians and amplified through media discourse but remain weak in their application and consequence. "International human rights have become the universal morality and ideology of the age," Douzinas had already concluded rather skeptically in 2007 (181). Likewise, Pheng Cheah (2006) critiques the universal assumptions in human rights discourse. He identifies capitalism as setting the structural and essentially unequal terms on which humans can claim certain rights. In other words, human rights neither have a universal basis to be claimed, nor do they construct persons on the margins the same as persons in the center (Cheah 2006; Hopgood 2013; Schultheis Moore 2016). Rancière summarizes it in these clear words: "They seem to be of no use. [. . .] Those rights that appear to be useless in their place are sent abroad, along with medicine and clothes, to people deprived of medicine, clothes, and rights" (2004, 307).

Cheah's and Rancière's conclusions seem to apply to the Uyghurs, at least in part. Up until 2018, Uyghurs had been largely ignored and yet ready to be used as a playing card by governments against an economically and politically rising China. Amnesty International, Human Rights Watch, and Uyghur diasporic organizations like the World Uyghur Congress have lobbied for years for governments to acknowledge human rights violations in Xinjiang but without much international traction. In addition to media reports about internment camps in Xinjiang, states were important in the human rights debate through tangible economic pressure they put on China. In 2018, former president Trump declared a trade war against China. Uyghurs became an important playing card again in this trade war through imposed tariffs on Chinese goods and boycotts of Xinjiang cotton and products created through forced labor. In 2020, the Uyghur Human Rights Policy Act became a US federal law that requires government actors to report human rights violations against the Uyghurs in XUAR. President Trump signed the bill and passed it into law on June 17, 2020.[1] The act requires various government agencies to identify any Chinese officials who are held responsible for detention, torture, and inhuman treatment of Muslim minority groups (not only Uyghurs), who are then subject to sanctions. The irony of this act has to be highlighted. It was a former US political leader, President G. W. Bush, who put Uyghurs in detention in Guantanamo Bay in the name of national security and went to war against the Muslim-majority nations of Afghanistan and Iraq.

In early 2021, the European Union followed with sanctions, and travel bans and asset freezes were implemented against Chinese officials in early 2021 by the European Parliament (European Parliament 2021). The private sector took action as well. H&M banned the sourcing of cotton in Xinjiang in March of 2021, with the consequence of Chinese netizens calling for the boycott of H&M products, among others, and the erasure of the firm from e-commerce platforms in China. Meanwhile, China remains one of the most important markets in the world for many companies including Volkswagen. The German company was the market leader in car sales in China in 2018 (4.21 million cars sold) (Volkswagen Group 2019) and has a factory in Urumqi/Xinjiang, among several others in China. The German government has ratified a law, to be in effect from 2023, which requires companies to be transparent in their supply chains in order to ensure human rights standards, including the ban of forced labor (Deutscher Bundestag 2021). For the companies, internal and external audits become increasingly difficult in China, however, as interviews with German companies in Xinjiang suggest (Heide

2021). In the future, transnational corporations in China will feel the squeeze even more to adhere to the legal standards set by China, on the one hand, and those by governments outside the country, on the other.

Despite the critique of human rights as a mere discursive legitimation for all types of universalizing projects, human rights cannot be pushed aside on the basis of a moral critique alone. The latter would play into the hands of governments that want their own nationalized rights frames recognized without accountability to an international community. With the rise of populist and autocratic governments calling for restrictions to freedom of information and the media, human rights have to remain part of the political process and of international legal frameworks. At the same time, human rights experts, NGOs, civil society, academics, and the media have the task of pointing to misappropriations and the usage of human rights as a proxy for ulterior political purposes.

SOCIAL MEDIA AND TRANSGRESSION

Uyghur organizations have used social media platforms for their advocacy for a while. Since at least 2010, Uyghurs in Germany and in the United States have been active on YouTube, Facebook, and Twitter (e.g., Chen 2014; Nur-Muhammad et al. 2016). NurMuhammad and colleagues (2016) illustrate how Uyghurs used Facebook to create transnational community through political messages as well as popular culture. Clothey and colleagues' (2016) research showed how Uyghurs play with sarcasm, metaphor, and Uyghur sayings as euphemistic means to comment on issues like unemployment of Uyghur youth or surveillance. In sum, the internet was and is essential for a transnational Uyghur identity, as Reyhan (2012) had already pointed out. According to Butler and Athanasiou, names are part of a performative politics and collective identity and can challenge social realities (2013, 99). Self-naming is key with regard to determining the parameters under which the uttering of a name is possible, argue Butler and Athanasiou (2013, 137). Members of the Uyghur diaspora and their supporters set those parameters on digital platforms like Twitter.

The following analysis traces Twitter discourse from 2011 to early 2021 with the goal of identifying keywords in Uyghur advocacy. Twitter was chosen as it is an important platform for Uyghur diasporic communication and as the public accounts are available for analysis. The search_users function from the

R package *rtweet* was employed to find users whose usernames or Twitter biographies contained the terms "Uigur," "Uighur" or "Uyghur," which yielded 189, 185, and 1,000 accounts respectively.[2] (The API [application programming interface] was limited to 1,000 accounts per query.) Account names, follower counts, and locations were extracted from the downloaded data. Accounts were kept that had more than one hundred followers. The final set contained 453 accounts, with a total of 602,136 tweets. The most recent tweet in this sample was posted March 8, 2021, and the oldest January 21, 2008.

To facilitate more accurate language recognition, the data were cleaned by removing hyperlinks, @ mentions, hashtags, and emojis from the tweet text, resulting in several empty entries, which were removed from the dataset. The remaining dataset contained 520,974 tweets. Out of those, 344,796 (66 percent) were in English (posted by 410 out of 453 accounts, including both tweets and retweets). While the tweets were largely in English, other languages used were Chinese and Uyghur as well as Japanese, French, Arabic, German, Indonesian, and Malay. Tweets in German amounted to only 1.5 percent. The high percentage of English tweets can be explained by the fact that most Uyghur advocacy is conducted in English as the lingua franca to increase global reach. Another explanation is that Uyghurs in Germany are not as active on Twitter and thereby continue the trend of lower social media engagement compared to their diasporic counterparts that Reyhan noted in 2012.

In order to focus on the more influential accounts within this Twitter network, the minimum number of followers was adjusted to 1,000. The filtered data contained 295,664 tweets posted by 158 accounts. The most recent tweet in the sample was posted March 8, 2021, and the oldest April 15, 2009. Seventy-four percent of tweets in this group were in English. The top ten accounts with followers' count and indicated location (in parentheses) were: Luke de Pulford (105,438, London), WUC (36,741, Munich, Germany), Arslan Hidayat (29,599, Urumqi, Uyghuristan), Uyghur Human Rights Project (26,528, Washington, D.C.), Uyghur from E.T. (20,200, no location), Abdugheni Sabit (16,331, Aksu, Uyghuristan), Voice of Uyghur (15,843, Washington, D.C.), Tahir Imin Uyghurian (15,127, Washington D.C.), Rian Thum (14,076, England), and Aydin Anwar (14,007, no location).

The World Uyghur Congress (WUC) account is the number two account in terms of followers. It is analyzed in more depth here as the WUC is the umbrella organization for Uyghur diasporic advocacy worldwide and sets the discursive terms for political mobilization. Luke de Pulford, the number one account in terms of followers, works for Arise, a registered nonprofit organization in the UK and the United States, which fights to end slavery and human trafficking with a global reach. He was left out of the analysis because of the general human rights mission of his NGO and only partial focus on the Uyghurs over the years. As there were very few posts by the WUC from 2009 to 2010, the analysis starts with the year 2011.

A close reading of the extracted tweets revealed a focus on *China* as a place where serious problems occur in relation to the Uyghurs. These problems were termed *camps* and *genocide*. So far, the insight is not surprising. In order to obtain a more precise understanding of the key terms and the meanings, as well as their change over time, words like *China, Chinese, Uyghur, Uyghurs, China's, people, Uigur, Uigurs,* and retweets were removed. The results indicate that the name *Xinjiang* was very present from 2011 to 2014, with *East Turkistan* being highly visible as well. The analysis of the tweet content showed that the term *Xinjiang* predominantly occurred in news media texts, which were circulated by the WUC. The WUC therefore acted as a clearinghouse for the circulation of media content critical of China. The media sources included Reuters, the BBC, the *Financial Times*, *Al Jazeera*, *Le Monde*, the *South China Morning Post* (Hong Kong), and Deutsche Welle. They also included US-funded media broadcasters, including Voice of America and Radio Free Asia, and think tank–affiliated news outlets, such as the *Diplomat* by the Lowry Institute, an Australian foreign-affairs think tank. In the circulated media reports, *Xinjiang* was a descriptor for the historical, cultural, and geographical limits imposed on Uyghur life. Moreover, the results shown in Figures 1–6 illustrate that *human_right* is either the most frequently used term over the years or the second-most frequently used term in the WUC account's discourse. The chart for 2011 is displayed in Figure 1 to exemplify that *human_right* was second to *xinjiang*, with *xinjiang* being related to critical media reports about the province, as explained above.

By 2015, the term *human_right* had taken over. This shift could be linked to the "Strike Hard Campaign against Violent Terrorism," effective in XUAR since May of 2014, followed by the introduction of a Counterterrorism Law in 2015 (ILO 2015) and increasing media reports on arrests of

World Uyghur Congress-20 Most Frequent Words 2011

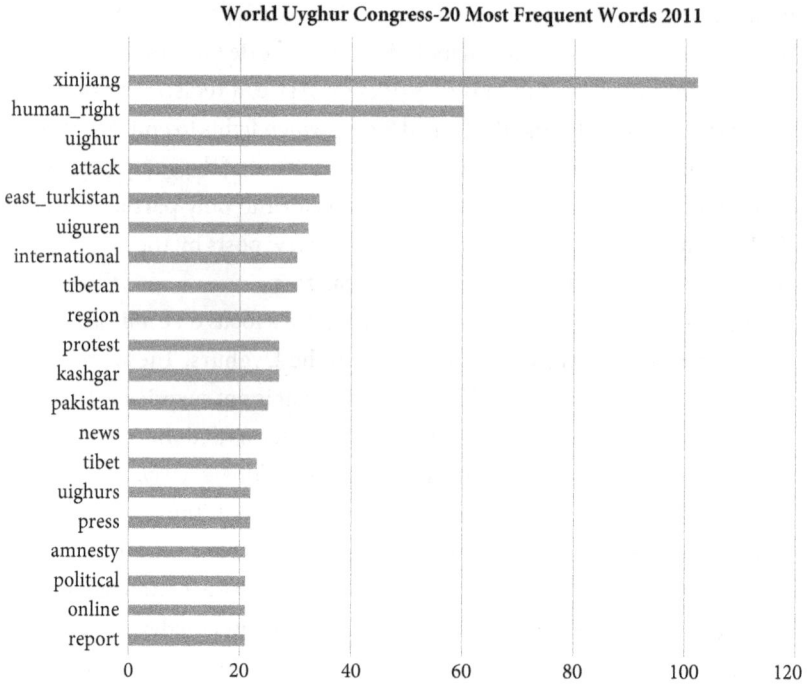

FIGURE 1. Twitter word frequency WUC 2011. Source: From author.

Uyghurs, culminating in allegations of detention camps. The WUC tweets and retweets from 2018 to 2021 make clear reference to these camps and the debate on whether mass detention of Uyghurs constitutes genocide. *Human_right* becomes the semantic and moral anchor for the digital debate on social and legal justice for the Uyghurs, confirming the core mission of the advocacy organization. Figures 2–5 show the wordclouds from 2015, 2017, 2019, and 2021, which represent the centrality of the term. Wordclouds are visually compact summaries of terms occurring in a body of text, with size indicating frequency (Mathews et al. 2015). In other words, the larger the word size in the cloud, the higher the frequency. Wordclouds can appear as crude visual representations with somewhat predictable outcomes. At the same time, a wordcloud can be a useful starting point to show the most frequently occurring key terms in a body of text—the WUC Twitter account text in this case—providing the empirical starting point for further analysis (see Mathews et al. 2015). *Human_right* is the most important key term in

2015 and all the way up to 2021, as the wordclouds, beginning with Figures 2 and 3, demonstrate.

FIGURE 2. Twitter wordcloud WUC 2015. Source: From author.

FIGURE 3. Twitter wordcloud WUC 2017. Source: From author.

In 2019, the terms *camp*, *detain*, and *internment camp* emerged (Figure 4), pointing to an increasingly alarming situation in the region.

FIGURE 4. Twitter wordcloud WUC 2019. Source: From author.

Genocide is very present in the Twitter discourse in 2021 (Figure 5), reflecting discussions on the government level of various countries of whether the treatment of the Uyghurs in China constitutes genocide or not.

FIGURE 5. Twitter wordcloud WUC 2021. Source: From author.

The Figure 6 chart on word frequency is another visual representation of the call for *human rights* and *action* in 2021 based on allegations of *genocide* against the Uyghurs in *East Turkistan* (mentioned key terms in italics).

World Uyghur Congress -20 Most Frequent Words 2021

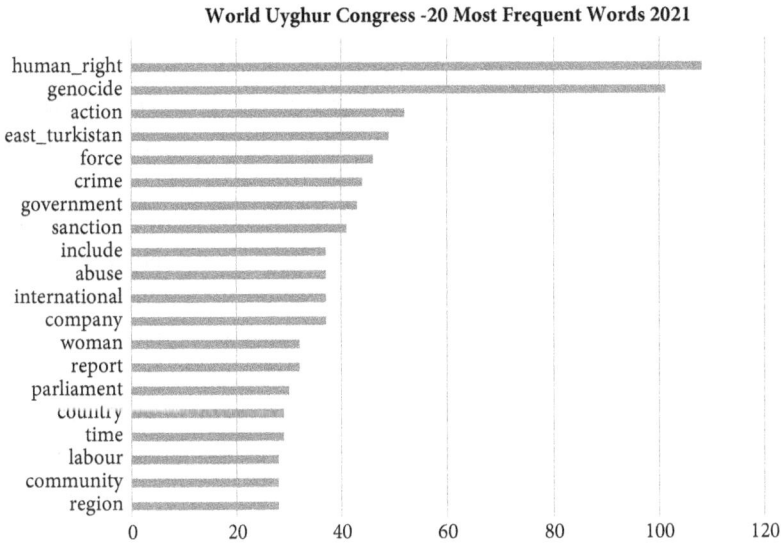

FIGURE 6. Twitter word frequency WUC 2021. Source: From author.

In sum, human rights have been the focal point of Uyghur advocacy for years and took center stage in 2021. Human rights are tightly linked to the imagination of Uyghur self-determination in the form of *East Turkistan*. The ways *East Turkistan* is imagined and presented to the world has changed, however. On the 2021 WUC website, *East Turkistan* has hyperlinks with topics like internment. This is different from earlier versions. In 2010–11, for example, the landing page of the website included the map of *East Turkistan* as an imagination of the cultural nation. There were hyperlinks to Uyghur history, religion, language, and culture and an archive of photographs about the natural beauty of the province, its history, architecture, food, and social life. Digital space created and archived the lost homeland and represented the nation online.

In 2021, the World Uyghur Congress' discourse has shifted from a nostalgic representation of culture to a decisive politicized humanism and the appeal to save life in the name of human rights. Sovereignty might remain an unfulfilled aspiration for the Uyghurs, given the strong stance by the Chinese government, which is in line with other governments who have fought hard against independence movements. Examples are Spain in the case of the Catalans or Turkey in the case of the Kurdish people. Nevertheless, *East Turkistan* remains a transgressive naming practice to express aspirations for self-determination—for some independence—in the language of humanism and rights, thereby making the international community answer the injustices in the region.

The discussion so far has centered on more traditional approaches to political advocacy and defiant speech. Uyghurs made use of the legal mechanisms for free speech guaranteed in the Constitutions of the United States and Germany and created a communicative space dominated by the discourse on rights. Diasporic organizations in particular have spearheaded the advocacy discourse. Unlike promoting independence, advocating for human rights was not subversion or a deliberate challenge of the status quo (see Jenks 2003). It stayed within accepted political and moral frameworks. Art, to the contrary, did challenge the status quo and became another unruly practice to expose social injustice. It will be addressed next.

ART AND CREATIVE POLITICS

Uyghur advocacy ranged from traditional lobbying strategies with governments and United Nations organizations to social media mobilization. There were some activists who felt that these approaches were too schematic. They pushed the limits of traditional advocacy and engaged the arts as a way to educate about the Uyghurs. I use one case by a female artist, whom I call Anargul, to illustrate how alternative types of advocacy were transgressions in two ways: the form of advocacy and the person doing the advocacy. Art is an unusual genre in Uyghur political work and can point out the social and moral limits of what is acceptable in a given society at a given time. Anargul herself was a symbol of social and moral unruliness as she was single and an artist. She pushed the limits of how advocacy could be done and who was allowed to speak for the nation.

Anargul lived by herself in Munich. For her, freedom of expression was based on creativity and social bonds beyond the Uyghur community, especially with other intellectuals and artists across Germany and Europe. As an artist and a woman having grown up in a heavily gendered culture, she was very aware of the consequences of going against the status quo, which she did with her art and living by herself. She had attended arts school and had been at the Xinjiang Arts Academy for twelve years. She described herself as one of the third-generation artists in Xinjiang. Her unconventional life in Urumqi had made her a keen observer and critic of conventions and a culture in which men told her what to do. She knew about the power of labeling. In Urumqi at the Arts Academy, so she told me, she remained *the female* and *the Uyghur* but never the artist, despite having had an exhibition in Beijing in 1994, which was an accomplishment for an artist from the border provinces.

When we met for an interview and the conversation came to the question of Uyghur culture and the limits of the acceptable, Anargul immediately answered that she had not been invited to Meshrep. Meshrep is an event practiced in Uyghur communities and across Central Asia after harvesting. It includes social gatherings and entertainment through food, songs, dance, and traditional poetry. Anargul assumed that she had not been invited because she was a single woman. Meshrep was a family affair. She felt alienated from Uyghurs, she said, and felt closer to her German friends. "I have arrived in Germany" was a phrase to express this state of being and feeling. Anargul thought of herself as an educated woman but it was difficult for her to find a well-educated Uyghur man, she said. She estimated that 99 percent of Uyghurs, most of whom were men, had come to Germany as refugees. The problem was, in her opinion, that these men sent for "mail order brides from home." She laughed while uttering this phrase. Hers was the language of art but not politics, a fact that other Uyghurs could not understand in her opinion.

Anargul had been in Germany for fourteen years and was a German citizen. Like many other Uyghurs in Germany, she came to seek asylum. In the beginning, she stayed in a shared asylum seeker accommodation in Munich. The room was small and painting helped her to stay positive. She painted what she called "my homeland" as she still missed it dearly. I interviewed her in German in her spacious home, which was full of her paintings. She shared the following observations about her nontraditional advocacy and her biographic details:

> Uyghurs here do not understand the worth of art and paintings. I don't want that much contact with Uyghurs. I want to talk about art and art history. Most of the Uyghurs here don't like that. There is no academic life here among Uyghurs. My friends back home were all artists. I was the only Uyghur artist in Germany and maybe Europe when I arrived in the late 1990s. And I don't like boxing myself in. I am not Uyghur, not European, not Chinese. I am not an easy one. I am a difficult woman. I listen to Radio Free Asia every day and also write in internet forums about art. My biggest wish is to have Uyghurs be treated like other people on this earth. That they should be able to speak their own language and practice their culture. I organized a cultural evening, not to showcase Uyghur culture but to show our children the beauty of culture and art. Some teens did not come. They said, "We do not have time." That was disappointing. But I would like to continue and organize a cultural evening with a bazaar, food, information center, painting walls, and so on. I would also like to see more art in politics. I think Germans and the other people around the world get a bit tired of Uyghur demonstrations and people shouting slogans and walking in the streets. I think art can be powerful and reaches the hearts of people more than an assertive type of politics that frightens people who are not interested in the politics of a faraway place. (my translation from German into English)

Anargul thought of herself as a freethinker, not attached to religion or other ideologies. But she cared deeply about what she called the "homeland" and wanted to contribute to making it known in Germany through her art. She insisted that she was an artist and not a politician although she emphasized that she felt connected to the Uyghur community through the desire to live freely, which meant to her to have a home where she could practice her art and live without fear of persecution and censorship. Her desire for freedom of expression and information became apparent in her listening to

Radio Free Asia, painting, educating the young about the power of art, and writing in digital fora.

Freedom of expression also meant for Anargul "not boxing herself in" and transcending received ethnic and gender limits. Implicitly, Anargul argued from the position of human rights, such as freedom of opinion and expression and the right to creativity as enshrined in Article 15 of the United Nations' International Covenant on Economic, Social and Cultural Rights (ICESCR) (OHCHR 1966). Artistic expression is one alternative to received ways of doing political advocacy. However, the Uyghur community was still in need of learning about how to make use of art in their collective lives, in Anargul's view. For Anargul, art meant aesthetic appreciation without a necessary purpose. She used the example of the heart as the sensory place that art speaks to and that makes people open up to the other and the matter at hand. In her view, this was in contrast to the commonly practiced type of diasporic politics based on verbal indignation and anger, emotions that shut down interactions. Those emotions were difficult to mirror in people and groups not having had similar experiences.

Anargul was one of the few Uyghurs I met who used her art as a form of disobedient expression. She crossed the limit of what was expected in diasporic politics at the time of the interview in 2010, which was mobilizing for protest and using verbal and written means. She suggested an alternative path to political advocacy through the aesthetic and affective grammar of art. She wanted to reach people through beauty and aesthetic appreciation and not through tired political slogans. Others have shared her argument that seeking pleasure and beauty through art is not a self-serving act. Protest art, including paintings, photography, graffiti, and performance, intervenes into established orders of aesthetics and participation by moving art and social commentary into public space. From street artist Banksy to the Russian punk rock band Pussy Riot, protest art activates people to participate in social processes and to shape public space through aesthetic and political commentary (Monachesi and Turco 2017).

Anargul never talked about herself as a female artist but as an artist who told the story of cultures under pressure in a visual way. Brian Holmes describes art as a way for a collective to reflect on its imagination and its central tropes (Holmes 2006). This understanding of art was also Anargul's. She tried to tease out collectively shared tropes that were important for Uyghurs living in the diaspora and to combine them with a universal humanism. Her paintings merged physical nature with traditional Uyghur life, such as old men riding donkeys, people selling watermelons in the market, and girls dancing, their long braids swinging around their bodies. The paintings spoke to key imaginations, such as the ancient art of trading, aestheticized female beauty, and the balance between humans and nature. While the paintings depicted an idealized local that was on the verge of disappearance, they also transcended a local way of life and evoked universal themes, such as the preservation of nature, the tension between globalization and local traditions, and the struggle of women to reorder gendered formations. For Anargul, art was democratic as it spoke to fundamental human creativity, desires, and fears with the potential for social change. Anargul did not want to see her art as political, and yet political it was. The tropes and cultural practices she (re)presented spoke precisely to the fear of loss as well as to the desire for social change. The freedom to express those fears and desires through artistic creativity was the basic premise shaping her disobedience against systems of power, including autocratic governance and patriarchy.

In sum, Anargul argued for "unhomeliness" (Bhabha 1994, 9), for being rooted and yet working against the totalism of those roots. This can be done through thinking and acting from a place "where 'presencing' begins" (Bhabha 1994, 9) and people form new relationships and alliances. For Anargul, those alliances were connections to other artists in Germany and Europe, support for her exhibitions, and work with young people. Art was the universal language to create communities who rally around the beliefs of artistic freedom of expression, the courage to try new ways of seeing the world, and acceptance of different ways of living. Art could induce change, in the artist's view. Art was the site to merge different cultural and ideological positions and to create something unexpected in which people find beauty and a sense of togetherness. Anargul's art was thus different in its unruliness from the conventional advocacy as practiced by the World Uyghur Congress, for example. She created social interactions beyond a rights discourse and around universal themes, which people from different backgrounds could relate to, including beauty, well-being, and artistic play. The themes speak to the conditions of displacement and emplacement and yet are an alternative take on dislocation, suffering, and exile. Artistic approaches to Uyghur identity politics are still rare. A recent publication composed by artists, poets, and scholars, *The Contest of the Fruits* (Ha, Slavs and Tatars 2021), provides a refreshing angle on Uyghur culture and resilience through the lenses of poetry, hip-hop, and calligraphy, among others. The collection is an example of the productive alliance of scholarship and art to gain new insights into identity politics through creative and humoristic boundary-crossing. A different type of creativity can be detected in another approach to identity politics, namely its digital control, discussed next.

SURVEILLANCE

The networked nature of social media, relatively easy access in 2021, and the digital literacy of diasporic members made social media a fertile ground for unruly speech and collective self representation. Prediction and preemption are part of networked logics (Amoore 2011, 2013), and the limits of speech need to be continuously adjusted in digital space (Bratich 2012). Three-quarters of all existing servers enabled for deep learning were based in China in 2018, according to Jon Cropley, senior principle analyst at HIS Markit (*Bloomberg News* 2018). Data-rich, innovative AI development is linked to a broader agenda of data-intense AI technology, which could be used for population control inside China as well as in the Belt and Road Initiative states, or for the health sector or the military. Eventually, so Beraja, Yang, and Yuchtman (2020) argue, massive datasets collected from jurisdiction-poor populations could be a strategic advantage in trade policies. An iteration of the argument has been made by other scholars who have pointed to the importance of migrant populations in jurisdiction-poor areas for digital experimentation (Daly et al. 2019).

Technology experts have found increasing evidence over the years of long-term targeted digital attacks against the Uyghurs and their advocates such as the Scarlet Mimic campaign (Stone 2016). This cyber-espionage campaign targeted human rights organizations as well as other entities knowledgeable about the work of those organizations and individuals, including academic institutions and governments. Malware and trolls are key to sowing uncertainty through disinformation among diasporic Uyghurs. The University of Toronto's Citizen Lab (Munk School of Global Affairs and Public Policy) studied the use of malware by China to target diasporic Uyghurs and Tibetans (Citizen Lab 2014; Whittaker 2019). The technology was developed by the China Electronics Technology Group Corporation (CETC), a defense manufacturer run by the Chinese state. The company grew out of military research labs in China and a defense-based mission to include civilian securitization, which means that Chinese military surveillance technology is tightly linked to civilian surveillance technology (Buckley and Mozur 2019).

Mobile security firm Lookout has estimated malware to be working on diasporic Uyghurs' Android phones since 2013 (Lookout 2020). The researchers surveyed four surveillanceware families, including GoldenEagle, SilkBean, DoubleAgent, and CarbonSteal. Malware can imitate virtual private networks (VPNs) to discover prohibited content access and to imitate apps. Examples of apps that are mimicked are Sakuy (Uyghur music service), Tawarim (e-commerce site), or Tibbiyjawhar (pharma app). Some apps mimic real ones from third-party platforms, including Twitter, Facebook, and Baidu. The apps collect information on people's behaviors, including shopping, beauty, music, and news consumption in the diaspora. Some of the malware is able to delete itself when the chance of detection is high as a result of its using too much phone battery. The apps are able to turn on a phone's microphone, record location and conversations, export photos, or even record calls, according to the Lookout report.

Malware apps are intended to reach a large international target group. They present Uyghur in four scripts (Arabic, Latin, Cyrillic, and Chinese) and are available in many languages, including English, Arabic, Chinese, Pashto, Turkish, Persian, Malay, Bahasa Indonesia, Uzbek, Hindi, and Urdu. Targeted countries range from Afghanistan to Egypt, Turkey, Indonesia, Pakistan, Malaysia, and France, among many others. The Lookout report concluded that apps have specifically targeted Uyghur-reading and speaking communities and that surveillance of Muslim groups was also carried out through the technology (Lookout 2020). A peak of the surveillanceware was 2015, which suggests that the malware has been part of the "Strike

Hard Campaign against Violent Terrorism," which started in XUAR in May of 2014.

Internet security and governance sources have reported on the surveillance of diasporas from China at least since 2010. In 2009, when I interviewed staff of the UAA in Washington, D.C., I encountered information technology (IT) experts who were busy identifying malware from suspected mainland Chinese sources and who installed protection devices on computers. The communication among the offices of Uyghur advocacy organizations had been interrupted by viruses in the email system, and emails were sent out in the name of staff members who had not written them. These observations are confirmed by extant research (Blasco 2013). Digital attacks on Uyghur organizations have been frequent and have targeted prominent advocacy organizations such as the WUC and UAA. In September of 2012, the UAA and the UHRP websites were down for two weeks (UHRP 2014). Spear phishing is also common. In 2013, Kaspersky Lab and AlienVault identified a technical issue in Microsoft Office for Mac when email users downloaded files on Uyghur human rights that were infected with malware (Blasco 2013; UHRP 2014). DDoS (distributed denial of service) attacks are frequent on advocacy websites like the UAA or the UHRP, as reported by the organizations' staff as early as 2009 and confirmed by the UHRP in its 2014 report on the "digital cage" Uyghurs are living in.

Surveillance of the diaspora happens in the name of national security. The rationale by the Chinese government is that Uyghurs living outside China are in danger of being radicalized and spreading terrorism to and in Xinjiang and across China. Therefore, any person returning to China, especially from a designated sensitive country, including Egypt, Turkey, Malaysia, Indonesia, Syria, Pakistan, or Afghanistan, has to be detained and checked (Allen-Ebrahimian 2019, referring to Bulletin No. 2, June 16, 2017, of the *China Cables*, published by the International Consortium of Investigative Journalists 2019). Moreover, relatives living abroad have become a liability for Uyghurs in China. Those family relations can be found out based on phone calls. Metadata like time of phone call received, duration, and international country code are fed into the IJOP database, and police officers can make the decision to detain or not (Allen-Ebrahimian 2019). Interviewees in Germany and the United States have spoken out frequently about their fears of relatives being safe. Even people who lived a rather apolitical life were very cautious as they were afraid of being spied on by fellow Uyghurs. Already in 2010, Rushangul, a woman in her thirties in Munich, said, "We know that Uyghurs do not necessarily volunteer to spy on us. But we also know that anybody who was able to see family in China could be a potential informant." She explained that Uyghurs living in Germany can be blackmailed by Chinese officials: "If you want to see your family, you can, but you need to give us information on your Uyghur friends." Some people, so Rushangul suspected, accepted the offer as they were desperate to see a dying father or mother or attend a sister's wedding. In addition to the "travel in exchange for information" bargains, a person could be in danger because of the ignorance of others. This seemed to be the case for Dilnaz. She had just finished a research degree when I interviewed her in Washington, D.C., and her US supervisor had allegedly sent her thesis to a professor in China upon request. Dilnaz's thesis was about the Uyghurs and she knew that her piece could be used against her and her family living in Xinjiang. After that incident, she applied for asylum in the United States and planned on staying there.

Fear was present in other Uyghur diasporic groups, such as the ones in the Netherlands. Franken (2019) shows in his thesis how Uyghurs used social media for political advocacy but also regarded them as unsafe and untrustworthy. The reasons were alleged spread of misinformation by the Chinese government and a lack of transparency of sources. Franken points to the problem of privacy concerns for Uyghurs and the subsequent use of aliases, which made the verification of social media claims even more difficult. Nevertheless, Uyghurs in Franken's study and elsewhere did something that Uyghurs could not or would rarely do before. They testified openly on social media and in human rights tribunals, as discussed in the next chapter, despite the fear for relatives still living in China.

CONCLUSION

Diasporic Uyghur organizations, Uyghur activists, the international media, and human rights organizations have focused international attention on the plight of the Uyghurs and other minority groups in Xinjiang province. The pressure on China has increased, with the Uyghur Human Rights Act passed by the United States and sanctions by European countries. Social media and news media provide a communicative space for defiant speech to happen, including the call for *East Turkistan* in the name of human rights. Human rights were endorsed in the name of minority protection, for humanitarian purposes, or for an expansionist democracy project by organizations like the National Endowment for Democracy. Human rights enacted discursive alliances between Uyghurs, human rights organizations, and political actors through promoting a culture of political participation and disobedient speech. The disobedient practices differed, from interest-driven, global political lobby-work, as represented by the World Uyghur Congress or the Uyghur Human Rights Project, to art. Art had the potential to open up communication spaces that allowed for an intimate reflection on collective identity.

East Turkistan was a catalyst for sociopolitical alliances, transgressing established legal and political codes in China. Unity, participation, and inequality, the main premises linked to *Xinjiang* as used by Uyghurs in China, are mirror images of the premises of belonging and human rights that *East Turkistan* encompasses. Uyghurs in China regarded culture and language policies as well as limited access to resources as reasons for inequality and restricted participation in the economic and sociopolitical life in XUAR. Although not every Uyghur in China wanted more autonomy or even independence from China, the younger generation desired more participation in society, from education to work. Inequality and lack of participation were also embedded in the premise of human rights, which was transported through the name *East Turkistan*. In the diaspora, this desire for social participation shifted to belonging in the sense of political participation and recognition. Digital platforms like Twitter assisted the Uyghur leadership to push the premise of human rights. As Mezzadra and Neilson (2013) write, conflicts "generate geographies-in-the-making" (58) and moments in which we can witness the creation of spaces that counter geographical and cognitive borders. The shift to human rights is indicative of such a moment in which people under duress are trying to move received geographical, political, and cultural borders, retain a sense of belonging, and yet escape another fixed identity. The discussion on suffering and testimonio in chapter 4 illustrates this point further.

The name *East Turkistan* crossed the limit of other-representation into self-representation. The name questioned China as a place where ethnic and social harmony was declared as the normative vision under the leadership of the Chinese Communist Party. It was also a mirror that could be used to imagine Uyghurs as a collective. The form of expression matters, as de Certeau (1997) emphasizes with regard to political protest. Naming is a form of resistant speech that highlights how Uyghurs want to represent themselves, to think and act on their own. Naming also highlights the tensions in diasporic representation. The diversity in ideas ranged from independence to autonomy, from a separate nation to being part of China but highly autonomous in culture, and in economic and political systems.

Moreover, the conditions enabling digital unruly speech need to be understood from a critical perspective. On the one hand, social media discourse threatens to result in hyper-communication in lieu of action. In his essay on the shift toward smart power, control, and psycho-politics in the age of information, Byung-Chul Han (2017, 14–15) writes:

> Smart power cosies up to the psyche rather than disciplining it through coercion or prohibitions. It does not impose silence. Rather, it is constantly calling on us to confide, share and participate: to communicate our opinions, needs, wishes and preferences—to tell all about our lives.

Digital space has become a designated space of the affirmative in which oppressed voices can speak and be heard. There is a circuit of information that gives endless leads for discussion and debate. Herein lies the danger of digital communication for human rights purposes: discourse without action, clicktivist indignation without consequence. Clicktivism is "low-risk, low-cost activity via social media, whose purpose is to raise awareness, produce change, or grant satisfaction to the person engaged in the activity" (Rotman et al. 2011). Halupka (2014) identifies key features of clicktivism, including being an impulsive gesture and spontaneous response by an individual to a political object. It is easily reproduced, noncommittal, and does not require specialist knowledge. Hence, clicktivism has been criticized as lazy activism (Morozov 2009, 2011).

On the other hand, social media like Twitter afford a space in which human rights violations can be circulated and documented. Digital platforms assist Uyghurs and their supporters to proactively engage in horizontal connective action, which means grassroots participation and everyday engagement without dependency on institutionalized advocacy (Bennett and Segerberg 2013; Halupka 2018, Dwonch 2019). The next chapter on testimonio elaborates on this point.

4 | TESTIMONIO AS EMBODIED AND DIGITAL PRACTICE

AS EXPLAINED IN THE INTRODUCTION and chapter 1, I use testimonio to refer to a political genre that has grown out of the persecutions, civil wars, and violence experienced by different populations in Latin America since the 1960s. Testimonio is a personal narrative about traumatic experiences told as an eyewitness account and originally presented as a written text (Beverley 2005). Testimonio was an important genre through which Uyghurs bore witness to collectively experienced injustices. Suffering was the main premise for testifying and transforming witnesses from victims into survivors. Within these logics, Haig-Brown (2003) refers to testimonio as political with the goal of inducing action against injustices. It creates an interactional space in which people "become subjects by virtue of addressivity and response-ability" (Oliver 2001, 90). Testimonio is not about winning an argument but about "[f]inding common ground" (Villenas 2019, 153). Testimonio crosses the limits of silence and taboo and seeks coalition as it stands for the lives of many others (Figueroa 2015). As a survivor, the witness usually does not have a voice in the sociopolitical, economic, and ideological makeup of the state but is driven by the urgency of the situation to speak out.

Uyghurs have served as legal witnesses to events in China for at least two decades now, such as in front of the Congressional-Executive Commission on China, the US Commission on International Religious Freedom, and the US House of Representatives Committee on International Relations. For example, on March 2, 2000, Reyila Abudureyim, a daughter of Rebiya Kadeer, bore witness to her mother's imprisonment and advocacy work for the Uyghurs in front of the House Committee on International Relations.[1] On April 8, 2014, Jewher Ilham, the daughter of imprisoned academic Ilham Tohti, testified to the Congressional-Executive Commission on China about repression against her father (see Tohti 2022).[2] Rebiya Kadeer, together with other Uyghur American Association and UHRP leaders like Nury Turkel have also provided witness accounts in front of the US Commission on International Religious Freedom.[3] Over time, testimonios were given in other contexts and in different formats, in part because of the changing situation of the Uyghurs in China.

Testimonio has been explored in depth as a verbal genre with a long tradition in feminist, decolonial, religious, and legal debates. Faithful witnessing is a term coined by Lugones (2003) to describe witnessing by the oppressed. Like Lugones, Figueroa (2015) discusses faithful witnessing as a subversive act as it actively takes on power through the narrating body. As such, faithful witnessing can be dangerous (Lugones 2003). This is especially true when witnessing happens on digital platforms and the visibility of the witness increases the threat to the witness's physical and psychological safety. The collaborative production and representation of collective experiences are described as key characteristics of the genre (Das et al. 2001; Figueroa 2015; Latina Feminist Group 2001; Lugones 2003; Menchú 1984; Oliver 2001; Smith 2012; to name just a few).

Testimonio has been theorized as an unruly practice and speech event with the potential for change on a collective level (Das et al. 2001). Testimonios are "surrogate sense organs of the absent" (Peters 2009, 25). As surrogate sense organs, they break down experience, archive it, and make it available for sharing and verification. Witnesses have a difficult task to accomplish as they need to straddle the tensions between experience, mode of narration, and evaluation of the truthfulness of accounts by the audience. Ashuri and Pinchevski (2009) conclude that witnessing is "a game of trust" (136). This game of trust is played between the witness, the medium and its gatekeepers, the audience, and preceding discourses. The medium and its gatekeepers play a key role as they create the order of witness discourse, meaning the audience, the conditions of witnessing, the timing, and the consequences of narrating and listening. As an unruly practice, testimonio has the potential to wrest power from the perpetrator, break the taboo related to collective violence, and illuminate the limits and conditions for speaking about trauma. While there is a large body of literature on testimonio in face-to-face settings, digital space has been neglected. Benmayor (2012, 507) has identified the importance of digital testimonio as "the creative multimedia languages of digital storytelling." Digital platforms afford intertextuality and mediated visibility, which are part of the multimedia language Benmayor mentions. They are explored later.

The main differences between embodied and digital testimonio include the purposes of testifying, narrative form, and the affordances of the communicative setting, including intertextuality and visibility. What is called *embodied testimonio* here was presented to me in the form of a personal narrative to share experiences of suffering. *Digital testimonio* refers to eyewitness accounts and related content digitized on websites and social media platforms. Digital testimonios are composed of a multi-genre, intertextual, and multimodal prism of evidence for the purposes of documentation, archiving, and potential future legal action. Those purposes are reminiscent of the witness accounts collected in other rights-abuse contexts in Asia, as in the case of the Khmer Rouge in Cambodia (Sankey 2016), in postwar Sri Lanka (Höglund 2019), or in the case of the Korean women violated by the Japanese military during World War II (Howard 1995; Nozaki 2005; Yang 2008). Witness accounts have to be adapted to the affordances of digital technologies, including to the ways of seeing, hearing, and sharing that those enable. Stefanie Quakernack (2016, 2018) points to this adaptation in her work on digital testimonio of undocumented youth in the United States. She analyzed the media logics that enabled digital witness stories to take shape and be circulated. She cautioned not to oversimplify the shift from embodied to digital testimonio but to illustrate how genre content and form are shaped by digital media and platforms like YouTube. One such difference, as previously identified by Benmayor (2008, 2012), is the different actors involved in the collective production of digital testimonio, including narrators, facilitators, technological experts, digital administrators, and a commenting global audience.

The question of the truthfulness of witness accounts is a reappearing topic (Ashuri and Pinchevski 2009; Frosh 2009; Frosh and Pinchevski 2009; Peters 2009; Schankweiler, Straub, and Wendl 2019). Truthfulness has gained renewed importance in social media contexts (Frosh 2018) and small stories research in the echo chambers of Facebook and Twitter (Georgakopoulou 2016). Frosh and Pinchevski (2009, 1) point to the role of technology in witnessing when they write: "[E]very act of witnessing implies some kind of mediation, [. . .] every act of mediation entails a kind of witnessing, particularly the use of technology as a surrogate for an absent audience." The truth question has to be asked anew in the context of digital technologies where text, pictures, and sound can become a "simulacra without reference" (Han 2015, 41). Short attention span, source credibility, and the oversaturation of audiences with human suffering command the witness to speak in certain ways, as shown later in the section on digital testimonios.

METHODOLOGICAL NOTES

I collected testimonios in face-to-face settings, called embodied testimonios here, and from websites and digital platforms like YouTube and Twitter (digital testimonios). The embodied testimonios were gathered in the United States and in Germany. Uyghurs told me their witness narratives in small cafes, in Uyghur and Turkish restaurants, on benches in the parks of Washington, D.C., and Munich, or in barrack accommodations for asylum seekers in Munich, Germany. Methodologically, it is important to emphasize again that the testimonios were unelicited, which means motivated neither by expectations about narrative style on the part of the interviewer, nor by witness expectations about possible material or symbolic rewards. I have selected four of those testimonios that represent the most common narratives about traumatic experiences, the reasons to leave China, political awakening, and the types of advocacy Uyghurs are involved in. The testimonios represent experiences before Uyghurs received international attention in the wake of the internment and detention allegations against the Chinese state. In other words, they are historical traces, grounding the debates on Uyghurs and rights in the early 2020s in a longer history of difficult experiences.

In addition to in-person testimonios, I discuss digital testimonios based on three sources, that of Rebiya Kadeer, the former WUC president; the Xinjiang Victims Database; and the Uyghur Transitional Justice Database.

Rebiya Kadeer's digital testimonial fragments in the form of YouTube videos and still images are witness to her international advocacy for the Uyghurs based on her personal experiences in China. The digital fragments relate to her autobiography *Himmelsstürmerin* (German version), or *Dragon Fighter: One Woman's Epic Struggle for Peace with China* (English version), which are discussed later. In addition, digital testimonios were collected from the Xinjiang Victims Database that was initiated through crowdfunding by activist Gene Bunin in the United States. The other example, the Uyghur Transitional Justice Database, is a project funded by the National Endowment for Democracy. The two databases present recent projects aimed at gathering and archiving Uyghur witness accounts that could be used in potential legal cases. Overall, the more recent digital testimonios can be seen as a continuation of the testimonios told in the personal interviews based on the premise of suffering.

Narrative analysis is helpful for exploring testimonial form in depth and illuminating its transgressive elements. I built on Koven's (2002) framework for analyzing speaker roles in narratives about personal experiences. The interactional nature of narrating and collaborative knowledge production is not unique to testimonio, as the analysis shows; rather, it has a long tradition in language and communication studies. It is true that the digital interface requires more technical, editorial, and digital literacy competencies. Nevertheless, narratives have always been collectively produced because language and imagination are dialogic in the synchronic and diachronic sense (Bakhtin 1981, 1986). Bakhtin observes: "Our speech [. . .] is filled with others' words [. . .]. These words of others carry with them their own expression, their own evaluative tone, which we assimilate, rework, and reaccentuate" (1986, 89).

Koven's framework is based on several scholarly traditions and concepts in narrative analysis: the functional approach (e.g., Labov 1972), conversation analysis (Sacks, Schegloff, and Jefferson 1974; Schegloff 1997), footing (Goffman 1974), and voicing (Bakhtin 1981, 1986; Jakobson 1957; Voloshinov [1929] 1973). The framework enables researchers to analyze how narrators perform their roles as authors of a story and as interpreters between their story of personal experience, audience, and truthful witness (Witteborn 2007a). In the interpreter role, a speaker can use laughter or evaluative word choices to signal to the listener how a particular character or event should be understood (Koven 2002, 180–184). Narrators can also speak from the perspective of story characters. Linguistically, this can be achieved through reported speech and coming alive as particular "types of people" (Koven 2002, 188). Reported speech can provide insights into the group identification of a narrator and as proof of authenticity of what is being said (Voloshinov [1929] 1973). Other purposes of reported speech are flagging the agency of the characters (De Fina 2003) and providing evidence (Holt 1996, 2000). Similar to Voloshinov, Hill and Irvine (1993) propose that reported speech holds speakers accountable for the utterance, something that is key in the act of bearing witness.

Koven's frame draws from the notion of intertextuality addressed by Kristeva (1986), Bakhtin (1986), and Fairclough (1992). Kristeva (1986, 36) distinguishes between horizontal and vertical dimensions. Horizontal intertextuality refers to the relationships between utterances—or what Fairclough calls "texts" (1992, 271)—and those that came before and after. Kristeva writes that "any text is a mosaic of quotations; any text is the absorption and transformation of another" (1986, 37). An example would be reference to or verbatim quotation of reported speech from a verbal witness account in the print media. Vertical intertextuality means relationships between texts and context, such as the hashtags #MeToo and #MeTooUyghur referring to and creating the context of protest and activism in the early twenty-first century. Testimonio can be constituted through multimodal genres (written text, images, maps, video) and intertextual chains (Fairclough 1992) enabled through hyperlinks, comments, and "likes," thereby creating a historically situated speech situation that points to rights violations. In the following, I analyze embodied and digital testimonios according to their form, what they make visible, and how. The goal is to illustrate an adaptive shift in activist testimonio projects toward quantifiable information in the name of human rights.

EMBODIED TESTIMONIO

The witnesses in the embodied testimonios were *superstes* (Fassin 2008, 535), meaning survivors who speak about a crisis from personal experience. This is different from the observer, who is a third person reporting about conflict from a neutral standpoint. The survivors I have listened to spoke in an urgent voice, commanding the listener through a radical ethics of solidarity and intervening in violence by documenting it (Fassin 2008). The testimonios told in face-to-face settings presented here cannot be found on digital platforms or in the records of congressional hearings. They were told outside of the international limelight. The narratives illustrate how personal and structural factors like political activism in China, violation of the female body, and guilt by association amplify each other and group people around the desire to belong. Belonging did not always refer to the imagined nation. Belonging also referred to being recognized as a political subject (Fassin 2008).

In other words, the suffering animated people to testify and transform a sense of victimhood into narrative ownership with the potential for political action. By challenging established limits on speech and action, the witnesses transformed themselves in the interaction from a displaced person with difficult experiences into an advocate for the right to culture, language, and the body. The testimonios have many similarities in that they talk about an early political awakening, often constituted by parents or family members who had experienced political persecution and prison. In addition to expressing suffering, testimonio addressed rights, specifically the right to one's body, the right to language, freedom of (creative) expression and religion, and gender equality. Some of those rights are enshrined in the Universal Declaration of Human Rights from 1948. However, the witnesses neither referred to legal codes in their testimonios nor to the autonomous self. They referred to aspirations of collective safety from violence and collective justice in light of the violation of the mentioned rights.

In the following section, I present four testimonios that are representative of the testimonios I recorded. Rayida represents the person seeking asylum whose suffering is based on her family's history and persecution. Her legal status and future remained uncertain at the time of the research. Maryam is the acknowledged refugee who has family and engaged in occasional political advocacy. Roshan is the emancipated woman who escaped systemic and familial violence and was active in German politics and Uyghur advocacy at the time. Tursun is the highly educated lawyer who practices human rights advocacy and links the struggle and suffering of his family to the struggle of a larger Uyghur collective.[4]

Rayida

Rayida was a woman in her late forties who, like many other Uyghurs, had arrived in Germany as an asylum seeker. I met her in a shared accommodation in Munich. She had lived in the place for several years with the status of *Duldung*, meaning that she had permission to stay temporarily in Germany on humanitarian grounds. Rayida lived with her teenage son. The shared accommodation had taken a toll on her and she talked about the stress caused by uncertainty. She had some Uyghur friends in Munich and was liked in the accommodation as she was a good cook and shared her meals with others. The friends and the political and cultural events sponsored by the WUC and other organizations in Munich were a brief respite from her monotonous life in the accommodation (Witteborn 2012a, 2012b). The emotional pain experienced in China resurfaced in different ways in Germany through the loneliness and social isolation produced by an institutionalized system in which asylum seekers were confined to an asylum accommodation during the lengthy processing of their asylum claims. And even though they might be allowed to find an apartment and work after several months, the emotional and social isolation remained for years (Witteborn 2012a, 2012b).

Rayida's isolation and emotional vulnerability revealed itself in her immense sadness. There was an urgency in her voice as she proceeded to talk about the trauma of collective cultural erasure. Suffering had shaped her personal life and had become the motor to keep her desire and advocacy for the "country," as she called it, alive. For Rayida, the loss of home and family and a sense of helplessness against the injustice that had brought her to live in this environment instilled anger, sadness, and contempt but also a desire for a better life, especially for her son. Suffering in relation to the lost home had an additional important dimension for her, which was to keep the pain of forced migration alive and use this pain to speak out against the experienced injustices on a personal and collective level. As a woman who had to witness the death of her husband during the Baren Township conflict, she still dreamed of going back home.

The premise of belonging figured strongly for Rayida in her speaking the Uyghur language, socializing with Uyghurs, and demanding equal treatment of Uyghurs in China. When I arrived, Rayida greeted me with a smile. She was an educated, strong, and outspoken woman. While telling her story, she code-switched between English and Uyghur, with German terms sprinkled in. Her son helped to translate from Uyghur to English. When she started crying, her desperation punctuated the words of her testimonio:

Me and my son fled from Urumqi to [. . .] and to Germany. We were scared [starts to cry]. Until 1949, East Turkistan was a free country. My great-grandfather was a businessman. My mother went to the Russian school in Kashgar. In March 1949, the Chinese came to my country. "Women bangzhu ni [We will help you]," the Chinese said. My grandfather came from Russia in '51 to China with 500 horses. They took him and threw him into jail. When he came out, he died. I come from a rich and educated family. My mother got married and moved to Urumqi. Every second day people died there. People were hanging from the electric cable masts. Disappeared. My husband was a soldier and participated in the Baren county 1990 uprising. He died. End of April it was. Can a person change his name? What is this? The Chinese call our Kashgar Kashi. No! The name is Kashgar. Wulumuqi? No! It is Urumqi. My Uyghur name is Rayida. Is this so difficult to say? This is my country. I am so full, so full with emotions! No freedom, no life. Freedom comes first. At the moment, I am weak. There is hope. Before 1949, it was East Turkistan, Uiguristan. You cannot just wipe out history. Until my last breath I will pray, every day, to see my country again. I love this country. People here in Germany know little about it. When they say, I come from China, I tell them that is not true. I cannot accept this. From China? No, no. It hurts.

The narrative is typical of forced migrants with a vested political interest. A range of practices composes the affective household of those migrants as well as their daily practices, ranging from nostalgia to active political participation (Bob 2005; Cetin 2020; Gertheiss 2019). In her authorial role, Rayida recounts the events in her life in chronological order, ending with the death of her husband in the month of April. She uses the character role only once in this first part of the testimonio, imitating a collective voice in Putonghua: "Women bangzhu ni." The reenacted collective offers assistance, the nature of which is unknown until the following sentence, which addresses jail time and death for family members and other Uyghurs. The direct speech enacts authenticity (Holt 2000), performing Uyghurs as being dependent on the helping Other. Rayida shifts into an interlocutory role in her second sentence to provide her own interpretations of events for the listener ("We were scared"). In her interlocutory role, Rayida projects her future actions, which position her as a survivor: "At the moment, I am weak. There is hope." The premise of suffering is directly linked to the historical memory of an "East Turkistan" and its disappearance. As Forbes (1986) explains, the Soviet-backed Second East Turkistan Republic from November 1944 to December 1949 was led by Soviet-educated Uyghur rebels and those from other ethnic groups like Kazakh, as well as Soviet agents. The leaders demanded equality for all ethnic groups in the region, recognition of their languages, and the curbing of Chinese migration to the area.

The memory of the past is one of suffering for Rayida. When mentioning the death of her husband, she quickly shifts to the topic of linguistic erasure and invisibility and the hegemony of the Chinese language, either because the death of her husband is still too painful or because linguistic and cultural identity is a metaphor for the erasure of Uyghur life for her. "My country" is depicted as a place of semiotic invisibility for groups like Uyghurs. Chinese becomes a sign system occupying and governing space as in the examples of city names (calling Uyghur-named *Kashgar* by the Chinese name *Kashi*). Rayida sums up linguistic and cultural invisibility and systemic control in the catchphrase "No freedom, no life."

She establishes vertical intertextual linkages between the role of language and her testimonio. She meta-communicates about language by referring to the imposed Chinese iterations of the places she feels connected to. Rayida emphasizes the obligation of Uyghurs and non-Uyghurs alike to honor people's sense of being-*in*-place as a person ("The Chinese call our Kashgar Kashi. No! The name is Kashgar. [. . .] My Uyghur name is Rayida. Is this so difficult to say?"). Place names become the symbolic announcement of a collective's existence. Claiming this existence and identity is a transgressive act, with the name "East Turkistan" calling out a space where collective memory and political actions can be negotiated.

Rayida highlights how language itself can function as epistemic control when used as the language of victory to overwrite other languages and ways of life. In her exclamation "It hurts," naming becomes a physical act, which resonates with and through the body and exacerbates the experience of being out-of-place. In her last sentence, she moves from her authorial role to proclaim her purpose in exile, which is to promote Uyghur identity. Her physical pain of being misidentified as Chinese gestures to the body as a place where suffering and history are inscribed. The individual and the social body merge through the pain of not being seen. This pain of invisibility and lack of voice are addressed by the other witnesses as well.

The call for emplacement contrasts with Rayida's own displacement and her feeling out of place in the asylum shelter. In order to feel at home, she had recreated the local through photographs and reproductive prints of social interactions in the capital Urumqi and in the old towns and villages situated on the fringes of the Taklamakan desert. She gestured toward the images while telling her story, describing the places and people she missed. There were the old neighbors who got together on the stoop of the house to chat every evening, enjoying tea and homemade snacks. There was a print of village life and the intimate sociality expressed through festivities. Smells and sounds figured prominently in the memories associated with the images, like the smell of kebabs suffusing the streets, the smell of fresh peaches, or the sound of vendors praising their goods. The warehouse characteristics of the asylum shelter were detrimental to notions of belonging. The sense of displacement and invisibility created through shelter life was amplified through the fact that Rayida had told her testimonio to immigration officers as evidence of her right to be granted asylum. At the time of the interview, she was not an accepted refugee yet, remaining a number in the asylum statistics in Germany and living in fear of deportation.

Maryam

Maryam came to Germany as an asylum seeker and at the time of the interview was living with her family as a recognized refugee. She was in her thirties. She spoke Uyghur at home but tried to speak German outside when she went grocery shopping or talked to the teachers of her daughter. She was afraid for her family members in China, as she feared they would get punished for her political activities, like the brother who was in jail. Nevertheless, she also mentioned how she had found a home in her neighborhood in Munich. She was working, cared for her daughter and husband, and watched German media to be up to date on politics and to improve her language skills. Like the testimonio by others, hers moves beyond a personal biography toward the experience of a similarly engaged group of people. Here is Maryam's testimonio:

> I thought much about the tragic situation of the Uyghur mothers. Our religion and language and culture are marginalized and there is birth control. Eighty percent of women are sick due to birth control devices.

So I spoke out about Uyghur women, birth control, and forced abortions. One evening, there was a knock on the door of my brother's home. Oh, so many police. They searched everything. He is in prison. I was so, so scared. My husband had a shop, which was doing well. But I took my daughter and my husband, and we went to Kazakhstan in a truck. We stayed there with relatives. Always at home as we had no visas. My daughter was eight and a half years old. She was sick [moaning]. We paid 14,000 US dollars to smugglers to get out. They gave us passports and train tickets. We got out in Germany but we needed to call the people I knew. I had my period on that day but I did not have anything. I found some newspapers and used them. I did not know where I was and did not have money. Then a man came who was not German. [She starts crying.] He said, "Come." He brought us to an internet cafe and he gave us change so that I could call Karlsruhe [registration center for refugees]. When we had our interview, we did not have any evidence or papers and our request was declined. Then we gathered evidence and my activism was part of the evidence and the reason we fled. Then we got the papers to stay in Germany for a period of time. We are content. I bake bread and like cooking and do internships. I also learn German. "Wenn ich ein Vogel wäre, flöge ich in meine Heimat und küsste die Erde [If I were a bird, I would fly to my homeland and kiss the earth.]" I have written this sentence in my German class when we learned the subjunctive [sobbing]. I talk with Germans about my home. I once talked in front of 500 people about our flight and told my story. The local newspaper reported on it but the larger newspapers declined writing about it. The pressure is strong on Uyghurs. In the villages people cry and cry and pray and pray and say, this is God's will [moaning].

Maryam creates intertextual linkages through the reference to her transgressive speech in China, the German language, newspapers, and the phone and internet. Those expressive means are the base for her acts of defiance, including speaking about forced abortions. Legal papers paved the way for remaining in Germany, and the press was a symbol of personal protection in the form of the newspaper. In their vertical intertextuality (Fairclough 1992), speech, language, the newspaper, and the call she had to make to announce her asylum claim turn silence into voice to speak truth to an overwhelming power. Through speech, Maryam addresses the topic of forced abortions in China and Germany; through the German language, she expresses her desire to go home; through the newspaper, she saw her story reported; and through the internet cafe call, she claimed asylum. At the same time, the voice of Maryam does not resonate yet with a larger audience, and the visibility of the group she advocates for remained low.

The figure of the woman who demands the right to her body is central to this testimonio. Maryam tells the events in chronological order in her authorial role, starting with her activism as the reason for being surveilled, followed by her flight, arrival in Germany, and current situation. The only time she slips into reported speech is when she performs herself as yearning to go back home. She uses the subjunctive grammar form from her German class to express a desire that might not be fulfilled. By doing so, she claims agency through a thought experiment in the face of helplessness. Like Rayida, she reveals her deeply distressed state through moaning and sobbing. And like Rayida, she explains her political engagement in Germany, educating Germans about Uyghurs and mediating her story. The talk about police searches in the early 2000s anticipates the securitization of Xinjiang province and the danger of political work.

As an explanatory note, it should be mentioned that the one-child policy in China was introduced in 1979 and was abolished in 2015. The three-child policy that began in 2021 is an answer to a demography problem in China, with more males than females and an aging population, as the most recent census in China shows (Ning 2021). In the past, the one-child policy did not apply to ethnic groups apart from Han Chinese. Uyghurs could have two children. Herders and farmers could have three. In the Uyghur society, which favors boys, very much like the majority population of Han Chinese, this policy can be lethal to women and their female fetuses. Despite the advantages that the one-child policy has brought to China, such as reduced overpopulation and conservation of limited resources, the trauma of forced abortions is alive in Uyghur collective memory, as Maryam's testimonio illustrates.

Through the figure of her menses Maryam evokes an existential fact of life. Her leaking body is a metaphor for its vulnerability, especially under conditions of flight. The last resort of privacy is opened up to the world for everybody to see. She, who spoke out about the violation of the woman's body in China and the suffering related to it, sees her own body scrutinized and vulnerable. A newspaper comes to her rescue and is used to cover up her body. The right to freedom of expression Maryam demanded back in China becomes a literal part of her, one that is indispensable at a moment of pain. The newspaper becomes the thread running through her testimonio as she recounts how she told her story to journalists in Germany, thereby asserting her right to expression. Maryam has made it her task to report on the violations of the female body and of the unborn child, and of the consequences for the whole family and society. Her displacement, along with some of the guilt of a survivor, fueled her passion (Witteborn 2007a). Maryam explained that she knew women who fell into deep depression after a stillbirth at eight months as a result of the effects of the injected abortion drug. Uyghur women told these stories repeatedly. The testimonios given in the Uyghur Tribunal in the United Kingdom in June of 2021 confirm the population control of the Uyghurs in China (Uyghur Tribunal, Witness Evidence, 33b, December 2021, 10).

Maryam paid for her unruliness with exile and the pain that comes with it, such as loneliness and feeding off the imagination of a home that might not exist anymore. In addition to the newspaper, it is a stranger who comes to her help, honoring the fact that he was different from other Germans and that his solidarity assisted her when she needed help the most. While telling the story, she is still moved by his compassion and sharing of resources, which was a crucial lifeline for her and her family. Maryam's moaning and sobbing created an affective scene in which the spoken word retreated into the background and the inexpressible made itself known. The moaning and sobbing by Rayida and Maryam stayed in my memory. The sounds announced the space of the limit, which Foucault (1977) talks about; a space apart from rationalized language and arguments. Moaning created a space of resonance that was hard to endure in its liminality and affective urgency.

Roshan

Half of the men and women whose testimonio is presented here have used this genre in newspapers, public speeches, or human rights fora in Germany and the United States. This was also true for Roshan. Roshan was a Uyghur activist and single mother of two at the time of the research, living in Munich. Like Rayida and Maryam, she had come to Germany as an asylum seeker.

And like Maryam, she was a recognized refugee. She claimed agency through becoming the author (Koven 2002) of her testimonio:

I arrived in Germany in 1996 via Kazakhstan and Kyrgyzstan. I met my ex-husband in the asylum accommodation and had two children. I was married for seven years. My father did not want me to marry him. He did not tell me why. I saw his true face after some time. Violence. He did not have an education and an emancipated woman was a problem for him. He wanted me the traditional way: woman at home, men outside. I left. After seven years we separated. I am mom and dad for the children now. I had worked for an organization[5] in East Turkistan and distributed flyers. We went on a business trip to Kyrgyzstan and my friend got called back. She was arrested, tortured, and put in prison. I also received a call while being abroad saying that my mother had fallen sick and I should return. I became suspicious and stayed. I had no contact with home for about a year. The organization helped me to go to Germany. I arrived at Frankfurt airport and took the train to Nuremburg and Munich. Somebody from the organization had been with me the whole way. After arriving at the train station, I was alone and did not know where to go. I talked to a Turkish man who helped me get to the right office. I spent three months in the shared asylum seeker camp for registration and then was distributed to another one. I was scared and felt very lonely. I prayed five times a day and read the Qur'an for support. I learned German and kept working on making the problems of Uyghurs public through translations. For example, there was a demonstration in [place name], an ancient town. I put the story online at three o'clock in the morning. My contribution is working with the media and making things public such as the forced abortions where the women get an injection and the child dies before being born. In Germany you feel like a human being when you are pregnant. My father worked as a cook in a prison in Khotan. He saw how Uyghurs were tortured. Political prisoners. My father has seen and heard it all. I always asked him. At night. During the day it was too dangerous. He always said, "You should not get involved. It is too dangerous. You have to study. We need more educated people." I am Uyghur and I want to do something for my people. I want to give them courage. So I learned a profession here in Germany. My daughter goes to the Gymnasium [high school in Germany, ending with a qualification to go to university]. Uyghurs abroad need to speak up more. Books need to be translated into several languages so that the world knows. We need press conferences and public protest. The Uyghurs suffer at home, but nobody listens. We can move freely here. My children understand that home is somewhere else. I tell them about Uyghurs, about the culture, traditions, religion. I tell them about heroes. Women heroes. I cook Uyghur food and they learn about the festivals and Islam. "Mama, where do we come from?" they ask. They don't believe I am coming from China. "Mama, I am not Chinese," they say. I tell them, "You are Uyghur."

Like many of her compatriots, Roshan acquired a political awareness early in life, nourished by her father's testimonios about torture in prisons. Her political work in China put her at risk but was formative for her activities in Germany, something she expresses through her tireless efforts to bring awareness about the situation of Uyghurs to local and international audiences. Roshan's work focuses on women and politics, equality in relationships, and the right to the body. In her testimonio, she speaks of the violence against the body in prisons in China, while relegating violence against the female body mostly to the cultural and domestic spheres. Her husband beat her, as she did not play her traditional role as the submissive housewife. Roshan is concerned about the treatment of the female body as the property of the state and a tool to engineer social and economic relations. Similar to Tursun, who is heard from later, she emphasizes education as the way to claim rights.

There are several intertextual linkages in the testimonio. The texts in their physical and content form are political or serve as the supporting infrastructure for Roshan's political work. The flyers and the father's witness accounts, her digital media posts, the Qur'an as a moral source, and language competency to engage in advocacy are examples. Roshan uses reported speech twice, first to talk about violence against Uyghurs, and second to perform her role as an educator of the new generation. Through reported speech, she claims authenticity and establishes the truth-value of the claims. She reenacts her father's prison work experience and his warning about the consequences of political work. The need for education addressed in chapter 2 is reiterated through the voice of her father: "You should not get involved. It is too dangerous. You have to study. We need more educated people." The second slippage into character happens when Roshan performs her children's question about identity and her firm reply that they are Uyghur. Reported speech underlines a truth that Roshan wants to be known in the family and in public. Justice for the Uyghurs requires courage as well as education and a firm sense of belonging. The reported speech exposes suffering as the main premise of the testimonio as well as the tools to address it. Suffering is caused by systemic violence, which seeps into families. For Roshan, the power of speech is essential to address this suffering and morph it into a productive force, such as education and advocacy.

Roshan stands for the visionary who politicizes gender and genders politics. Like Maryam and Rayida, Roshan defines herself as a survivor of violence and as a political actor. Roshan puts into practice what other Uyghurs and advocates have demanded. She enables the younger generation to receive a better education than their parents for at least two reasons: to stand up for the collective rights of those who are silenced and to change traditional values to the benefit of women. She sets an example by distancing herself and her children from a violent father, learning a profession, giving her children an education, and making the Uyghur story visible through digital media posts.

She told me that she sometimes felt lonely as a single mother and divorcee, feeling looked down upon by her Uyghur friends. Roshan spoke fluent German and had been working all along in Germany, taking evening classes, and completing a trade traineeship with a qualifying certificate. As a divorced woman who is professionally successful, speaks her mind, and envisions strengthening the role of women in politics, Roshan seemed suspicious to some members of the Uyghur diaspora. She felt somewhat marginalized by some people in her own community but persisted in her political work with the help of her friends and colleagues.

Women like Roshan are embodiments of the political in that they strategically address received symbolic orders of gendered relations and look for allies to challenge them (Mouffe 2007). Those allies come from within the Uyghur diaspora and outside, such as in the form of women's coalitions or support from politicians in the Green Party in Munich. Roshan had found a position in the offices of the Green Party, working with people who had just arrived in Germany. She felt excited, as she hoped to raise the profile of Uyghurs in local politics and on the national level. She engaged in unruly speech through her testimonio as well as by actively disseminating information about the

Uyghurs on digital media and through her work. Roshan claims participation in diasporic advocacy, which tends to be dominated by males. As such, she is similar to women like Aynur from chapter 2 who question gendered expectations about women, work, and public visibility. Roshan's witness account has many similarities with the grievances of other females from the region. The women are survivors of various types of violence, which turned them into political subjects, highly conscious of repressive forces wanting to victimize them again. The specter of morality was threatening to them, and they were suspicious of historical narratives celebrating female morality.

There are many examples of such historical narratives. There is the story of Nuzugum, for example, a Kashgari woman who paid with her life for killing the oppressor she was forced to marry. This narrative has shaped the moral and political imagination of Uyghurs and continues to shape Uyghur advocacy and Han-Uyghur relations (Abramson 2012; Brophy 2005). Nevertheless, cracks started to show in the narrative of the suffering heroine sacrificing herself for the cultural nation. Women like Roshan or Anargul, the artist living in Munich, challenged the relation between the female body, morality, and the nation, even at the cost of being excluded from the Uyghur community. Theirs is an uphill struggle: people who question honor, shame, and endogamy are still being sidelined in the first generation of Uyghurs that migrated to Germany and the United States.

Tursun

Tursun stands for the educated and well-connected legal professional living in the United States. As a Uyghur human rights activist and attorney, he speaks regularly on the state of Uyghurs in China, is cofounder of the Uyghur Human Rights Project in Washington, D.C., and has written on East Asia and China policy in the *Wall Street Journal*, the *Washington Post*, and for the BBC. I met with him in a coffee shop not far from the Uyghur American Association office and the White House. Tursun went through the Chinese education system and spoke Uyghur and Chinese fluently. He is part of the highly educated group of Uyghurs in the United States, which acts as the intellectual figurehead of the diaspora and represents it legally and politically. I have heard several times in Germany and in the United States that Uyghurs need highly trained, multilingual, and rhetorically savvy people to represent themselves to a national and international audience. Tursun was one of those people. As a lawyer residing in the United States, he makes ample use of his right to expression. Even brief testimonios like his are important to give difficult histories a face (Butler 2009):

> In 1995, I left Kashgar. My dad had relatives in the Soviet Union, my mom was the daughter of a nationalist. She was six months pregnant when they got her because she came from a nationalist family. I was born in Chinese captivity. My mother and I, she was only nineteen, were six months in prison. I studied at Kashgar High School and then the Chinese language in [place name]. In 2001, I went to law school in the United States. In my second year, I joined the Uyghur American Association. The UAA is the most well-organized and recognized in the Uyghur diaspora. We have a lot of Uyghur intelligentsia here in the region and the US. The organization was initially thought to promote the interest of Uyghurs and educate Uyghurs and others on East Turkistan history and culture. Starting in 2003, the National Endowment for Democracy has supported us through grants.

Tursun's testimonio, albeit short, stands for the experience of the collective. In his authorial role, he systematically recounts events in a brief and to-the-point fashion. He uses few interlocutory shifts explaining the events, except for interpreting his mother's fate for the audience: "She was six months pregnant when they got her because she came from a nationalist family." Intertextuality is kept to a minimum. The narrative focuses on dates and facts. Tursun's testimonio is one of early political awakening, educational migration, specialization in law and human rights, and supporting Uyghur advocacy. The spatial and temporal distance enables him to go beyond personal hurt and to testify to the persecution of people who were not in line with the respective political establishment of the time.

The premises of political participation for Uyghurs in China and social justice drove his human rights law career. He represents those Uyghurs who converted their early suffering and personal biographies to serve the collective good. Their linguistic abilities and knowledge of Uyghur, Chinese, and US culture and politics as well as their ability to engage in public and legal discourse were significant advantages. Tursun represents the educational elite, which is rhetorically versed in lobbying for a diasporic cause in the Western center of political power, Washington, D.C. His testimonio constitutes the

Uyghur nation as a historical, cultural, and political fact that demands international attention.

Tursun shifts into transgression through mentioning *East Turkistan* as the name for the rightful nation. The latter is legitimized through a continuous history, collective memory, and culture that needs to be shared with younger generations. For him, the Uyghur intelligentsia has a particular role to play in leading the Uyghur diaspora and mobilizing its members around shared knowledge of the history of the region and Uyghur culture. In this line of reasoning, knowledge leads to awareness and political action, which is supported by organizations like the National Endowment for Democracy. The importance of education has been addressed by other interviewees in Germany and in the United States. Language competence, public speaking skills, and an extensive knowledge of political lobbying are components of a solid education that could serve Uyghur advocacy, in their view.

In the United States, Uyghurs had created an outspoken lobby, supported by Uyghur lawyers and international relations experts, among them several PhD holders. In Germany, the situation was different, as discussed before, with many Uyghurs not being proficient in the German language and coming from less privileged social strata. Those people who worked in Turkish restaurants[6] and cleaned trains or windows were particularly nostalgic about the homeland as they had lived in the countryside and missed the close connections, the space, and cultural networks. Without being prompted, the people emphasized, several of them shyly, that they felt unable to talk publicly about Uyghurs and China as they lacked language competence in either German or English. They also doubted that anybody in Germany would be interested in the Uyghurs. In addition, the majority of Uyghurs came as asylum seekers to Germany and lived in shelters for years without having their refugee status recognized. As a result, they were ineligible at the time to attend paid language classes. Interactions with society were limited. However, despite the obstacles, Uyghurs engaged in advocacy, as the examples of Maryam and Roshan illustrated.

To conclude, all four witnesses have one common denominator. They are survivors and yet "guilty" by association. Tursun was born in prison because of his mother's family background. Rayida had to flee China because of her husband's political actions. Even after settling in Germany, Maryam and Roshan still feared for their families in China as they could be punished for the women's political work in Germany. *Guilt by association* dates back to ancient imperial China, as mentioned in chapter 1 (McNeill and Sedlar 1970). It means that family members are targeted for questioning, are detained, and are forced to admit guilt publicly. The principle has shaped the witnesses as survivors. The people and their families have not only outlived the period of hunger in China between 1958 and 1961 (*sannian kunnan shiqi*), during which 45 million people are estimated to have found an early death (Dikötter 2010), but also the political turmoil in Xinjiang province in the 1990s. Surviving political and social upheaval was common to the majority of Uyghurs in this study, especially those in Germany and the United States who came to seek asylum. The experience of survival solidified the premises of suffering and longing for a home, on the one hand. On the other hand, being a survivor also meant creating visions for a better personal and collective life, whether through political work, talking to the media, or practicing human rights law. The survivor was a survivor precisely because he or she was not the victim of circumstance but was playing an active role in overcoming established political and social limits. Unruly speech such as bearing witness, writing for the traditional and digital media, and challenging gendered communication was key to the process.

DIGITAL TESTIMONIO

Uyghur advocacy is carried out in partnership with political and lobby organizations and by promoting shared goals in the media and on digital platforms. Organizations like the NED provide the financial backbone for Uyghur diasporic work; political parties like the Green Party in Germany promote human rights in the name of the Uyghurs; and media like *Al Jazeera*, *The New York Times*, *The Guardian*, the BBC, and *Die Zeit* report the Uyghur story. In addition, social media and activist websites present, archive, and circulate Uyghur testimonios. Uyghur activists and activist databases collect witness accounts, create links to other protest movements (e.g., through hashtags), and set the technological parameters for testimonial presentation. YouTube was an early platform of choice for activists as it was understood as a starting point for content circulation on other platforms (Jenkins 2009). The early activists on YouTube already understood the danger of decontextualization, making them create their own sites (Jenkins 2009). The difficulty of controlling narratives about politically contested events arises from the reframing and resignification of these narratives (Goffman 1981; Jackson 2012). The standardized form of Uyghur digital testimonio counters resignification and serves to control the Uyghur narrative about persecution through factual, biographical, and otherwise verifiable information.

Bakhtin writes about text, audience, and historical context as being in dialogue with each other. Referring to Bakhtin's work (1981, 1986), Kristeva discusses the "intersection of textual surfaces" (1980, 64–65). The question is not what a speech event means but how it came to be developed in and as an interface with other visual, auditory, and metapragmatic practices and traditions. The digital testimonios discussed in this chapter are examples. Hashtags place the digital testimonio into a discursive synchronic and diachronic order of activism as in the tradition of #MeToo or #IamCharlie. The testimonios create textual coherence (Briggs and Bauman 1992) through their link to preceding discourses on social justice and use of their aesthetic symbolism for maximal attention.

Digital testimonios relied on an activist mode of narrating, including the call to social action through retweeting or a hashtag. What sounds like an invitational rhetoric (Foss and Griffin 1995) is a strategic move by activists to collect evidence of human rights abuses. On the basis of feminist principles, an invitational rhetoric does not aim at persuading but at understanding and promoting equality, dialogue, and self-determination. Activists have created platforms for Uyghurs to self-represent their plight, and viewers are invited to understand events in Xinjiang, China, through first-person witness accounts and to amplify the reach of these witness accounts. The latter is enabled through the connective function of social networks, such as the retweet of hashtags. While there is an invitation to stand up for human dignity, anti-violence, and freedom of expression, the main purpose of Uyghurs' digital testimonio is persuasive and a call to action, instead of an invitation to dialogue.

Moreover, the intertextuality of digital testimonios is amplified by the visible mode as one main affordance of digital media. Affordance refers to the perceived and real properties of a digital object that prompt people to use it in certain ways, such as interface icons and the sharing function (Nagy and Neff 2015; Norman 1988). Visibility becomes "a site of strategy" (Brighenti 2007, 326). As stated in the Introduction, mediated visibility can foster social recognition through making unrecognized groups hypervisible (Brighenti

2007). Digital testimonios are examples of mediated visibility, giving Uyghurs international exposure. Those testimonios are enabled by the technological and political support of organizations and individuals who create websites and social media channels, moderate them, and gather testimonial evidence. At the same time, the digital surveillance of the Uyghurs, as discussed in chapters 2 and 3, controls their mediated visibility and attempts for social recognition (Brighenti 2007). I present three examples to illustrate the relationship between form, intertextuality, and visibility in digital testimonios and their functions. The first is the online presence of Rebiya Kadeer, former president of the World Uyghur Congress. The second example is digital testimonios in the Xinjiang Victims Database. The third example engages with digital testimonios in the Uyghur Transitional Justice Database. The examples show how digital testimonio challenges political codes and creates spaces for connective visibilities and solidarities.

TESTIMONIAL FRAGMENTS: REBIYA KADEER

Tapping into normative scripts of maternal care, sacrifice, and nurture, the Uyghur leadership has resurrected a universally appealing archetype of the suffering mother who comes to the rescue of her family.[7] In this role, Kadeer seeks alliances with celebrities and politicians, which are highly mediated. Rebiya Kadeer, the president of the World Uyghur Congress from 2006 to 2017, entered the international media stage in 2006 when she made her witness accounts public on YouTube and established herself as a leader of Uyghurs in exile. Kadeer's testimonio gave suffering a personalized face. "Trauma demands a body," states Nayar (2011, 94). Kadeer presented herself as such a traumatized body, which she transformed into an agent of Uyghur advocacy. She inserted herself into public discourse through various testimonial formats, including an autobiography, YouTube videos, and digital photo collections. Her testimonial presentation pushes several limits: the limit of what was known about Uyghurs outside China at the time and the limit of analogue testimonial scripts.

When Kadeer went into exile in Washington, D.C., in 2005, social media platforms were not well developed yet. Advocacy was done through organizational websites and linked discussion fora as well as press releases, conferences, other types of direct lobby work, media reports, and books. Kadeer's autobiography is an example. As mentioned before, the book is called

Himmelsstürmerin (Kadeer and Cavelius 2007) in German, with the English version known as *Dragon Fighter: One Woman's Epic Struggle for Peace with China* (Kadeer with Cavelius 2011). The mission of Rebiya Kadeer is clear: "I want to be the mother of the Uigurs, the medicine for their sufferings, the cloth to wipe their tears, and the shelter to protect them from the rain" (English translation from German, Kadeer and Cavelius 2007, 18). In the German and English versions of the book, Kadeer provides a traditional witness account of her political awakening, her release from China with the help of US Secretary of State Condoleezza Rice in 2005, and her advocacy work. Kadeer's written witness account was produced in collaboration with a professional writer and constitutes an example of testimonio in the tradition of Rigoberta Menchú (1984). Through the amplification of traditional gender roles, Rebiya Kadeer mobilized suffering and sacrifice as values for an identity politics scripted for a transnational audience.

Kadeer's story is one of success and resurrection through political alliances, from laundry owner to millionaire to a media-savvy international advocate. In 1992, Kadeer became a delegate to the National People's Congress of China. In a meeting in 1997, she criticized the policy of the Chinese Communist Party toward Uyghurs in the wake of riots in Xinjiang. She subsequently lost her seat in Congress. Kadeer was arrested in 1999 on her way to meet a US congressional delegation and has been advocating for the Uyghurs in Washington, D.C., since her release in 2005. In a 2009 interview, Kadeer maintained: "I have become the No. 1 enemy of the Chinese authorities because I am the voice of my people" (Lowrey 2009). The gendered details of Kadeer's narrative, her arranged marriage, divorce, being a mother of eleven children, imprisonment, emigration, and political advocacy construct her as a body in pain (Nayar 2011) and as a symbol for Uyghur international advocacy.

This body in pain has increasingly been circulated in digital form. Examples are online photographs depicting alliances with celebrities and streaming videos in a quest to become a globally recognized human rights activist. Kadeer herself has cultivated the image of a lone woman struggling against China, an image that has been eagerly taken up by the media. One interviewer described her on the website of the Swiss-Tibetan Association: "A short, fragile woman with soft facial features sits in front of me. [. . .] Somebody unfamiliar with her could assume her to be a simple grandmother from somewhere in Central Asia" (Chompel 2007). This Orientalist image of Rebiya Kadeer from a no-place, a "somewhere," has turned her into a symbol of gendered resistance, on the one hand, and of nonthreatening endearment, on the other.

Kadeer has used the figure of motherhood to promote her campaign at least since 1997 when she initiated the Thousand Mothers Movement. This movement attempted to create solidarity among Uyghur women and to provide support to female-run businesses. It was soon dissolved by the Chinese government (Kadeer and Cavelius 2007). However, it continues to have a presence on Uyghur websites[8] where picture galleries offer photographs of Kadeer as Mother of the Nation and draw attention to the Thousand Mothers Movement as one of her key accomplishments and memories. The humanitarian image of Kadeer in the United States stands in contrast to the one in China, where she has been criticized as a shrewd businesswoman turned political defector with the help of the United States. In 2021, she seemed retired from international political advocacy after fifteen years of intense engagement.

The trope of the suffering and caring mother ready to sacrifice herself for the nation has become the main trope of advocacy for Kadeer and those who ask for her help. YouTube had early, emotionally charged videos where alleged young torture survivors in China reach out to Rebiya Kadeer as "Mother," pleading for help.[9] These testimonios about violence invoked the mother trope as an anchor for collective survival. The self-sacrificing mother is linked to the trope of the heroine prevalent in Uyghur history and art through the act of suffering with a moral purpose (Huang 2009; Tursun 2017). Suffering with a moral purpose firmly places the Uyghur woman in a narrative of moral obligations to the nation. These obligations range from endogamy to chastity to sacrifice for the Uyghur national family. Rachel Harris (2005) describes this topic in relation to symbolism in Uyghur music and song. The self-sacrificing mother is the emotional, weeping mother, ready to take on the sorrows of the personal and national family. The mother figure has clear ethno-nationalistic connotations, symbolizing a nation under threat and in need of protection. As Harris points out, Uyghur singer Omarjan Alim's "Lament for the Mother" song in the 1990s merged the expression of grief for the mother with grief over the death of the nation.

Rebiya Kadeer herself testified to the difficult experiences of the Uyghurs through digital photograph collections, streaming videos, and an autobiography, as mentioned before. The digital testimonial pieces are posted on websites of Uyghur advocacy organizations, social media platforms, and in media reports. Visuals are tied to written explanations about the characters presented and their historical and political positioning, thus creating vertical intertextual links to showcase political alliances in the wake of persecution. Pictures on websites and social media portray Kadeer alongside symbols of spiritual and political importance like the Dalai Lama, Kofi Annan, or former US president G. W. Bush. The latter was responsible for the creation of the detention camp at Guantanamo Bay, where twenty-two Uyghurs were incarcerated in 2002 and over time set free. Strategic positioning of the Uyghur story and gaining the support of powerful allies seemed more important to Uyghur diplomacy at the time than political inconsistencies (Witteborn 2011c).

Specifically, Kadeer has related the Uyghur narrative of persecution and resistance to that of Tibetans. Photographs of Kadeer and the Dalai Lama, such as the ones on Pinterest or by Getty Images,[10] create visual evidence that testifies to a shared history of oppression and a political and moral alliance between Uyghurs and Tibetans. Both figures, usually portrayed as standing next to each other, are symbolic for a people living with an overpowering Chinese state. Other testimonial pieces of the shared resistance of the Uyghurs and Tibetans against the Chinese state include images portraying Kadeer and the US actor Richard Gere, an important celebrity supporter and public relations catalyst for the Dalai Lama and the Tibetan cause in North America. These images can be read as a metacommunicative commentary on extending international sympathies for the Tibetan cause to include the Uyghur cause.

Visuals have always been important in Uyghur advocacy as they create textual chains that document the human rights advocacy of the Uyghurs while maintaining authorial voice. A Google image search in 2009 resulted in ninety-one different photographs of Rebiya Kadeer,[11] seventy-nine of which showed her with the traditional four-cornered Uyghur cap, the *doppa* (Witteborn 2011c). The photos create a collage of pictorial evidence that becomes a digital witness to Kadeer's international recognition as a human rights leader. The same search in 2018 produced 387 images, 373 of which had the *doppa*. The increased number of visuals related to the cultural representation of Kadeer is notable. Few pictures on the internet and in her biography show Rebiya Kadeer with traditional clothes before she went into exile. She was usually portrayed in a white headscarf or the *tomak*, a fur hat that symbolizes modernity and wealth. After she went into exile and became active on the political world stage, her public image transformed. She is represented with the traditional Uyghur cap and sometimes in braids, a traditional hairstyle that can still be seen in the towns and villages of Xinjiang. Kadeer's pictorial presentation as an elderly woman with braids and local clothing radiates kindness, peace, and compassion. The image encourages an affective sociality that sympathetic audiences and human rights defenders can relate to. The culturalized body performs moral integrity and the peaceful intentions of a native woman fighting for the preservation of her people. As a young Uyghur woman I interviewed put it: "Kadeer has had a huge influence on Uyghurs. No one has ever had it. She brings people together" (personal interview, May 19, 2009 in Washington, D.C.). One can even go so far as to claim that suffering demands the ethnicized body to individualize this emotion and to make suffering relevant to audiences around the world.

Rebiya Kadeer herself has been routinely portrayed in the Chinese media as a terrorist disrupting national unity. For example, the English edition of *People's Daily Online*, launched by *People's Daily*, the official newspaper of the Communist Party of China, identified Kadeer early on as a member of the "East Turkistan" terrorist forces and a "great terrorist threat to China at present and in the future" (*People's Daily Online* 2005). By calling Xinjiang "East Turkistan," the Chinese press constructed the Uyghur diasporic leadership as supporting an ethno-nationalist and secessionist project, state subversion, and politicized Islam. *The Uyghur* is confirmed as a deviant symbol, justifying "different technologies of disciplining, regulation, and pastoral care" (Ong 2006, 7). Framing the diaspora in this way ensures that *the Uyghur* remains deviant through continuous disciplining, a negative role model that the state can use to control other groups.

Kadeer created a sensory appeal of the homeland as a feminized and protective space, hoping to forge bonds with a dispersed Uyghur community and to evoke the support of global publics. Feminist scholars have long argued that the homogenization of social groups tends to naturalize gendered categories, which obscures power relations and hierarchies (Gajjala 2019; Hegde 1998, 2011; Yuval-Davis 1997; Yuval-Davis and Anthias 1989). For Kadeer, gendered symbols such as motherhood seem to break the mold of *the Uyghur* and reveal power hierarchies. The premise of suffering becomes the affective key in testimonio, gesturing to overwhelming political structures. The positive connotations of the family, femininity, protection, and care also assist with separating Uyghurs from any form of militant Islam (compare Vergani and Zuev 2015). Rebiya Kadeer has expanded the image of the silently suffering mother into the image of a peaceful advocate for human rights for Uyghurs, critiquing not only the Chinese government but also Islamist militants trying to instrumentalize the Uyghur struggle.

However, the premise of suffering also conceals power relationships as suffering is linked to loyalty and morale. Anne McClintock has noted how "women are typically construed as the symbolic bearers of the nation but are denied any direct relation to national agency" (1997, 90). Kadeer appropriates the logic of women as protectors of culture as a way of reaching out to women in the Uyghur community. She frequently talked about how Uyghurs have been reduced to a position where they have lost their moral coordinates. By inserting an essentialized idea of Uyghur womanhood into a script of cultural values and moral behavior, Kadeer calls on women to protect Uyghur culture in face of the passing of a way of life and the fading dream of an independent motherland. Kadeer reclaims domesticity as a location from where to articulate a politics of recognition through cultural, social, and political rights. Her role model is appealing to some Uyghur women as it emphasizes traditional values and yet shifts the traditional role of the female from the local, domestic world of the house to the global world of international advocacy. At the same time, female voices that rebel against the notion of purity and the nuclear or extended family are in danger of being suppressed. This marginalization could prove counterproductive for Uyghur advocacy as there are Uyghur women in China and outside who do not feel included or represented. The analysis of the name *Xinjiang* in chapter 2 illustrates how young Uyghur men and women have started questioning received gender, age, and religious hierarchies and adopted a transnational outlook beyond China.

Early Uyghur advocates like Rebiya Kadeer and her supporters presented their experiences in autobiographies, in interviews, the print and broadcast media, and testimonial fragments on various digital platforms. More recently, digital testimonio by and about Uyghurs has appeared on YouTube, Twitter, and activist websites. The curated digital testimonios break with received images of suffering in order to archive evidence and use it for potential legal action. There is a shift from emotive toward evidence-driven language, which means the language of rationality that relies on data and factual information. The latter does not allow for ambiguities. Uyghur testimonio collected by activists co-opts the mechanism of transparency (Han 2015, 2017), which means relying on calibrated information to ensure truth value. The latter is very important in the volatile context of social media where disinformation and deep fakes create fragmented audiences and make conspiracy theories thrive. I demonstrate these claims by the example of two testimonio databases: the Xinjiang Victims Database and the Uyghur Transitional Justice Database (UTJD).

DATA-BASED EVIDENCE AND CROWDFUNDED ACTIVISM

The Xinjiang Victims Database documents various forms of detention and disappearances of different minorities in Xinjiang, including Uyghur, Kazakh, Kyrgyz, and Hui. The database, created by human rights activist Gene Bunin in 2018 (Baptista 2021)[12] and crowdfunded, is a monitor of rights abuses. It states: "The goal of this database consists in documenting the aforementioned individuals, so as to both protect them now and hold the Chinese authorities accountable later, by creating the foundations for future legal action and reparations" (https://shahit.biz/eng/). The name "Xinjiang" in the database points to the region and governing political system in which people of all ethnic groups, not just Uyghurs, can disappear or be detained for alleged "crimes" like "contact with outside world." In March of 2021, crowdfunding had raised USD 104,127, with 926 donors, 1,100 shares, and one thousand followers. Donations and spending are publicly accessible and governmental funding is not allowed (https://shahit.biz/eng/#faq). The database website is complemented by social media platforms like Twitter, Facebook, and the YouTube channel Uyghur Pulse. As of June 2021, there were 15,338 victim entries. By February of 2022, the number had jumped to 26,143 reports. Figure 7 is a screenshot of the landing page. The "Victim in Focus" changes whenever one opens the website. We see the screenshot of Nigare Abdushukur, a twenty-six-year-old Uyghur student from Ghulja,

FIGURE 7. Screenshot of the Xinjiang Victims Database landing page. Source: https://shahit.biz/eng/#2396.

sentenced to nineteen years in prison. The suspected reasons are "sending money abroad, being in contact with people abroad."

On the screenshot, one can see several genre formats that compose the testimonio. There is the "Victim in Focus" box resembling a bureaucratic-legalistic-type ID document with basic data on the detained person, including picture, name, age, gender, ethnicity, profession, likely current location, detainment date and reason, and others. There is a "Primary-Evidence Report," including eyewitness accounts, letters from detention, court documents, and media reports. Below, and not captured in the screenshot, is a "Facilities Report" about the type of detention facility, geolocation, GPS coordinates, and address if available. There is also a "Victim Map" to the right, which can be partially seen, with dense geotagged locations of the victims' homes.

Moreover, for each "Victim in Focus," there is a template for testimonios that serves to verify the legal identity of the witness, including "testifying party" and "about the victim." There is also a line for "how testifier(s) learned of the victim's situation." The template concludes with supplementary materials, including official court verdicts, media coverage, streaming testimonios, and photos; thus, it presents a dense collection of factual evidence and its verification (https://shahit.biz/eng/#view). For Nigare Abdushukur, the student from Ghulja, the testifying parties are her brother who lives in Munich, a former neighbor, a cousin in Turkey, and an anonymous and unknown source, with verified identities for each (https://shahit.biz/eng/#2396). Moreover, there is Urumqi police record evidence. According to the information, Nigare is in a prison in Ghulja city and was taken from her home in 2017 in her senior year of university.

One central element of the database is the "Victim-Centered Primary Evidence" report, linked to the "Primary-Evidence Report" on the landing page (https://shahit.biz/xjvictims_primary.pdf). There were fifty-three eyewitness accounts at the time of the research, the majority from former detainees. Those were collected through interviews and are therefore elicited, unlike the testimonial accounts in the personal interviews analyzed before. The eyewitness accounts were collected by organizations such as the Atajurt Kazakh Human Rights organization in Almaty, Kazakhstan, or they are testimonios published by international media like *Die Zeit* in Germany, *Believer Magazine*, and *Russian Reporter*. They also originate from interviews with Radio Free Asia. There are six letters from detention, among several other sources.

The letters from detention are a separate genre from the first-person testimonios, yet they complement the testimonial density. Mehmud Muhemmet (Entry 4964), for example, is associated with a letter written in Uyghur and displayed in English with the following excerpt: "Under the Party's correct guidance, the wise leaders have, to ensure the people's bright future, provided us with a comfortable environment, clean and comfortable dormitories, and three excellent, delicious, and timely meals a day, as well as knowledgeable teachers and brave people's police to be with us night and day." Several other letter excerpts praise the party for its forgiveness, such as one from Memet Ismayil (Entry 4959), a seventy-seven-year-old herder and village imam: "In the past, because of my low awareness of the law, I had gone on a pilgrimage to Mecca. [. . .] I am now studying at this school, under the care of the Party government. I am very grateful for the forgiveness the Party has shown me" (https://shahit.biz/eng/#evidence). Ismayil was released in 2019, according to the testimonio by his grandson who lives in Japan, and is under house/town arrest. The stylized party-speak in both letters hints at forced confessions.

The digital medium affords intertextual linkages and loops where texts and images are added continuously into existing templates to condense the testimonial evidence. Intertextual loops create dense evidence formats, such as the "Victim Map" with clusters of pins. Those pins, in turn, establish intertextuality through visual representation of physical places where victims lived and by turning those places into markers of collective suffering. Moreover, the testimonial evidence is interpreted through metacommentaries like graphs and summaries. Under "Tools" and "Statistics" (https://shahit.biz/eng/#stats) one can see data categories that interpret the text-based witness accounts and include the age of the detained and imprisoned people (the majority between 35 and 55), gender (20,715 males and 5,445 females), estimated year of detention/prison (the majority of reports give a year before 2017), and suspected detention reasons (e.g., relatives or endangering state security). The "Statistics" category is comparable to Koven's (2002) narrative interlocutory role where a speaker interprets a text for his or her audience. Summaries and graphs are analytical metacommentaries on demographic clusters, frequencies, and trends that help the reader make sense of the written testimonios (https://shahit.biz/xjvictims_primary.pdf). The database is transparent about its sources, crowdfunding, and "Quality of Victim Entries," ranging from high, to medium, to low, and unrated. The majority of victim entries are rated "medium." This rating enhances the self-presentation of the project as being transparent about the credibility of its collected evidence.

The Xinjiang Victims Database is a multimodal collection of texts that is linked to another multimodal collection, the Uyghur Pulse on YouTube. Gene Bunin, the founder of both the database and the YouTube channel, says the idea was based on the Kazakhstan grassroots organization *Atajurt* that collects testimonial evidence in Kazakhstan on detained Kazakh relatives in Xinjiang. Bunin and his team gather testimonios submitted by Uyghurs about relatives and friends and upload them on the YouTube channel as well as Twitter and Facebook. By March 15, 2021, the YouTube channel, founded on August 6, 2019, had 892 subscribers and received 103,958 views, according to *socialblade.com*. By February 5, 2022, the channel subscribers had slightly increased to 1,010 and views to 121,840. The Twitter account had 2,208 followers by February 5, 2022, and 939 tweets (socialblade.com). The languages of the testimonios were English, Kyrgyz, Arabic, Uzbek, Dutch, Turkish, German, Chinese, Japanese, Kazakh, Russian, French, and Uyghur, with the majority in the English playlist (846), followed by Uyghur (346), Turkish (89), French (48), Kazakh (41), Chinese (38), Russian (22), German (17), and Japanese (10) as of February 5, 2022.

Testimonios delivered in English are by far the most numerous. This could be because Gene Bunin has closer connections with Uyghurs in the English-speaking world and because Uyghurs living in the United States, Canada, and Australia were more willing to testify than those living in Central Asia or Turkey. Another reason could be legal protection, including from extradition to China, from countries like the United States, Canada, Australia, and the UK. In addition, Uyghurs fluent in English may feel more comfortable to testify and to reach an international audience without translation.

From an analytical point of view, those who provide testimonio on the YouTube channel maintain their interlocutory and character roles in their digital witness accounts but are only partial authors. They do not select the format of the presentation, which is a short video in which they testify about a disappeared person. A speaker introduces him- or herself by name, city of origin in Xinjiang, and time spent abroad and describes the person she or he testifies about, which is announced through a photo held up to fill the camera screen. After the witness and main character of the testimonio are introduced, the witness narrates the relationship type and provides information about the detained or imprisoned person like name, age, and profession. The witness is turned toward the camera, sitting in a living room, a kitchen, or an advocacy office.

In order to understand the inter-platform circulation on YouTube and Twitter as well as the viewer uptake of the testimonios, the Twitter dataset from chapter 3 was used for analysis, which included 295,664 tweets posted by 158 accounts. To further evaluate the views of the testimonios, the number of retweets and views of each unique entry were determined. In the overall dataset there were 1,052 mentioned unique video testimonios. The most-viewed video had a view count of 15,400 (Beat 216: Asiye, from the Netherlands). The video is embedded in the following tweet:

> @AsiyeUyghur asks the obvious question: "if everything is so great in XJ, why can't the people there communicate freely with the outside world and say so themselves?" She hasn't had contact with her relatives in 3 years. #uyghurpulse https://t.co/N7l49P3mci.

The video was retweeted 101 times. The least-viewed video—seventy-nine times—is from the United States and is a testimonio about religious scholars. It is linked to the following tweet:

—Beat 928: Maya, USA (English)—Maya does a support testimony for 10 religious scholars who are arrested and missing, including the 92-year-old Abidin Ayup (https://t.co/bhsIX1uaE6), taken in 2017. #uyghurpulse https://t.co/6pmHyc2X3k.

This video is only retweeted once, which is surprising as it refers to a whole group of people who might have been prominent in their communities as religious authorities. Overall, Uyghur activists, advocacy organizations, Uyghur Aid, Uyghur Bulletin, and Uyghur scholars tweeted about individual testimonios. There were 1,920 tweets from the activist Twitter handle @uyghurpulse. Of these tweets, 895 are original entries posted by @uyghurpulse and 1,025 are retweets. This number of retweets seems minor in the entire Twitter network of influential users. Nevertheless, the circulation of the videos and comments suggests horizontal connective action (Halupka 2018) between activists, Uyghurs, crowdfund supporters, and other types of audiences. Moreover, the purpose of the testimonial evidence goes beyond circulation and clicktivism. It creates an archived data pool that can be used for analytics and pattern recognition, according to database founder Gene Bunin:

> Over the past two years, these goals have evolved. To some extent, we've become a very analytical platform, which is not really the goal but a very positive side-benefit, as you can use our data to study different patterns, trends, and nuances, and a lot of things become apparent that would not be apparent otherwise. (Bunin 2021)

The digital testimonios are different in form, visibility, intertextuality, and function from the embodied testimonios collected in interpersonal settings. Unelicited first-person testimonios told in the interviews followed traditional narrative structures in terms of authoring the testimonio, performance of characters, and interpretation of the plot for the listener (Koven 2002). Digital testimonios, in comparison, had a format curated by the initiators of the witnessing space. Data on the disappeared person as well as the witness testifying to the disappearance could be linked to ID documents, GPS data, and the embodied person on the ground, thereby increasing the chances for truth verification. Nevertheless, like in the embodied testimonios, digital witnesses were survivors and not just impartial observers (Fassin 2008) as they testified to the detention of loved ones from exile and with the knowledge of having escaped psychological and potentially physical violence.

DATA-BASED EVIDENCE AND ORGANIZATIONAL ACTIVISM

The Uyghur Transitional Justice Database (UTJD) is an example of organization-supported eyewitnessing. It was founded by Bahtiyar Omer, head of the Norway Uyghur Committee, and supported by the National Endowment for Democracy (NED). The project is situated in Norway and acts independently, according to the NED website (NED 2020). In particular, the project

> documents, analyzes, and presents meaningful analysis of human rights violations in East Turkistan to uphold justice and accountability. Acting independently, UTJD [. . .] played a key role in submitting an official request to Norway's Council of Ethics for government pension investment funds to be divested from Chinese companies involved in the human rights atrocities. (NED 2020)

In addition to the collection of eyewitness accounts, the project gathers data on the number of disappeared and interned Uyghurs, with 5,031 Uyghurs reported missing as of January 2020. The UTJD also has the goal of offering victim support and pushing for sanctions. Unlike the Xinjiang Victims Database, it uses the name "East Turkistan" in its description, thereby openly opposing the political code implemented by the Chinese government and creating resistant interaction space. The website only displays data up until January 21, 2020, and is linked to YouTube, Facebook, Instagram, Pinterest, and Twitter. The number of subscribers on YouTube (638) was rather low at the time of the research.

In early 2021, three sample witness accounts were displayed under "Recent Testimonies." Each is presented in the form of a black-and-white-square, diagonally divided in half. The upper-left part displays the image of a disappeared or detained family member, while the lower-right part shows the picture of the person bearing witness. One example is Yashar. Double-clicking on the square leads the viewer to a page that displays the heading "Intellectuals" in large font and the subheading "My dad is missing." There is an upper-body photo of Yashar, the son, who holds a tablet computer with the photo of his father. The father, Hemdulla Abdurahman, is sitting on a chair in a dress shirt and formal jacket. He is smiling into the camera. A text explains that

Yashar lost contact with his father, a Uyghur-language researcher, in 2018. As in the description of the overall UTJD project ("About us"), Yashar uses the transgressive term *East Turkistan* in his written witness account, which is an indicator that he lives outside China. He had contacted police and other services in Urumqi to ask about the whereabouts of his father. His mother told him in a brief WeChat conversation to leave the parents alone as they could not talk on the phone. In the testimonio, the son wonders where the father was and, if he was sent away, the reasons why.

The UTJD project makes a clear call for action in the name of a politicized humanism, exemplified by the four sentences on the landing page: "We are your fellow human beings. We are not numbers. We are . . . We are Uyghurs." The quotes appeal to the compassion of readers and respect for human life in face of violence against a people. The project's mission therefore aligns with the NED's support of the Uyghur struggle in the name of basic human rights, as discussed in chapter 3.

Hashtags are an important means to create vertical and horizontal inter-textuality and multimodal bridges, connecting the website to other platforms, including Twitter. Clicking the "Register" link on the landing page brings up an image with small squares, with each square containing a shot of the upper body and face of a person, holding a sign with missing people or the hashtags #IamUyghur and #CloseTheCamps. Hashtags consist of a string of characters (without a space) for sorting, finding, and archiving topics. The embedding of hashtags into the handheld signs and the website is an example of intertextual and multimodal linkages, which strengthen the testimonial message and amplify the visibility of Uyghurs. Hashtags like #IamUyghur reference previous protest events through semantic similarities (#Iam). Figure 8 is a screenshot of the described hashtag images.

The hashtag "#IamUyghur," which figures prominently in the screenshot, is semantically similar to hashtags with global traction, such as #IamCharlie (#JeSuisCharlie). In other words, the hashtag creates a ritualized communi-cation event (Goffman 1981) through the recontextualization of protest. The original hashtag started in January 2015 right after the attack on the editorial team of the French satire magazine *Charlie Hebdo* in Paris (Giglietto and Lee 2017). Recontextualization occurred when the slogan and hashtag were used to condemn violence in other deadly incidents, such as the attacks in November of 2015 in Paris, where many were killed and wounded in the

ABOUT US   ≡

Uyghur Transitional Justice Database (UTJD) is an ongoing project that focuses on the registration of the disappeared and extrajudicially interned Uyghurs in East-Turkistan. We are building a comprehensive database to document the ongoing atrocities being committed by the Chinese Communist Party toward the Uyghurs since the revision of its legislation in 2017 (amended Oct. 9, 2018) to "allow" local governments to "educate and transform" people influenced by extremism at so called "vocational training centers", also effectively known as concentration camps by their extrajudicial nature in East-Turkistan (aka. Xinjiang Uyghur Autonomous Region (XUAR)).

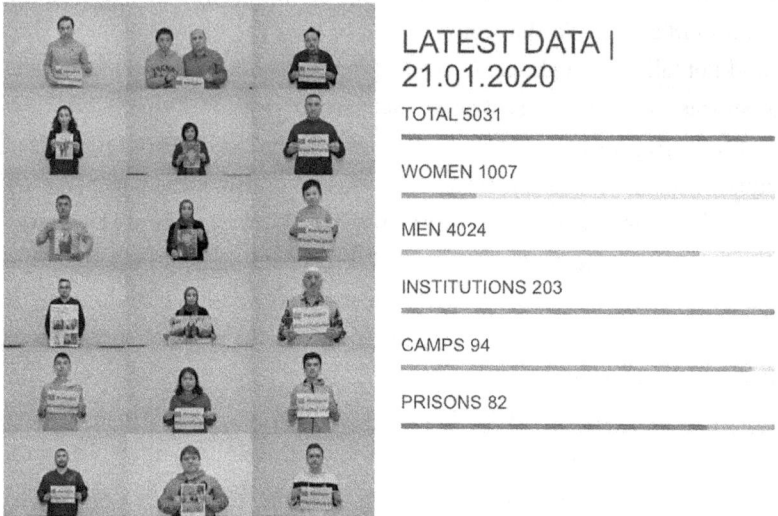

**LATEST DATA |
21.01.2020**

TOTAL 5031

WOMEN 1007

MEN 4024

INSTITUTIONS 203

CAMPS 94

PRISONS 82

FIGURE 8. Screenshot of the Uyghur Transitional Justice Database. Source: https://www.utjd.org.

Bataclan concert hall and in other places in Paris. A countermovement, "Je ne suis pas Charlie" ("I am not Charlie"), formed on Twitter and Facebook against "I am Charlie" supporters. While "I am Charlie" supporters argue mostly in the name of freedom of expression and portray it as the foundation of Western democracy, "I am not Charlie" supporters counter this discourse by raising the topics of systemic racism, Islamophobia, and hate speech that in their view created the conditions for the violent attack (Sutkutė 2016). An article by Onishi and Méheut (2020) in *The New York Times* states that "Charlie" supporters tend to be white while opponents tend to be the Other, citing sociologist Vincent Tiberj (2017), who maintained that the discourse on religious extremism fueled by the media and political figures had divided French society more than the attack itself.

#IamUyghur is thus an example of horizontal intertextuality and a symbolism that borrows its discursive strength from previous successful group mobilizations. It links to an established string of words that calls for individual positioning in the name of tactical collective solidarity based on suffering. The hashtag #CloseTheCamps alludes to this suffering and the internment of Uyghurs in China. Identity politics is a common denominator in the semantics and pragmatics of #IamX. Diasporic Uyghurs use the hashtag to mobilize for nonviolence and freedom of cultural expression and against the actions by the Chinese state. The "I am Charlie" hashtag supporters also mobilize for nonviolence and defend freedom of expression against a perceived religious threat. Therefore, both hashtags gesture to an overwhelming power and aim at amplifying the voice and visibility of those who have suffered under it. Diasporic Uyghurs recontextualize a dominant Western position through the established symbolism of #IamX to secure alliances and save lives at the possible cost of being marginalized themselves as Muslim and cultural Other, now and in the future.

There are other hashtags amplifying the visibility and suffering of the Uyghurs by making use of the intertextual force of ritualized formats for political mobilization. The #MeTooUyghur hashtag is an example. It was launched in 2019 as an advocacy campaign to create international attention about Uyghur disappearances in China through collecting personal testimonios. Halmurat Harri Uyghur, who lives in Finland and is the founder of Uyghur Aid, is credited with creating the hashtag and a social media campaign on Twitter and Facebook (Ramzy 2019). He initiated the hashtag campaign following the temporary disappearance of his parents and a video he posted on Facebook in May of 2018. The campaign gained traction after the Uyghur diaspora became ignited over news about the well-known Uyghur folk musician Abdurehim Heyit, who had allegedly died in detention in Xinjiang according to Turkish media reports. Chinese state media contradicted this claim by posting a twenty-eight-second YouTube video showing Heyit on February 11, 2019. In this video, Heyit proclaimed he was in good health and was being investigated for the violation of national laws (Heyit 2019). The authenticity of the confession video was questioned (Handley and Li 2019). The campaign by Halmurat Uyghur is another example of the growing digital presence of the Uyghurs. "People have started to stand up," said Halmurat Uyghur in an interview with *The New York Times* (Ramzy 2019).

#MeTooUyghur recontextualizes the protest to publicly name an unnamed problem. The unnamed problem is violence against women in the original case and violence against the Uyghurs in the context of this study. As a reminder, the phrase "Me Too" was coined by Tarana Burke in 2006 on MySpace against sexual harassment and abuse of African American women (Hill 2017). The slogan gained traction in 2017 after Harvey Weinstein was outed as an abuser with a long history of sexual harassment and Alyssa Milano wrote her famous tweet asking women to speak out if they had been harassed. #MeToo quickly turned into a highly mediatized global protest movement, with women replying to and retweeting the hashtag. By doing so, the women either made a gesture to share an experience of abuse, identifying with experiences thus described, and/or invited others to be disobedient by speaking out. Halmurat Harri Uyghur explicitly mentions how he and his co-activists were initially worried about offending women in their struggle against sexual violence but eventually selected the hashtag with a gesture to #MeToo in order to show that Uyghurs are abused. Resonance with those who have been silenced becomes a ritualized act, which gives the hashtag "MeTooUyghur" discursive force.

There is emerging research in sociolinguistics on social media posts as mini-narratives. The goal of the research is to understand the digital circulation of stories, multimodal storytelling, and the dimensions of semiotic group formations (Georgakopoulou 2016; Schapp 2014). Georgakopoulou (2016), for example, writes about narrative stance-taking, which refers to routines that precede and frame events and characters, evaluate events and story characters, and highlight characters by tagging them. The functions are to produce "likes" and to create a space for groups and their allies within a public forum. In the curated testimonial space of the UTJD, the hashtag #IamUyghur is part of creating a multimodal and intertextual space for transgressive communication in which participants mobilize for tactical solidarities. The intertextuality of the space enables dialogic interactions with other networked spaces through the curated witness account, the visual and textual recontextualization of suffering, and the transformation of this suffering into an act of defiance.

CONCLUSION

The chapter discusses embodied and digital testimonios as forms of unruly communication that appeal to an audience to take action. In the unelicited testimonios in personal interviews, which were rather unscripted, the narrators were the authors of their stories. The desire to actualize the right to their bodies, to participate in society, and to think and speak without fear manifests itself in the transgressive act of witnessing. The testimonios were told to educate and to advocate. The visibility remained low, however, since intertextual linkages were limited in analogue storytelling.

Some Uyghur activists linked suffering to received gender scripts such as the woman as the moral preserver of culture and nation. Received gender scripts can be in tension with Uyghur women's calls for social participation, however. Some of the female witnesses were skeptical about whether received values like being the reproductive guardian of the nation could be the way forward for Uyghurs, whether in China or abroad. The testimonios are therefore built on variants of the premises of social and political participation discussed in chapters 2 and 3 and are evidence that a quest for rights—political, gender, and others—can be traced across historical time and geographical space.

In contrast, digital testimonios were collected by Uyghur activists to document and archive human rights abuses for potential legal action. The accounts were testimonios, as survivors witnessed to collectively experienced injustices in order to create alliances and to gain international attention. The digital format was a curated template and emphasized factual information, intertextual links, and networked visibility afforded by the digital medium (Brighenti 2007). The images of Rebiya Kadeer are an early example of networked visibility to increase social—and potentially political—recognition. The images tell a narrative of transnational solidarity with other oppressed groups dear to the international imagination like Tibetans. Digital testimonios enhance networked visibility through recontextualized versions of hashtags that align with preceding protest movements in the struggle for nonviolence and accountability. In contrast to the suffering displayed in some human rights discourses through a surplus of affect, the digital testimonios shifted to the language of biographical data, statistics, and abstracted metacommentary. Grassroots efforts and activists were important for the initiation of crowdsourced platforms for horizontal action, as in the case of the Xinjiang Victims Database.

From a diachronic perspective, so the chapter argues, genres and texts cannot stand by themselves as they are inherently dialogic (Bakhtin 1986; Briggs and Bauman 1992). This was also true for YouTube videos, comments, and tweets that gestured to previous utterances and events. As Goffman explains: "Often when we [. . .] engage in "fresh talk," that is, the extemporaneous, ongoing formulation of a text [. . .] it is not true to say that we always speak our own words and ourself take the position to which these words attest" (1981, 146). Talk is dialogic in that it latches onto previous utterances, characters, and words that sediment through ritualized participation frameworks and create new communication events (Goffman 1981). In the case of the Uyghurs, a ritualized participation framework is the hashtag with a commentary like "MeToo(X)" or "Iam(X)." The hashtag and the ritualized terms are the intertextual hinges that enable networked transgression through sociopolitical and moral positioning.

Interlinked platforms, from YouTube to Twitter, created intertextual flows of information and thereby the chance for heightened visibility of Uyghur grievances. The Twitter analysis illustrated the circulation and uptake of testimonial videos through mentions. There were 1,052 mentioned testimonios, with the most-viewed video receiving 15,400 views but only 101 retweets. Of the 1,920 tweets from the activist Twitter handle @uyghurpulse, there were more than one thousand retweets, amplifying the mediated visibility of suffering. At the same time, there is the danger that with waning international media attention over time, digital testimonios will reach fewer people and Uyghurs themselves might be less inclined to upload video testimonios and engage in digital networks. While the overall number of reports in the Xinjiang Victims Database had increased from 15,338 entries in early 2021 to 26,143 in early 2022, the uploaded YouTube testimonios on Uyghur Pulse had only slightly increased in number. Likewise, subscriber numbers increased only from 892 to 1,010 and view numbers from 103,958 by March of 2021 to 121,840 by February of 2022. Violence against the Uyghurs in China and sanctions are still part of the international media, political, and legal debate, but viewer and format fatigue, a shift of attention to other global events, and lack of funding could impede the circulation and uptake of testimonios. The Uyghur Transitional Justice Database, for example, only displays data up until January of 2020.

The evidence-driven approach to transgressions in networked spaces is different from the traditional mediated human rights discourse, where the persecuted narrate their difficult experiences "as apolitical subjects without agency" (Hesford and Lewis 2016, viii). There are problems with this mediated rescue narrative, endemic to Western historical codes of conduct as it creates a transnational imaginary of the marginalized person as being either a victim or a threat (Chouliaraki 2013, 2017; Eberl et al. 2018; Georgiou 2018; Ozduzen, Korkut, and Ozduzen 2020). Identification with the victim and her suffering is a powerful mechanism that obscures the historical conditions that make this identification possible (Gruenewald and Witteborn 2022; Lyon 2013). Hesford's *Spectacular Rhetorics* (2011) comes to mind as it addresses how narrative frames shape socio-legal recognition and public responses. Hesford illustrates how visual images construct bodies in pain and package them as generalized victims of human rights abuses for Western indignation. In particular, the author demonstrates the commodification of female testimony for a global audience and how visual spectacles of rape, torture, genocide, and the sex trade engage historical narratives and produce the human rights subject. Hesford talks about a crisis of testifying and the risks of witness accounts being commodified.

Something similar is happening in some of the representation of Uyghur testimonio by the international media. The BBC, for example, has reported on rape of Uyghur women in detention (e.g., *BBC News* 2021b). Gene Bunin, the aforementioned founder of the Xinjiang Victims Database, has criticized the article as it suggested systemic rape practice, a claim that lacked evidence (Baptista 2021). He emphasizes that the instrumentalization of witness accounts undermines the credibility of survivors as well as the efforts of human rights campaigners. In other words, sensational reports are in danger of using witness accounts for affective performances (e.g., indignation) and distracting from action in the form of collaborative fact-finding missions. Vulnerabilities are mapped onto the bodies of people marked by gender, race, and class (Hesford and Lewis 2016) who briefly gain a face though their affective presence but then fade away as an image "from somewhere" soon to be replaced by another grieving person.

There is the danger of the Uyghurs' digital testimonios being repurposed for a politics of affect. Hashtags like #IamUyghur or #MeTooUyghur can create ideological echo chambers. At the same time, digital technologies provide opportunities for a testimonial infrastructure hinging on connective logics (Bennett and Segerberg 2013) and checks-and-balances mechanisms. Grassroots human rights advocacy, supported by academic and think tank research, is one dimension of this testimonial infrastructure. Interlinked platforms archive visual, textual, and audio data that can be the basis for evidence verification beyond a fleeting affective presence. Digital testimonial evidence can be complemented by actual legal processes. For example, the NGO Coalition for Genocide Response helped launch the Uyghur Tribunal on September 3, 2020. The tribunal, supported by the WUC and independently chaired by Sir Geoffrey Nice, aimed at investigating human rights violations against the Uyghurs and other minorities in XUAR, China. (Sir Nice, a professor of law, was the lead prosecutor at Slobodan Milošević's trial in The Hague.) The Uyghur Tribunal witnesses included Uyghurs, human rights advocates, and academics, and sessions were open to the public (June 4–7, 2021, and September 10–13, 2021, https://uyghurtribunal.com/about/). The Uyghur Tribunal announced in December of 2021 that it was "satisfied beyond reasonable doubt that the PRC, by the imposition of measures to prevent births intended to *destroy* a significant part of the Uyghurs in Xinjiang as such, has committed genocide" (Uyghur Tribunal 2021, section 190, 57). The tribunal jury "considered only the clearest breaches of international standards and law to which the PRC is fully committed, acting with caution and care to reach its decisions" (63). The impact of the trial is unknown but can be guessed to be minimal. China's veto power in the UN Security Council will likely block any further legal proceedings at the highest international level, such as in the UN's highest court, the International Court of Justice.

CONCLUSION

Unruly Speech and the Production of Difference

THE ARGUMENTS IN THIS BOOK are driven by the questions of how transgressive communication practices challenge and dislocate established social and political limits, how the practices travel across geographical space, and how they create opportunities for sociopolitical change. The book analyzes unruly speech as a code of defiance as well as an embodied and technological practice. Against the backdrop of Uyghurs in China, the book illustrates how the shift of premises associated with the practice of naming were signposts for a social body under change. Young Uyghurs pushed for social participation while others argued for more unity in the face of social and religious diversity. Within the context of the Uyghur diaspora, the book shows how transgressive practices move from China to the US and Germany and are strategically adapted to advocate for human rights and the cultural nation. Unruly speech illuminates the social and political moorings of the limit in political systems, the law, technologies, and transnational organizations. The chapters vividly illustrate that naming sociopolitical and physical place and exposing historical injustices are crucial to the process of imagined futures.

The shift toward communication practice is important in times of a retreat into essentialisms and nationalisms. Communication is not only a tool but the main symbolic process that creates social realities and relations. In the tradition of the ethnography of communication, a researcher starts with observable terms for practices and then moves to the analysis of their meanings and properties, enabling claims about sociocultural and political premises in and across locales. By taking practice as a unit of analysis, one can escape the lure of culturalism by looking at how difference is produced. If we understand communication in this way, *practice and process* become the center of attention. They enable a critique of conceptually frozen notions of migration and displacement as a demographic problem or opportunity to be managed or an ethno-national group to be examined. Looking at communicative practice and the elements sustaining this practice questions notions of an ethnically predictable migrant body and mind. It opens up the view toward a politics of participation and trans-spatial alliances through grounded practice. As the late Arif Dirlik maintained, "[W]hat is needed is a more precise consideration of the units of culture in their seemingly ceaseless historical motions" (2003, 287). This book offers empirically based examples of those "units of culture" through the concept of *practice*. Tracing practices across space and time illustrates their breaches and the emerging spaces of interaction that have the potential for social change.

The analytical focus on unruly communication practice presents a counter-perspective to the cultural essentialism lingering in the discourse about the Uyghurs and their advocacy. Claiming rights is essential for those who are denied rights. Transgression might only be a momentary accomplishment but the experience can be carried forward into the future and conserve itself in collective memory. This study includes several examples of these moments, such as the young man in the carpet store uttering *East Turkistan* under his breath or the young woman Aynur learning participatory practices through her NGO work. Courage had moved the young man to say the unutterable, creating a moment of trust. Recognition as a competent equal, able to participate in decision-making and problem-solving, had motivated Aynur to work in the NGO.

Names like *Xinjiang* and *East Turkistan* announced the transgression of a limit through the premises of inequality, unity, participation, belonging, and human rights. Uyghurs in China called for unity in face of generational, urban-rural, and spiritual diversity, thereby pushing social and cultural limits within Uyghur communities. The call for unity disrupts stereotypes about the Uyghurs and an imagination of Uyghurs as a homogeneous entity. In

2006, young Uyghurs were keen on imagining social change from within, expressed in music and through transnational media consumption and work in international environments. Some even found it important to relegate Uyghur culture and religion to the realm of the private. This vision proved to be useful for the state and its surveillance mission to create the new Uyghur as a loyal citizen of China. Overall, the tension between unity in face of diversity and strong assimilation pressures by the state illustrate the complex forces Uyghurs already had to cope with in 2006. Uyghurs who imagined participation talked about ways of *having* (Tarde [1895] 1999). They talked about rights: the right to speak and be heard, the right to practice one's language and culture, the right to be mobile, the right to speak one's mind without fear, and the right to question cultural hierarchies. Debate, feedback, and asking questions are practices that create the grounds for critical reflection and eventually the critical, questioning citizen. They were also practices that helped people imagine a more open, inclusive society. However, the opening that seemed possible in 2006 is put on hold.

The highly politicized name *East Turkistan* proved to be an important resource in diasporic mobilization in the name of human rights. The name can be understood as an inverse mirror image of *Xinjiang* through the call for basic rights, such as the right to free speech and information. While uttering *East Turkistan* constitutes a political breach in China, it was the name of choice for many diasporic Uyghurs. The name was realized through digital networks and self-presentation of the digital nation. This insight strengthens Diminescu and Loveluck's (2014) observation that digital networks shape visibility and through this visibility the ways to self-represent as a diasporic body.

The premise of belonging pushed the idea of self-determination. It positioned the speaker in China in the risky legal territory of secession and terrorism, which the Chinese government had staked out through the "Strike Hard Campaign against Violent Terrorism" in May of 2014 and the Counterterrorism Law in 2015 (ILO 2015). Belonging did not only refer to culture or an ethno-nationalistic imagination. Belonging positioned the political subject. The political subject did not only present herself in the language of trauma and the genealogy of a damaged self. In the words of Didier Fassin (2008, 533): "Thus, to speak of political subjectification is not in any way to predicate a Cartesian 'I' or a Freudian 'ego' but, rather, the production of subjects and subjectivities that hold political significance within the framework of social interaction." Uttering *East Turkistan* and testifying were part of this subjectification. The witness became an interpellated subject whose telling of difficult experiences was a political act. The name *East Turkistan* challenged the political sovereignty of China, and the social media analysis showed the circulation and amplification of the Uyghur human rights discourse over time. Meanwhile, the Chinese government, via its government media, denies any allegations of violence against the Uyghurs. The discourse is assertive, attacking any evidence of human rights abuse as the use of a double standard in view of US aggressive foreign policy in Muslim-dominated nations and treating Muslims in the US and Europe as security threats (e.g., *China Daily* 2021).

In addition to naming, digital testimonios circulated the call for human rights through the language of data, creating intertextual links between social and traditional media, activist platforms, and an international audience. Digital testimonio aligned with the legalistic tradition and delivered evidence for truth verification. The primary objective and message was not the affective narrative but the triangulation of verifiable data. Unruly speech engages the political structure, to rephrase de Certeau (1997). Using the name *East Turkistan* instead of *Xinjiang* is a prime example of the capture of speech, which de Certeau (1997) discusses so vividly in the context of social protest in France. *East Turkistan* created a resonance space to reflect on some of the varying goals of politically active Uyghurs. Some argued for more political and cultural autonomy for Uyghurs and other minorities alike, others for cultural recognition, and yet others for independence.

Technology co-created the conditions for resistant speech to be performed. Diasporic Uyghurs have built the digital nation over time and kept it alive through the premise of belonging circulated on advocacy websites and platforms like Twitter, Facebook, and YouTube. This insight adds to the large body of literature on digital diasporas lobbying for the nation (e.g., Dwonch 2019; Keles 2016; Oiarzabal 2020). Digital networks maintain transnational imaginaries, especially in the case of displacement and statelessness, as Aziz (2022) shows by the example of the Rohingya. Chapter 4 argues for the importance of networked technologies for visualizing suffering through curated formats. The testimonios posted in digital space had a more complex intertextual, inter-genre, and multimodal character than the "analogue" testimonios. Written and oral accounts, photographs and streaming videos, maps, geolocation data, hashtags, and retweets created a testimonial infrastructure driven by the connective logics of networked actors (Bennett and Segerberg 2013). These actors included Uyghurs in various parts of the world, activists, human rights supporters, and financial donors. Horizontal and vertical intertextuality (Fairclough 1992; Kristeva 1986) was created through hashtags and reference to protest movements. By doing so, Uyghurs positioned themselves as victims of violence and used the momentum of global anti-violence movements like #MeToo to amplify their mediated visibility and their demands for collective justice.

Grassroots activism played an important role in the mobilization for collective justice. Uyghur Aid, the Xinjiang Victims Database, and the Uyghur Pulse are part of a well-curated human rights defenders network that makes rights violations visible through crowdfunding and wide-ranging organizational support, including academic institutions. The discussed digital testimonio projects are part of a larger network of human rights activism for the Uyghurs, such as the Xinjiang Documentation Project (University of British Columbia and Simon Fraser University, n.d.). This information-rich project gathers, evaluates, and archives information on the "extrajudicial detention" of Uyghurs and ethnic groups in Xinjiang, as the home page of the website states (https://xinjiang.sppga.ubc.ca). The project includes testimonios by Uyghurs, academic sources, and teaching syllabi, as well as films, podcasts, and documentaries related to the topic. The networked infrastructure is an example of connective logics and the personalization of large-scale political action on the grassroots level (Bennett and Segerberg 2013). The mediated visibility of Uyghur testimonios can be scaled through these efforts, as exemplified by retweets and individual views of testimonial videos in chapter 4.

At the same time, this visibility does not automatically translate into other forms of protest and support and an improvement of the situation for the group in question. Connective visibility can have the positive connotation of interpersonal resonance (e.g., Hjorth and Lim 2012; Madianou 2016). On the flip side, consumption of victims' images and narratives can become an automated act that hinges on the "smooth communication of the Same" (Han 2015, 2). Exposure to repeated loops of victims' images and narratives can potentially dampen their resonance (Chouliaraki 2013; Nayar 2011). Lazy clicktivism (Morozov 2009, 2011) due to oversaturation could be the consequence, slowing the uptake of the Uyghur rights discourse over time.

Technology also played a crucial role in controlling transgressive speech. Malware programs interrupted diasporic communication, and internalized fears of surveillance strengthened self-censorship. Digital surveillance turned the Uyghur diaspora and Uyghurs in China into data assets that could be used by the state to assess a person's risk potential. The datafied Uyghur has come to represent the ideal of the transparent counter-figure to an opaque cultural body. Even the last frontier of opaqueness and cultural reproduction—the family home—can now be used as an index of deviance. It can be technologically controlled and integrated into a surveillance infrastructure to preempt unruly action and disobedience. Chapter 2 illustrates the ways in which Uyghurs' speech and actions are turned into digital data for risk calculation through platforms and deep-learning databases. Chapter 3 highlights the digital surveillance of diasporic communication. These insights connect to the extant literature on the datafication of migrant mobilities and other behaviors, especially how technologies construct bodies and groups as alphanumerical entities in order to sort and categorize them according to inclusion and exclusion criteria (e.g., Ajana 2013; Fog Olwig et al. 2020; Pollozek and Passoth 2019; Ruppert and Scheel 2021; Tazzioli 2020; van der Ploeg and Pridmore 2016). Automated surveillance of everyday life in the name of security is the expanded version of biometric bordering, as described by the researchers mentioned above, who worked mostly in a European setting. Automated surveillance is expansive in China and works with immediate consequences, from public shaming on LED screens when jaywalking to digital content management and flagging of those who transgress discursive limits.

Byler (2019) observes that China's anti-terrorism strategies have boosted the growth of technology startups in China, a growth that in his opinion will continue, given the vast markets in the Belt and Road Initiative (BRI) countries and the fact that 60 percent of the Muslim-majority nations in the world are part of it. At the same time, the fact that countries which tend to condemn China for human rights violations attend the China-Eurasia Security Expo in Urumqi raises the question of whether the attendance is due to competitive interest or government technology visions, or both. Technology with the potential for surveillance shapes lives in most parts of the world.

Biometric borders, the technology enabling smart environments, and social media platforms are all examples (Zuboff 2019). The latter is not an argument to downplay the ubiquitous surveillance of citizens in China but a reminder to take the situation in Western countries into consideration before proposing a substantiated critique of the situation in China.

The affordance of visibility enabled through digital technologies recalls Lefebvre's observation about seeing as the primary mode of representation and abstraction. "In the course of the process whereby the visual gains the upper hand over the other senses, all impressions derived from taste, smell, touch and even hearing [. . .] fade away altogether, leaving the field to line, colour and light" (Lefebvre 1991, 286). The ideal of transparency in communication and work practice, which young Uyghurs in China admired in 2006, has become the digital yoke of the Uyghurs today. Control-type visibility (Brighenti 2007, 339) regulates visibility in the name of transparency and exposes the last remaining space of opaqueness. Byung-Chul Han (2015, 2) says that transparency calibrates a social system by sorting out difference: "This systemic compulsion makes the society of transparency a calibrated society. Herein lies its totalitarian trait." The participatory aspirations of Uyghurs have been crushed by a technologically enhanced surveillance system, which shines a light onto the most private aspects of their lives. Couched in the discourse of a war on terror, Uyghurs' personal and cultural autonomy has become fully restricted in China.

In addition to technology, transgressive speech is enabled by political and legal conditions and organizational actors. Freedom of expression and the press, as protected by Article 5(1) of the Basic Law of the Federal Republic of Germany and the First Amendment to the United States Constitution, enabled diasporic Uyghurs in Germany and the United States to call for self-determination. Chapter 3 on the name *East Turkistan* has illustrated this point. Likewise, organizational actors were crucial for supporting unruly speech. In China, younger Uyghurs felt encouraged to push cultural hierarchies through practices they had learned in the transnational workplace, such as participatory decision-making, feedback, and dialogic learning. Those ways of communication challenged existing cultural norms linked to age and gender hierarchies. In the United States and Germany, organizational and media support was vital for the Uyghurs' political advocacy and visibility. Examples are donor organizations such as the National Endowment for Democracy in Washington, D.C., transnational advocacy organizations like Amnesty International and Human Rights Watch, and reports by media organizations, including *The New York Times*, *The Guardian*, the BBC, Radio Free Asia, or *Die Zeit* in Germany. Organizations like the NED financed Uyghur advocacy through conferences and by supporting international networking of the diaspora related to human rights education and practice. The NED also assisted with amplifying Uyghurs' digital presence, as the Uyghur Transitional Justice Database project underlined.

Over time, national governments and intergovernmental organizations have become part of a human rights discourse that shifts uneasily between supporting Uyghur calls for human rights, protecting economic interests, and acknowledging the limits of international legal mechanisms. For example, in anticipation of its own limited impact, the Uyghur Tribunal called for grassroots voices to become active in the political process. The call is a moral reminder of citizens' duties, which activists did not need as they had long been involved in the research and documentation of the rights situation of Uyghurs and other minorities.

Unruly speech was also linked to tactical strategic essentialism (Spivak 1984/85). As a tactic in the advocacy for belonging and human rights, the Uyghur leadership resurrected a shared identity to represent the Uyghurs as a group worth supporting. Especially the premise of suffering has illustrated how political advocacy for a homeland demanded a culturally conservative repertoire to gain the sympathies of international audiences. The Uyghur leadership saw the need at times to publicly affiliate with political figures like former US president G. W. Bush to secure political support in its diasporic struggle despite the political and moral inconsistencies of some of those allies. This alliance-seeking can be seen as a response to a media-saturated environment as well. In a media-saturated environment, which thrives on powerful entities coming to the rescue of the oppressed, an advocacy campaign has to engage with an essentialized Other who suffers (Nayar 2011). The figure of the female heroine fighting for the resurrection of the nation was an important element in the strategic, culture-focused self-presentation of the Uyghurs. Rebiya Kadeer, for example, drew from received gender scripts that appealed not only to a Uyghur but to an international audience. The mother who courageously protects her suffering children is an affective commonplace that is universally appealing. Cultural essentialism ties in with contemporary audience tastes and a general preoccupation with the preservation of cultures under threat.

Strategic essentialism was a move that worked in tandem with the digital inscription of the nation. However, strategic essentialism was not without risk, as Payal Arora (2020) noted in her research about Oromo diasporic mobilization. Strong collective identification can mean exclusion of dissenting voices. This was also true in the case of the Uyghurs, as those who questioned received normative behavior and social roles could be sidelined in the diaspora. The divorced mother and the single artist became diasporic outsiders, forging their own advocacy for social and political rights. The struggle by these outsiders has similarities with the struggle of young Uyghur women in Xinjiang. There, young females were pushing for participatory ways of decision-making and the disruption of gender and age hierarchies. Excluding different points of view and approaches from advocacy might not be the most productive move. On the contrary, difference can be an added strength as those women and men who had crossed social and cultural limits created alliances around progressive values, such as gender equality and creativity. Those values, in turn, can assist with keeping the social and generational diversity of Uyghur communities in focus and prevent the freezing of culture in time. By learning new ways for organizational interaction or by engaging in political advocacy, Uyghur women gained confidence and transcended the domestic sphere. Women left unhappy marriages, raised children by themselves, and fulfilled their aspirations for education and skilled work. The women gendered transgression by emphasizing their needs for personal safety, creativity, education, and participation in society. The alliances growing out of female emancipation can be a further means of opening up new rights practices for the Uyghurs, as the current ones are in danger of being treated as ritualized by-products of international diplomacy.

There is also the danger that Uyghurs are corseted by the premises of a mythic homeland, which is currently overwritten by the discourse on human rights but might return more forcefully in the future. In other words, unruliness—when linked to strategic self-presentation—can activate mythic ways of thinking, which might be detrimental to the freedom an individual or group can experience in the moment of transgression. As Ernst Cassirer (1955) argues, mythic thinking is strictly patterned. It assigns value to names, people, things, and "modes of synthesis" (60) that emphasize unity of the multiple. In Cassirer's words: "Myth itself is one of those spiritual syntheses through which a bond between 'I' and 'thou' is made possible, through which a definite unity and a definite contrast, a relation of kinship and a relation of tension, are created between the individual and the community" (177). Mythic thinking and speaking means assurance of an ordered universe.

Names are an assurance of a designated place. *East Turkistan* can mobilize not only a Uyghur or pan-Turkic identity but also the logics of a totem according to which social groups are divided into strict categories with characteristics and taboos that represent the microcosm of being (Cassirer 1956). Mythical thinking takes fate for granted and provides security in the symbolic forms of a predefined cosmos. Richard Sennett ([1977] 2002) elaborates on that notion from a sociological perspective in the context of place politics. He argues that communal fantasies about collective personality can create an illusionary bondage to a fantasy of unique (cultural) closeness. In independence movements, this fantasy is tied to an essentialized idea about belonging, which nurtures itself through a preassigned order of space, people, and language. Independence movements driven by mythical thinking are in danger of making "local territory morally sacred" (Sennett [1977] 2002, 295). Morally sacred territory does not allow for difference. It has space for guests and tolerance but not members and acceptance. This territory is defined through the exclusion of those who are not part of the lineage and do not conform, be it those who are single, divorced, too politically progressive, or too religiously conservative.

It has to be emphasized that strategic essentialism is a tactical move that does not correspond to the historical realities of the Uyghurs inside and outside of China. The border regions of China have always been cosmopolitan in the contemporary understanding of the term and have developed their localized variants of culture, art, and religion with inspirations from Central Asia, North Africa, and Europe (Millward 2007; Newby 2007; Rudelson 1997; Schluessel 2007, 2009; Smith Finley 2007, 2013; Thum 2014a). Uyghurs and the place they call home have been heterogeneous and outward-oriented on account of contact with traders and pilgrims from Turkey, Iran, and India (Thum 2014a), religious soundscapes that connect local communities with transnational migrant networks from Central Asia to Turkey (Harris 2007, 2016, 2020), and the outlook and careers of Uyghurs in China and abroad (Grose 2015a, 2015b, 2019; Tursun 2017). Despite the tactical strategic essentialism, diasporic Uyghurs are an extension of this outward-oriented vision, exemplified by the women and men who challenged gender imaginations and engaged with difference in creative ways. In other words, the case of Uyghurs is another reminder for those studying migration and mobilities to engage with history and shift their gaze from centers of identity building, be it state, metropolis, or political leadership, toward the alleged periphery of place and social group, with all their complexities and rhizomatic relations.

The focus on communication practice has implications for migration and social interaction researchers. Analyzing ways of speaking reveals the heterogeneity of a place and the intersectionality of identity, spatiality, and temporality. This study suggests tracing practices across time and space. The call is made in response to the sedentary approaches to communicative practice and studying communities as being rooted in place, as explained in the Introduction. Tracing practices is not meant to imply a linear search for an origin or root. To the contrary, tracing assists with identifying spatial patterns of relationality and with providing a fresh look at groups beyond the primordial bond. Practice and process become the units of analysis and not the preconceived cultural trait. Put differently, a focus on practice highlights how migrants come into being as people being displaced through cultural, political, and legal processes as well as through the dislocating nature of language itself (Cooren 2010). Those who are displaced speak *in the name* of a group, principle, or idea, thereby authorizing those concepts and giving them discursive force with actionable consequences. Even more, the arguments highlight the role of transnational organizations in giving authority to particular ways of speaking and relating. Organizations introduce new practices into a place, which can be perceived as defiant by the state if they do not cohere with the political code. This was the case with Save the Children and the emphasis of its managerial staff at the time on participatory decision-making. In other words, transnationally operating organizations become part of the embodied and mediated circuits that impact notions of what it means to be a person in place (also Witteborn 2010).

The arguments in this book are also important for international relations and security researchers and those wanting to understand the complexities of contemporary China. In response to a focus on human rights, Chestnut Greitens, Lee, and Yazici (2020) raise the question of whether the Uyghur issue could be better addressed by the shared challenges that China and the rest of the world face, such as terrorism. In the view of the authors, human rights might not be an effective means to change China's course in relation to the Uyghurs:

> More broadly, examining external sources of China's domestic security policies in Xinjiang reinforces the analytical leverage and potential policy traction that scholars can gain by viewing CCP behavior not just through the lens of a repressive party-state, but as the behavior of a state that, despite its growing power, is simultaneously insecure at home and abroad, and that sees these insecurities as deeply interrelated. (Chestnut Greitens, Lee, and Yazici 2020, 47; Shirk 2007)

This view, in turn, raises the question of the context that gives rise to violence and the national and international treatment of a group as potentially dangerous; a process which continues the spiral of violence, blaming, and further stereotyping. Fuller and Starr (2003) pointed to other regions where groups are mediatized and treated as "terrorists," including in the Palestinian Territories, Kashmir, Chechnya, the Basque country, or Mindanao in the Philippines. "The claims of existing states against dissident minorities have been strengthened and are likely to remain so for the foreseeable future," Fuller and Starr had already concluded in 2003 (14).

The statement still holds. Most states show a strong hand in controlling defiant groups, from Russia, Israel, India, Spain, and China to the Philippines and Thailand. While Xinjiang is a border region with politically volatile neighbors, including Afghanistan and Pakistan, it is also at the crossroads between East and West, Central Asia, and South/East Asia, with major neuralgic infrastructural nodes. China will remain forceful in its response to dissident minorities, including the Uyghurs. Nevertheless, the government has to balance this approach with persuading the Uyghurs to play a productive role in the motherland. China needs the collaboration of Uyghurs to realize the Belt and Road Initiative projects, deliver an important workforce in Xinjiang province and in China, and raise standards of living.

Critics might suggest that the political advocacy by the Uyghurs and their allies solidifies the moral dominance of the rich, industrialized countries and its unreflective preaching about democracy and human rights to ascending countries, especially those with autocratic rule. The struggle of the Uyghurs nourishes the privileged northern multitude in their celebration of heroic rebels against a morally dis-preferred state. Symbolic orders of national, cultural, and moral hierarchy are maintained in this constellation. Such a concern has to be taken seriously, especially in the context of a human rights discourse that conceals the harsh realities of continuing neoliberal globaliza- tion, on the one hand, and the psychological and physical abuse of cultural and religious Others, on the other. Even more, embracing the role of an ethnic Other in need of cultural protection may distract from the call by Uyghurs for political representation. The call for human rights has proven ineffective to date despite the push for trade and political sanctions against China in the wake of allegations of forced labor in Xinjiang and detention camps. The 2022 Beijing Winter Olympics, which opened on February 4, 2022, illustrated how organizations like the International Olympic Committee can bracket human rights in the name of neutrality and apolitical sports-wo/manship.

Despite the digital surveillance in and militarization of Xinjiang province, one can speculate that the quest of young Uyghurs for international exposure and experience might be slowed down but will not be impeded. One can also speculate that unruly voices will eventually become part of Uyghur self-representation, complicating reductive essentialism. Uyghur collective memory will continue to be based on aspirations of unity and societal partic- ipation. With China forcing loyal citizenship, younger Uyghurs might decide to comply and take advantage of the promised economic prosperity. Fuller and Starr talked about assimilationists in 2003 and estimated this group to be small. The young people interviewed in chapter 2 were no assimilationists. They did look forward to economic prosperity and social mobility instead of looking back into a hurtful past. Nevertheless, economic prosperity was not enough for them. They wanted social participation and cultural reform. Especially urban Uyghurs in this study were deeply interested in sociocul- tural reforms, including a change of cultural values that override personal freedoms. The sociocultural desire for change was indicative of a desire for political change, including speaking one's mind freely. There was also the tension between the lure of migration for careers and a deep connection to the local. In the face of strict cultural and political regulation, the assimilationist group could grow, but stifling policies could also have the opposite effect. Witnessing the repression of parents, neighbors, and colleagues, people might be less inclined to accept cultural engineering and might demand social and economic participation. They could orient even more toward Central Asia,

Turkey, and other countries, taking every opportunity to migrate. Some of those people might join the diaspora from Central Asia to Europe, Australia, Japan, and North America to keep Uyghur identity alive.

In a further variant of speculation, one could present an internationally more challenging scenario. Governments and international audiences should ask themselves what happens if Xinjiang morphs into another volatile region in the world like Kashmir or Palestine, with intermittent uprisings, or if a more conservative form of Islam takes hold in Xinjiang province. Chances are low as the Chinese government exerts strict control over the territory. However, if it were to be the case, how would these developments affect the human rights discourse? Would European, North American, and Australian audiences still support Uyghurs, or would they start supporting surveillance and control practices by the Chinese government? Chouliaraki (2017) and Georgiou (2018) remind us that collaborative agency is only partially successful because it is embedded into larger symbolic regimes of ordering, which stop short of granting true sociopolitical recognition to particular groups. Given the strong anti-Islam rhetoric in North America and Europe since September 11, 2001, one could imagine a fast shift from a human rights discourse to an anti-Uyghur discourse in case a subsection of Uyghurs chose to radicalize in the face of ongoing injustices. Moreover, the topic of Uyghurs' grievances can be overshadowed by related topics of interest to an international audience, such as China's economic ascent and technological development. The Uyghur diaspora has actively raised awareness about the cultural and economic marginalization of the people in Xinjiang for at least two decades. However, the international community has only paid attention recently. At times, it seemed as if the debate on the technological advancement and digital surveillance in China, including during the Covid-19 pandemic, has stirred an international audience more than the reports of violence against the Uyghurs.

I would like to end this discussion on a personal note. Writing this book has been a cultural, political, and personal journey for me over several years. It was a journey that has left me humbled, energized, and disturbed. I am humbled by the trust of the people I had the privilege to journey with, by their witness accounts, and by their optimism to build a new life. I am energized and yet disturbed by the changes I have seen over more than a decade in China, from young Uyghurs anticipating travel, international study, and meaningful work opportunities, like so many other young people in China and around the world, to people becoming controlled datasets. For Uyghurs, life looks more challenging than ever. The definable and definite still dominates discourses on migration as can be seen in the commonplace of the *crisis* of forced migration, the figure of the *refugee* eliciting compassion as well as pity, or the figure of the *Uyghur* who is defined along the continuum of human rights and radicalism. Saturated figures like these feed public imaginations, serve as affective bolsters in arguments for border protection and surveillance, and are vehicles to further political agendas. Therefore, it remains important to keep reflecting on the temporally and spatially constituted nature of migration, culture, and belonging. Uyghurs push to gain attention, to take a seat at national and international tables, and to represent themselves in digital spaces. Communicative practice is key in these endeavors, from deliberation and decision-making to speaking one's mind without fear. The call for an anti-essentialist understanding of the group and the emphasis on collective rights and representation seem feeble calls to make in times of a global pandemic, displacement, technological militarization, environmental degradation, and punishment of people who speak out. And yet, those calls should be made by activists, politicians, media workers, and academics. They should be made from different theoretical and methodological perspectives and with the wisdom of the generative power of the right to disagree in nonviolent ways.

Notes

PREFACE

1. G.N. (E.) 72 of 2020, the Law of the People's Republic of China on Safe-guarding National Security in the Hong Kong Special Administrative Region, https://www.gld.gov.hk/egazette/pdf/20202448e/egn2020244872.pdf.

INTRODUCTION

1. The formal name, Xinjiang Uyghur Autonomous Region (XUAR), intro-duced in 1954, could rarely be heard in face-to-face interactions. It was a name on official documents in China, Germany, and the United States. *Xinjiang* was a more forceful signifier in and outside China and is therefore used in the fol-lowing chapters.

2. For a detailed account of Uyghur protest and measures taken by the Chinese government to surveil and control Uyghur mobility and life, see Sean Roberts (2018, 2020).

3. Darren Byler's book *Terror Capitalism* (2022) was not available in Hong Kong yet when I finalized the manuscript. The book *In the Camps* (2021b) was available in The Chinese University of Hong Kong library.

4. This study was funded through two grants from The Chinese University of Hong Kong. The first was a Direct Grant, entitled *Muslim Communities in China: The Discourse on Terrorism and the Construction of Muslim Collective Identity* (2006/2007) (Project ID: 2020851). The second was a Thematic Grant, entitled *Ways of Communicating Key Messages: An Analysis of Face-to-Face*

Communication and Media Strategies Used by Transnational NGOs Operating in Xinjiang/China (2006), collaboration with Political Science faculty, CUHK (Project ID: 2020883).

5. The study of Uyghur diasporas in Germany and the United States was funded by the General Research Fund of Hong Kong from 2008 to 2010 and entitled *Mobilizing Diasporic Identities: The Case of Uyghurs in the United States and in Germany* (PI, RGC Ref. No.: CUHK451908).

CHAPTER 1

1. *A Preface to Transgression* was first published as "Hommage à Georges Bataille," *Critique* ° 195–196 (1963).

CHAPTER 2

1. The Kuomintang was the first National People's Party of China, which founded the Republic of China in 1912 and had to retreat to Taiwan in 1949 during the Chinese Civil War.

2. In places like Hong Kong, *Chinese,* when used in relation to language, tends to refer to Cantonese as a major Chinese dialect. *Chinese* is sometimes also referred to as *Mandarin,* which gestures to a group of varieties, with the standard dialect of Beijing as the most important (Standard Chinese). In everyday language, Chinese speakers in the PRC tend to use the term *Putonghua,* which means *common language.* When speaking English with me, Uyghurs and Han Chinese used the term *Chinese.*

3. The discussion about the export of communication styles to the Global South is based on an article originally published in 2010 in the journal *Language and Intercultural Communication*: Witteborn, Saskia. 2010. "The Role of Transnational NGOs in Promoting Global Citizenship and Globalizing Communication Practices." *Language and Intercultural Communication* 10 (4): 358–72.

4. For a related discussion on the meaning of communication in US society, see Katriel and Philipsen (1981).

CHAPTER 3

1. Uyghur Human Rights Policy Act of 2020, June 17, 2020, Public Law No. 116–145, 116th Cong., https://www.congress.gov/116/plaws/publ145/PLAW-116publ145.pdf.

2. I would like to thank my research assistant for his work on the Twitter analysis. He shall remain anonymous because of the politically sensitive nature of the book's topic.

3. All figures were created by my research assistant, whose work I want to acknowledge here; see previous note.

CHAPTER 4

1. *Human Rights in China and Tibet: Hearing before the Subcomm. on International Operations and Human Rights of the Comm. on International Relations,* 106th Cong., March 2, 2000, serial no. 106-114, https://www.govinfo.gov/content/pkg/CHRG-106hhrg65151/html/CHRG-106hhrg65151.htm.

2. *Testimony of Jewher Ilham before the Congressional-Executive Commission on China,* April 8, 2014, https://www.cecc.gov/sites/chinacommission .house.gov/files/CECC%20Hearing%20-%20Human%20Rights%20Defenders %20-%20Jewher%20Ilham%20Written%20Statement.pdf. See also *Congressional-Executive Commission on China, 2005 Annual Report,* https://www.cecc.gov/publications/annual-reports/2005-annual-report.

3. *USCIRF Testimony at Capitol Hill Hearing on Uighur Muslims, Before the United States Commission on International Religious Freedom,* June 10, 2009, https://www.uscirf.gov/resources/uscirf-testimony-capitol-hill-hearing-uighur -muslims.

4. I need to reiterate that I have changed personal names and some place names to protect the identity of witnesses.

5. To protect herself and others, Roshan did not mention the name of the organization.

6. Turkish was a preferred language environment because of the similarities between the Turkish and Uyghur languages and many shared cultural traditions.

7. Some of the arguments made in this section on Rebiya Kadeer were originally published in a book chapter of mine, entitled "Gendering Cyberspace: Transnational Mappings and Uyghur Diasporic Politics." The chapter was published in *Circuits of Visibility: Gender and Transnational Media Cultures,* edited by Radha S. Hegde, 2011, New York: New York University Press, 268–83.

8. http://www.meshrep.com/Politicals.interview.htm (accessed December 15, 2008). Now defunct.

9. "China 'crushing Uighurs' (Rebiya Kadeer)," http://www.YouTube.com/watch?v=7sK8woLHKUo (accessed December 17, 2008). Now defunct.

10. https://www.gettyimages.co.uk/detail/news-photo/tibetan-spiritual-leader-the-dalai-lama-and-rabiya-kadeer-news-photo/90592296 (accessed September 2018).

11. Search terms were Rebiya Kadeer, Rabiye Kadir, or Rebiya Qadir (accessed January 10, 2009).

12. I am citing the journalist Eduardo Baptista from the *South China Morning Post* in Hong Kong to illustrate that the most important English-language newspaper in Hong Kong, which is owned by the Alibaba Group, cites Bunin as the founder of the Xinjiang Victims database. This contradicts a report by the Chinese state media, the *Global Times* (Fan and Chen, April 9, 2021), which mentions another person as the creator.

References

Abramson, Kara. 2012. "Gender, Uyghur Identity, and the Story of Nuzugum." *Journal of Asian Studies* 71 (4): 1069–91. https://doi.org/10.1017/S00219118120 01179.

Afolabi, Niyi. 2009. *Afro-Brazilians: Cultural Production in a Racial Democracy.* Rochester Studies in African History and the Diaspora. Woodbridge, UK: Boydell & Brewer.

Ahluwalia, Pal. 2006. "Race." *Theory, Culture & Society* 23 (2–3): 538–45. https://doi.org/10.1177/026327640602300298.

Ahmed, Sara. (2004) 2014. *The Cultural Politics of Emotion.* New York: Routledge.

Ajana, Btihaj. 2013. *Governing through Biometrics: The Biopolitics of Identity.* Basingstoke, UK: Palgrave Macmillan.

Ala, Mamtimin. 2021. *Worse than Death: Reflections on the Uyghur Genocide.* Lanham, MD: Rowman & Littlefield.

Alencar, Amanda. 2018. "Refugee Integration and Social Media: A Local and Experiential Perspective." *Information, Communication & Society* 21 (11): 1588–1603.

———. 2020. "Digital Place-Making Practices and Daily Struggles of Venezuelan (Forced) Migrants in Brazil." In *The SAGE Handbook of Media and Migration,* edited by Kevin Smets, Koen Leurs, Myria Georgiou, Saskia Witteborn, and Radhika Gajjala, 503–14. Thousand Oaks, CA: SAGE.

Allen-Ebrahimian, Bethany. 2019. "Exposed: China's Operating Manuals for Mass Internment and Arrest by Algorithm." *China Cables.* November 24,

2019. https://www.icij.org/investigations/china-cables/exposed-chinas-opera
ting-manuals-for-mass-internment-and-arrest-by-algorithm/.

Alonso, Andoni, and Pedro J. Oiarzabal, eds. 2010. *Diasporas in the New Media Age: Identity, Politics, and Community*. Reno: University of Nevada Press.

Amin, Ash. 2012. *Land of Strangers*. Malden, MA: Polity Press.

Amoore, Louise. 2011. "Data Derivatives: On the Emergence of a Security Risk Calculus for Our Times." *Theory, Culture & Society* 28 (6): 24–43. https://doi .org/10.1177/0263276411417430.

———. 2013. *The Politics of Possibility: Risk and Security beyond Probability*. Durham, NC: Duke University Press.

Anderson, Benedict R. 1991. *Imagined Communities: Reflections on the Origin and Spread of Nationalism*, rev. ed. London: Verso.

Andrejevic, Mark. 2020. "Shareable and Un-Sharable Knowledge." *Big Data & Society* 7 (1). https://doi.org/10.1177/2053951720933917.

Appiah, Kwame Anthony. 2006. *Cosmopolitanism: Ethics in a World of Strangers*. New York: W. W. Norton.

Arora, Payal. 2020. "The Oromo Movement and Ethiopian Border-Making Using Social Media." In *The SAGE Handbook of Media and Migration*, edited by Kevin Smets, Koen Leurs, Myria Georgiou, Saskia Witteborn, and Radhika Gajjala, 321–33. Thousand Oaks, CA: SAGE.

Ash, Timothy Garton. 2004. "Washington's Post-9/11 War on Terror Is Finished." *Guardian*, January 21, 2004. https://www.theguardian.com/world/2004/ jan/22/syria.usa.

Ashuri, Tamar, and Amit Pinchevski. 2009. "Witnessing as a Field." In *Media Witnessing: Testimony in the Age of Mass Communication*, edited by Paul Frosh and Amit Pinchevski, 133–57. Basingstoke, UK: Palgrave Macmillan.

Austin, John L. 1962. *How to Do Things with Words*. Edited by James Opie Urm-son and Marina Sbisá, 2nd ed. Cambridge, MA: Harvard University Press.

Awad, Isabel, and Jonathan Tossell. 2019. "Is the Smartphone Always a Smart Choice? Against the Utilitarian View of the 'Connected Migrant.'" *Informa-tion, Communication & Society* 24 (4): 611–26.

Aziz, Abdul. 2022. "Power Geometries of Mediated Care: (Re)mapping Trans-national Families and Immobility of the Rohingya Diaspora in a Digital Age." *Media, Culture & Society* 44 (5): 967–985. https://doi.org/10.1177/01634 437211065690.

Bakhtin, Mikhail M. 1981. *The Dialogic Imagination: Four Essays*. Austin: Uni-versity of Texas Press.

———. 1986. *Speech Genres and Other Late Essays*. Translated by Vern W. McGee. Austin: University of Texas Press.

Bamman, David, Brendan O'Connor, and Noah Smith. 2012. "Censorship and Deletion Practices in Chinese Social Media." *First Monday* 17 (3). https://doi .org/10.5210/fm.v17i3.3943.

Baptista, Eduardo. 2021. "Human Rights in China: Activists Say Sensationalist Reports on Xinjiang Do More Harm Than Good." *South China Morning Post*, May 24, 2021. https://www.scmp.com/news/china/politics/article/3134671/ human-rights-china-activists-say-sensationalist-reports.

Baranovitch, Nimrod. 2007. "Inverted Exile: Uyghur Writers and Artists in Beijing and the Political Implications of Their Work." *Modern China* 33 (4): 462–504. https://doi.org/10.1177/0097700407304803.

Barfield, Thomas. 1989. *The Perilous Frontier: Nomadic Empires and China 221 BC to AD 1757*. Studies in Social Discontinuity. Cambridge: Wiley -Blackwell.

Basso, Keith H. 1970. "'To Give Up on Words': Silence in Western Apache Culture." *Southwestern Journal of Anthropology* 26 (3): 213–30. https://doi .org/10.1086/soutjanth.26.3.3629378.

Bataille, Georges. 1986. *Erotism: Death & Sensuality*. Translated by Mary Dalwood. San Francisco: City Lights Books.

BBC News. 2021a. "Canada's Parliament Declares China's Treatment of Uighurs 'Genocide,'" February 23, 2021. https://www.bbc.com/news/world-us-canada -56163220.

———. 2021b. "Claims of Rape and Torture of Uighur Women in China Provoke Global Condemnation." YouTube video, 4:02, February 5, 2021. https://youtu .be/hh8QOh1aXRM.

Becker, Howard S. 1967. "Whose Side Are We On?" *Social Problems* 14 (3): 239–47. https://doi.org/10.2307/799147.

Bellér-Hann, Ildikó. 1991. "Script Changes in Xinjiang." In *Cultural Change and Continuity in Central Asia*, edited by Shirin Akiner, 71–83. New York: Kegan Paul, and London: Central Asia Research Forum, School of Oriental and African Studies.

———. 2007. "Situating Uyghur Life Cycle Rituals between China and Central Asia." In *Situating the Uyghurs between China and Central Asia*, edited by Ildikó Bellér-Hann, M. Cristina Cesàro, Rachel Harris, and Joanne Finley, 131–48. Aldershot, Hampshire, UK: Ashgate.

———. 2008. *Community Matters in Xinjiang, 1880–1949: Towards a Historical Anthropology of the Uyghur*. China Studies, vol. 17. Leiden: Brill Academic.

Bellér-Hann, Ildikó, M. Cristina Cesàro, Rachel Harris, and Joanne Finley, eds. 2007. "Introduction." In *Situating the Uyghurs between China and Central Asia*, 1–14. Aldershot, Hampshire, UK: Ashgate.

Bellér-Hann, Ildikó, and Chris Hann. 2020. *The Great Dispossession: Uyghurs Between Civilizations*. Münster, Germany: LIT Verlag. (English)

Benmayor, Rina. 2008. "Digital Storytelling as a Signature Pedagogy for the New Humanities." *Arts and Humanities in Higher Education* 7 (2): 188–204. https://doi.org/10.1177/1474022208088648.

———. 2012. "Digital Testimonio as a Signature Pedagogy for Latin@ Studies." *Equity & Excellence in Education* 45 (3): 507–24. https://doi.org/10.1080/10665684.2012.698180.

Bennett, Lance W., and Alexandra Segerberg. 2013. *The Logic of Connective Action: Digital Media and the Personalization of Contentious Politics*. Cambridge: Cambridge University Press.

Benson, Linda. 2004. "Education and Social Mobility Among Minority Populations in Xinjiang." In *Xinjiang, China's Muslim Borderland*, edited by S. Frederick Starr, 190–215. London: M. E. Sharpe.

Beraja, Martin, David Y. Yang, and Noam Yuchtman. 2020. "Data-Intensive Innovation and the State: Evidence from AI Firms in China." *NBER Working Paper No. 27723*. http://www.nber.org/papers/w27723.

Bebergal, Peter. 1998. "A Meditation on Transgression: Foucault, Bataille and the Retrieval of the Limit." *CTHEORY*. https://journals.uvic.ca/index.php/ctheory/article/view/14629/5495.

Bernal, Victoria. 2006. "Diaspora, Cyberspace and Political Imagination: The Eritrean Diaspora Online." *Global Networks* 6 (2): 161–79. https://doi.org/10.1111/j.1471-0374.2006.00139.x.

———. 2014. *Nation as Network: Diaspora, Cyberspace, and Citizenship*. Chicago: University of Chicago Press.

Bequelin, Nicolas. 2000. "Xinjiang in the Nineties." *China Journal* 44: 65–90. https://doi.org/10.2307/2667477.

———. 2004. "Staged Development in Xinjiang." *China Quarterly* 178: 358–78.

Beverley, John. 2005. "Testimonio, Subalternity, and Narrative Authority." In *The SAGE Handbook of Qualitative Research*, edited by Norman Denzin and Yvonna Lincoln, 3rd ed., 547–57. Thousand Oaks, CA: SAGE.

Bhabha, Homi K. 1994. *The Location of Culture*. Routledge Classics. New York: Routledge.

Blackburn, Kevin. 2009. "Recalling War Trauma of the Pacific War and the Japanese Occupation in the Oral History of Malaysia and Singapore." *Oral History Review* 36 (2): 231–52.

Blasco, Jaime. 2013. "Cyber Espionage Campaign against the Uyghur Community, Targeting MacOSX Systems." Blog. *AT&T Cybersecurity*. AT&T Business,

February 13, 2013. https://cybersecurity.att.com/blogs/labs-research/cyber-es
pionage-campaign-against-the-uyghur-community-targeting-macosx-syst.

Blinken, Antony J. (U.S. Secretary of State). 2021. "The Signing of the Uyghur
Forced Labor Prevention Act." *U.S. Department of State Press Statement*,
December 23, 2021. https://www.state.gov/the-signing-of-the-uyghur-forced
-labor-prevention-act/.

Bloch, Anne-Christine. 2001. "Minorities and Indigeneous Peoples." In *Economic,
Social and Cultural Rights*, edited by Asbjørn Asbjørn, Catarina Krause, and
Allan Rosas, 373–88. Dordrecht: Martinus Nijhoff.

Blommaert, Jan. 2001. "Investigating Narrative Inequality: African Asylum Seekers' Stories in Belgium." *Discourse & Society* 12 (4): 413–49. https://doi.org/1
0.1177/0957926501012004002.

———. 2005. *Discourse: A Critical Introduction*. Cambridge: Cambridge University Press. https://doi.org/10.1017/CBO9780511610295.

———. 2009. "Ethnography and Democracy: Hymes's Political Theory of Language." *Text & Talk* 29 (3): 257–76. https://doi.org/10.1515/TEXT.2009.014.

———. 2014. "Infrastructures of Superdiversity: Conviviality and Language in
an Antwerp Neighbourhood." *European Journal of Cultural Studies* 17 (4):
431–51.

Bloomberg News. 2018. "China Uses Facial Recognition to Fence In Villagers in Far
West," January 17, 2018. https://www.bloomberg.com/news/articles/2018-01-17/
china-said-to-test-facial-recognition-fence-in-muslim-heavy-area.

Bob, Clifford. 2005. *The Marketing of Rebellion: Insurgents, Media, and International Activism*. Cambridge University Press.

Bojadžijev, Manuela. 2012. *Die windige Internationale: Rassismus und Kämpfe
der Migration*, 2nd ed. Münster, Germany: Westfälisches Dampfboot.

Bojadžijev, Manuela, and Serhat Karakayali. 2007. "Autonomie der Migration:
10 Thesen zu einer Methode." In *Turbulente Ränder: Neue Perspektiven auf
Migration an den Grenzen Europas*, edited by Transit Migration Forschungs-
gruppe, 203–10. Bielefeld, Germany: Transcript.

Borkert, Maren, Karen E. Fischer, and Eiad Yafi. 2018. "The Best, the Worst,
and the Hardest to Find: How People, Mobiles, and Social Media Connect
Migrants in(to) Europe." *Social Media + Society* 4 (1). https://journals.sagepub
.com/doi/10.1177/2056305118764428.

Boromisza-Habashi, David. 2013. *Speaking Hatefully: Culture, Communication,
and Political Action in Hungary*. University Park: Pennsylvania State University Press.

Brah, Avtar. 1996. *Cartographies of Diaspora: Contesting Identities*. London:
Routledge.

Bratich, Jack Z. 2012. "Sovereign Networks, Pre-Emptive Transgression, Communications Warfare: Case Studies in Social Movement Media." In *Transgression 2.0: Media, Culture, and the Politics of a Digital Age*, edited by Ted Gournelos and David J. Gunkel, 224–39. New York: Bloomsbury Academic.

Briggs, Charles L., and Richard Bauman. 1992. "Genre, Intertextuality, and Social Power." *Journal of Linguistic Anthropology* 2 (2): 131–72.

Brighenti, Andrea. 2007. "Visibility: A Category for the Social Sciences." *Current Sociology* 55 (3): 323–42. https://doi.org/10.1177/0011392107076079.

Brinkerhoff, Jennifer M. 2009. *Digital Diasporas: Identity and Transnational Engagement*. Cambridge: Cambridge University Press.

Broeders, Dennis, and Huub Dijstelbloem. 2016. "The Datafication of Mobility and Migration Management: The Mediating State and Its Consequences." In *Digitizing Identities: Doing Identity in a Networked World*, edited by Irma van der Ploeg and Jason Pridmore, 242–60. London: Routledge.

Brophy, David. 2005. "Forced Marriages and Female Heroines in Uyghur Culture." *Harvard Asia Quarterly* 9 (1): 57–65.

———. 2016. *Uyghur Nation: Reform and Revolution on the Russia-China Frontier*. Boston: Harvard University Press.

Buckley, Chris, and Paul Mozur. 2019. "How China Uses High-Tech Surveillance to Subdue Minorities." *New York Times*, May 22, 2019. https://www.nytimes.com/2019/05/22/world/asia/china-surveillance-xinjiang.html.

Bunin, Gene A. 2021. "An Interview with Gene Bunin of the Xinjiang Victim Database & Uyghur Pulse." Blog. *Art of Life in Chinese Central Asia* (edited by Darren Byler), February 8, 2021. https://livingotherwise.com/2021/02/08/an-interview-with-gene-bunin-of-the-xinjiang-victim-database-uyghur-pulse/.

Butler, Judith. 2009. *Frames of War: When Is Life Grievable?* London: Verso.

Butler, Judith, and Athena Athanasiou. 2013. *Dispossession: The Performative in the Political*. Cambridge: Polity Press.

Byler, Darren. 2018. "China's Government Has Ordered a Million Citizens to Occupy Uighur Homes. Here's What They Think They're Doing." *China File*. October 24, 2018. https://www.chinafile.com/reporting-opinion/postcard/million-citizens-occupy-uighur-homes-xinjiang.

———. 2019. "China's Hi-Tech War on Its Muslim Minority." *Guardian*, April 11, 2019. http://www.theguardian.com/news/2019/apr/11/china-hi-tech-war-on-muslim-minority-xinjiang-uighurs-surveillance-face-recognition.

———. 2020. "The Digital Enclosure of Turkic Muslims." *Society + Space*, December 7, 2020. https://www.societyandspace.org/articles/the-digital-enclosure-of-turkic-muslims.

———. 2021a. "Anti-colonial Friendship: Contemporary Police Violence, Storytelling, and Uyghur Masculinity." *American Ethnologist* 48 (2): 153–66.

———. 2021b. *In the Camps: China's High-Tech Penal Colony*. New York: Columbia University Global Reports, London: Atlantic Books (2022).

———. 2022. *Terror Capitalism: Uyghur Dispossession and Masculinity in a Chinese City*. Durham, NC: Duke University Press.

Carbaugh, Donal. 1996. *Situating Selves: The Communication of Social Identities in American Scenes*. SUNY Series, Human Communication Processes. New York: State University of New York Press.

———. 1999. "'Just Listen': 'Listening' and Landscape Among the Blackfeet." *Western Journal of Communication* 63 (3): 250–70.

———. 2007. "Cultural Discourse Analysis: Communication Practices and Intercultural Encounters." *Journal of Intercultural Communication Research* 36 (3): 167–82. https://doi.org/10.1080/17475750701737090.

———, ed. 2017. *The Handbook of Communication in Cross-Cultural Perspective*. New York: Routledge.

Carbaugh, Donal, Michael Berry, and Marjatta Nurmikari-Berry. 2006. "Coding Personhood through Cultural Terms and Practices: Silence and Quietude as a Finnish 'Natural Way of Being.'" *Journal of Language and Social Psychology* 25 (3): 203–20. https://doi.org/10.1177/0261927X06289422.

Carbaugh, Donal, and Lisa Rudnick. 2006. "Which Place, What Story? Cultural Discourses at the Border of the Blackfeet Reservation and Glacier National Park." *Great Plains Quarterly* 26 (3): 167–84.

Cassirer, Ernst. 1955. *The Philosophy of Symbolic Forms. Volume 2: Mythical Thought*. Translated by Ralph Manheim. New Haven, CT: Yale University Press.

———. 1956. *Wesen und Wirkung des Symbolbegriffs*. Darmstadt, Germany: Bruno Cassirer.

Cetin, Kumru Berfin Emre. 2020. "Transnational Resistance to Communicative Ethnocide: Alevi Television during the State of Emergency in Turkey (2016–18)." In *The SAGE Handbook of Media and Migration*, edited by Kevin Smets, Koen Leurs, Myria Georgiou, Saskia Witteborn, and Radhika Gajjala, 563–73. Thousand Oaks, CA: SAGE.

Charalambous, Constadina. 2012. "*Republica de Kubros*: Transgression and Collusion in Greek-Cypriot Adolescents' Classroom Silly-Talk." *Linguistics and Education* 23 (3): 334–49. https://doi.org/10.1016/j.linged.2012.05.005.

Cheah, Pheng. 2006. *Inhuman Conditions: On Cosmopolitanism and Human Rights*. Cambridge, MA: Harvard University Press.

Chen, Yangbin. 2008. *Muslim Uyghur Students in a Chinese Boarding School.* Lanham, MD: Lexington Books.

———. 2019. "Uyghur Graduates' Ethnicity in Their Dislocated Life Experience: Employment Expectations, Choices and Obstacles." *Asian Studies Review* 43 (1): 75–93.

Chen, Yu-Wen. 2014. *The Uyghur Lobby: Global Networks, Coalitions and Strategies of the World Uyghur Congress.* New York: Routledge.

Cheesman, Margaret. 2020. "Self-Sovereignty for Refugees? The Contested Horizons of Digital Identity." *Geopolitics* 27 (1): 134–159. https://doi.org/10.1080/14650045.2020.1823836.

Chestnut Greitens, Sheena, Myunghee Lee, and Emir Yazici. 2020. "Counterterrorism and Preventive Repression: China's Changing Strategy in Xinjiang." *International Security* 44 (3): 9–47. https://doi.org/10.1162/isec_a_00368.

China Daily. 2021. "Things to Know about All the Lies on Xinjiang: How Have They Come About?" April 30, 2021. https://www.chinadaily.com.cn/a/202104/30/WS608b4036a31024adobabb623.html.

Chompel, Balok. 2007. "Interview with Rabiya Kadeer." *Tibetfocus.* November 19, 2007. http://www.tibetfocus.com/gm/archives/00000450.html (now defunct).

Chouliaraki, Lilie. 2013. *The Ironic Spectator: Solidarity in the Age of Post-Humanitarianism.* Cambridge: Polity Press.

———. 2017. "Symbolic Bordering: The Self-Representation of Migrants and Refugees in Digital News." *Popular Communication* 15 (2): 78–94. https://doi.org/10.1080/15405702.2017.1281415.

Chouliaraki, Lilie, and Rafal Zaborowski. 2017. "Voice and Community in the 2015 Refugee Crisis: A Content Analysis of News Coverage in Eight European Countries." *International Communication Gazette* 79 (6–7): 613–35. https://doi.org/10.1177/1748048517727173.

Citizen Lab. 2014. *Communities @ Risk: Targeted Digital Threats against Civil Society.* Toronto: Munk School of Global Affairs, University of Toronto. https://targetedthreats.net.

Clarke, Michael, ed. 2022. *The Xinjiang Emergency: Exploring the Causes and Consequences of China's Mass Detention of Uyghurs.* Manchester, UK: Manchester University Press.

Clothey, Rebecca A., Emmanuel F. Koku, Erfan Erkin, and Husenjan Emat. 2016. "A Voice for the Voiceless: Online Social Activism in Uyghur Language Blogs and State Control of the Internet in China." *Information, Communication & Society* 19 (6): 858–74. https://doi.org/10.1080/1369118X.2015.1061577.

CNNIC (China Internet Network Information Center). 2014. *33rd Statistical Report on Internet Development in China.* http://www1.cnnic.cn/IDR/Re portDownloads/201404/U020140417607531610855.pdf (now defunct).

Cohen, Ronen A., and Bosmat Yefet. 2021. "The Iranian Diaspora and the Homeland: Redefining the Role of a Centre." *Journal of Ethnic and Migration Studies* 47 (3): 686–702.

Conley, Tom. 1997. Afterword to *The Capture of Speech and Other Political Writings,* by Michel de Certeau. Edited by Luce Giard, translated by Tom Conley, 175–90. Minneapolis: University of Minnesota Press.

Consulate-General of the People's Republic of China in Toronto. 2021. *Main Data of Xinjiang Uygur Autonomous Region from the Seventh National Population Census,* June 16, 2021. http://toronto.china-consulate.gov.cn/eng/news/202106/t20210616_8990244.htm.

Cooren, François. 2010. *Action and Agency in Dialogue.* Dialogue Studies, vol. 6. Amsterdam: John Benjamins.

Costa, Elisabetta, and Jinxue Wang. 2020. "Being at Home on Social Media: Online Place-Making among the Kurds in Turkey and Rural Migrants in China." In *The SAGE Handbook of Media and Migration,* edited by Kevin Smets, Koen Leurs, Myria Georgiou, Saskia Witteborn, and Radhika Gajjala, 515–25. Thousand Oaks, CA: SAGE.

Coutu, Lisa M. 2008. "Contested Social Identity and Communication in Text and Talk about the Vietnam War." *Research on Language and Social Interaction* 41 (4): 387–407. https://doi.org/10.1080/08351810802467845.

Covarrubias, Patricia Olivia. 2002. *Culture, Communication, and Cooperation: Interpersonal Relations and Pronominal Address in a Mexican Organization.* Lanham, MD: Rowman & Littlefield.

Daly, Angela, Thilo Hagendorff, Hui Li, Monique Mann, Vidushi Marda, Ben Wagner, Wei Wang, and Saskia Witteborn. 2019. "Artificial Intelligence, Governance and Ethics: Global Perspectives." *SSRN Electronic Journal.* https://doi.org/10.2139/ssrn.3414805.

Das, Chaity. 2017. *In the Land of Buried Tongues: Testimonies and Literary Narratives of the War of Liberation of Bangladesh.* New Delhi: Oxford University Press.

Das, Veena, Arthur Kleinman, Margaret M. Lock, Mamphela Ramphele, and Pamela Reynolds, eds. 2001. *Remaking a World: Violence, Social Suffering, and Recovery.* Berkeley: University of California Press.

Das Gupta, Monisha. 2006. *Unruly Immigrants: Rights, Activism, and Transnational South Asian Politics in the United States.* Durham, NC: Duke University Press.

Dautcher, Jay. 2009. *Down a Narrow Road: Identity and Masculinity in a Uyghur Community in Xinjiang China.* Harvard East Asian Monographs 312. Cambridge, MA: Harvard University Asia Center.

de Certeau, Michel. 1997. *The Capture of Speech and Other Political Writings.* Edited by Luce Giard, translated by Tom Conley. Minneapolis: University of Minnesota Press.

Deeb-Sossa, Natalia, and Louie F. Rodriguez, eds. 2019. *Community-Based Participatory Research: Testimonios from Chicana/o Studies.* Tucson: University of Arizona Press.

De Fina, Anna. 2003. *Identity in Narrative: A Study of Immigrant Discourse.* Studies in Narrative 3. Amsterdam: John Benjamins.

Delgado Bernal, Dolores, Rebeca Burciaga, and Judith Flores Carmona. 2012. "Chicana/Latina Testimonios: Mapping the Methodological, Pedagogical, and Political." *Equity & Excellence in Education* 45 (3): 363–72. https://doi.org/10.1080/10665684.2012.698149.

Deutscher Bundestag. 2021. "Gesetz über die Unternehmerischen Sorgfaltsplichten in Lieferketten" [Law About Corporate Duties in Supply Chains]. *Bundesgesetzblatt* Teil 1 (46): 2959–69 [Federal Law Paper, Part 1, July 22, 2021]. https://www.bgbl.de/xaver/bgbl/start.xav?startbk=Bundesanzeiger_BGBl&#__bgbl__%2F%2F*%5B%40attr_id%3D%27bgbl121s2959.pdf%27%5D__1664796387392.

Dikötter, Frank. 2010. *Mao's Great Famine: The History of China's Most Devastating Catastrophy, 1958–62.* New York: Bloomsbury.

Dillon, Millicent, and Michel Foucault. 1980. "Conversation with Michel Foucault." *Threepenny Review* 1: 4–5. http://www.jstor.org/stable/4382926.

Diminescu, Dana. 2008. "The Connected Migrant: An Epistemological Manifesto." *Social Science Information* 47 (4): 565–79. https://doi.org/10.1177/0539018408096447.

———. 2012. *e-Diasporas Atlas: Explorations and Cartography of Diasporas on Digital Networks.* Paris: Éd. de la Maison des Sciences de l'Homme.

———. 2020. "Researching the Connected Migrant." In *The SAGE Handbook of Media and Migration,* edited by Kevin Smets, Koen Leurs, Myria Georgiou, Saskia Witteborn, and Radhika Gajjala, 74–78. Thousand Oaks, CA: SAGE.

Diminescu, Dana, and Benjamin Loveluck. 2014. "Traces of Dispersion: Online Media and Diasporic Identities." *Crossings: Journal of Migration & Culture* 5 (1): 23–29. https://doi.org/10.1386/cjmc.5.1.23_1.

Ding, Jeffrey. 2019. "The Interest behind China's Artificial Intelligence Dream." In *Artificial Intelligence, China, Russia, and the Global Order,* edited by Nicholas D. Wright, 43–47. Alabama: Air University Press.

Ding, Sheng. 2007. "Digital Diaspora and National Image Building: A New Perspective on Chinese Diaspora Study in the Age of China's Rise." *Pacific Affairs* 80 (4): 627–48. https://doi.org/10.5509/2007804627.

Dirlik, Arif. 2003. "Global Modernity? Modernity in an Age of Global Capitalism." *European Journal of Social Theory* 6 (3): 275–92. https://doi.org/10.1177/1368431003063001.

Dirven, René, Louis Goossens, Yvan Putseys, and Emma Vorlat. 1982. *The Scene of Linguistic Action and Its Perspectivization by SPEAK, TALK, SAY and TELL.* Pragmatics & Beyond, vol. 3:6. Philadelphia: John Benjamins. https://doi.org/10.1075/pb.iii.6.

Dolan, Jill. 2005. *Utopia in Performance: Finding Hope at the Theater.* Ann Arbor: University of Michigan Press.

Douzinas, Costas. 2007. *Human Rights and Empire: The Political Philosophy of Cosmopolitanism.* Abingdon, UK: Routledge-Cavendish.

Drissel, David. 2008. "Digitizing Dharma: Computer-Mediated Mobilizations of Tibetan Buddhist Youth." *International Journal of Diversity in Organizations, Communities, and Nations* 8 (5): 79–92. https://doi.org/10.18848/1447-9532/CGP/v08i05/39665.

Dubberley, Sam, Alexa Koenig, and Daragh Murray, eds. 2020. *Digital Witness: Using Open Source Information for Human Rights Investigation, Documentation, and Accountability.* Oxford: Oxford University Press.

Durkheim, Emile. 1982. "What Is a Social Fact?" In *The Rules of Sociological Method. Contemporary Social Theory,* edited by Steven Lukes, 50–59. London: Palgrave Macmillan.

Dutt, Mallika. 2001. "Reclaiming a Human Rights Culture: Feminism of Difference and Alliance." In *Talking Visions: Multicultural Feminism in a Transnational Age,* edited by Ella Shohat, 225–33. Cambridge, MA: MIT Press.

Dwonch, Albana S. 2019. *Palestinian Youth Activism in the Internet Age: Online and Offline Social Networks after the Arab Spring.* SOAS Palestine Studies. London: I. B. Tauris.

Dwyer, Arienne M. 2005. *The Xinjiang Conflict: Uyghur Identity, Language Policy, and Political Discourse.* Policy Studies No. 15. Washington, D.C.: East-West Center. https://www.files.ethz.ch/isn/26109/PS015.pdf.

Eberl, Jakob-Moritz, Christine E. Meltzer, Tobias Heidenreich, Beatrice Herrero, Nora Theorin, Fabienne Lind, Rosa Berganza, Hajo G. Boomgaarden, Christian Schemer, and Jesper Strömbäck. 2018. "The European Media Discourse on Immigration and Its Effects: A Literature Review." *Annals of the International Communication Association* 42 (3): 207–23. https://doi.org/10.1080/23808985.2018.1497452.

Elegant, Naomi. 2018. "Penn Removes Portrait of Former GSE Dean With Alleged History of Sexual Harassment." *Daily Pennsylvanian*, November 4, 2018. https://www.thedp.com/article/2018/04/gse-getup-sexual-harassment-dell-hymes-portrait-removal-upenn-penn-philadelphia.

Enteen, Jillana B. 2010. *Virtual English: Queer Internets and Digital Creolization.* New York: Routledge.

European Parliament. 2021. "MEPs Refuse Any Agreement with China whilst Sanctions Are in Place." *Press Release*, May 20, 2021. https://www.europarl.europa.eu/news/en/press-room/20210517IPR04123/meps-refuse-any-agreement-with-china-whilst-sanctions-are-in-place.

Fan, Lingzhi, and Qingqing Chen. 2021. "Xinjiang-related Databases Fabricated by Anti-China Think Tanks Based on False Testimonies, Purely Political Maneuvers." *Global Times*, April 9, 2021. https://www.globaltimes.cn/page/202104/1220654.shtml.

Fairclough, Norman. 1992. "Intertextuality in Critical Discourse Analysis." *Linguistics and Education* 4 (3–4): 269–93. https://doi.org/10.1016/0898-5898(92)90004-G.

Fassin, Didier. 2008. "The Humanitarian Politics of Testimony: Subjectification through Trauma in the Israeli-Palestinian Conflict." *Cultural Anthropology* 23 (3): 531–58. https://doi.org/10.1111/j.1548-1360.2008.00017.x.

Figueroa, Yomaira C. 2015. "Faithful Witnessing as Practice: Decolonial Readings of *Shadows of Your Black Memory* and *The Brief Wondrous Life of Oscar Wao.*" *Hypatia* 30 (4): 641–56. https://doi.org/10.1111/hypa.12183.

Fitch, Kristine L. 1998. *Speaking Relationally: Culture, Communication, and Interpersonal Connection.* Guilford Series on Personal Relationships. New York: Guilford Press.

———. 2003. "Cultural Persuadables." *Communication Theory* 13 (1): 100–123. https://doi.org/10.1111/j.1468-2885.2003.tb00284.x.

Fletcher, Joseph F. 1968. "China and Central Asia 1368–1884." In *The Chinese World Order,* edited by John K. Fairbank, 206–24, 337–68. Cambridge, MA: Harvard University Press.

Fog Olwig, Karen, Kristina Grünenberg, Perle Mohl, and Anja Simonsen, eds. 2020. *The Biometric Border World.* London: Routledge.

Forbes, Andrew D. W. 1986. *Warlords and Muslims in Chinese Central Asia: A Political History of Republican Sinkiang 1911–1949.* Cambridge: Cambridge University Press.

Foss, Sonja K., and Cindy L. Griffin. 1995. "Beyond Persuasion: A Proposal for an Invitational Rhetoric." *Communication Monographs* 62 (1): 2–18. https://doi.org/10.1080/03637759509376345.

Foucault, Michel. 1977. "A Preface to Transgression." In *Language, Counter-Memory, Practice*, edited by Donald F. Bouchard, 29–52. Cornell Paperbacks. Ithaca, NY: Cornell University Press.

———. 1998. *Aesthetics, Method, and Epistemology*. Vol. 2 of *Essential Works of Foucault, 1954–1984*. New York: New Press.

Franken, Michel. 2019. "Exploring the Role of Digital Technologies in Uyghur Political Activism." Master's thesis. Erasmus University Rotterdam. https://thesis.eur.nl/pub/49334/.

Frosh, Paul. 2009. "Telling Presences: Witnessing, Mass Media, and the Imagined Lives of Strangers." In *Media Witnessing: Testimony in the Age of Mass Communication*, edited by Paul Frosh and Amit Pinchevski, 49–72. Basingstoke, UK: Palgrave Macmillan.

———. 2018. *The Poetics of Digital Media*. Cambridge: Polity Press.

Frosh, Paul, and Amit Pinchevski, eds. 2009. *Media Witnessing: Testimony in the Age of Mass Communication*. Basingstoke, UK: Palgrave Macmillan.

Fuller, Graham E., and Jonathan N. Lipman. 2004. "Islam in Xinjiang." In *Xinjiang: China's Muslim Borderland*, edited by S. Frederick Starr, 320–52. Oxon, UK; Routledge.

Fuller, Graham E., and S. Frederick Starr. 2003. *The Xinjiang Problem*. Washington, D.C.: Central Asia-Caucasus Institute, Paul H. Nitze School of Advanced International Studies, Johns Hopkins University.

Gajjala, Radhika. 2019. *Digital Diasporas: Labor and Affect in Gendered Indian Digital Publics*. London: Rowman & Littlefield.

Gajjala, Radhika, and Yeon Ju Oh. 2013. "South Asian Digital Diasporas: Remixing Diasporic Youth Cultures." In *Media Studies Futures*, edited by Angharad Valdivia, 569–84. Vol. 6 of *The International Encyclopedia of Media Studies*. Chichester, UK: Wiley-Blackwell. https://doi.org/10.1002/9781444361506.wbiems162.

Garfinkel, Harold. 1967. *Studies in Ethnomethodology*. Englewood Cliffs, NJ: Prentice Hall.

Geertz, Clifford. 1973. *The Interpretation of Cultures*. New York: Basic Books.

Georgakopoulou, Alexandra. 2016. "Small Stories Research: A Narrative Paradigm for the Analysis of Social Media." In *The SAGE Handbook of Social Media Research Methods*, edited by Luke Sloan and Anabel Quan-Haase, 266–81. Thousand Oaks, CA: SAGE. https://doi.org/10.4135/9781473983847.n17.

Georgiou, Myria. 2013. *Media and the City: Cosmopolitanism and Difference*. Global Media and Communication. London: Polity Press.

———. 2018. "Does the Subaltern Speak? Migrant Voices in Digital Europe." *Popular Communication* 16 (1): 45–57. https://doi.org/10.1080/15405702.2017.1412440.

Gertheiss, Svenja. 2019. *Diasporic Activism in the Israeli-Palestinian Conflict.* London: Routledge.

Giglietto, Fabio, and Yenn Lee. 2017. "A Hashtag Worth a Thousand Words: Discursive Strategies Around #JeNeSuisPasCharlie After the 2015 *Charlie Hebdo* Shooting." *Social Media + Society* 3 (1). https://doi.org/10.1177/2056305116686992.

Gillespie, Marie, Lawrence Ampofo, Margaret Cheesman, Becky Faith, Evgenia Iliadou, Ali Issa, Souad Osseiran, and Dimitris Skleparis. 2016. *Mapping Refugee Media Journeys, Smart Phones and Social Networks.* Milton Keynes, UK: The Open University.

Gladney, Dru C. 2004. *Dislocating China: Reflections on Muslims, Minorities, and Other Subaltern Subjects.* Chicago: University of Chicago Press.

Goffman, Erving. 1959. *The Presentation of Self in Everyday Life.* Garden City, NY: Anchor Books.

———. 1963. *Stigma: Notes on the Management of Spoiled Identity.* Englewood Cliffs, NJ: Prentice Hall.

———. 1967. *Interaction Ritual: Essays in Face-to-Face Behavior.* Garden City, NY: Anchor Books.

———. 1974. *Frame Analysis: An Essay on the Organization of Experience.* New York: Harper & Row.

———. 1981. *Forms of Talk.* University of Pennsylvania Publications in Conduct and Communication. Philadelphia: University of Pennsylvania Press.

Gournelos, Ted, and David J. Gunkel, eds. 2012. *Transgression 2.0: Media, Culture, and the Politics of a Digital Age.* New York: Continuum.

Graham, Mark, Scott A. Hale, and Monica Stephens. 2011. *Geographies of the World's Knowledge.* Edited by Corinne M. Flick and the Convoco Foundation in cooperation with the Oxford Internet Institute, University of Oxford. London: Convoco!

Grauer, Yael. 2021. "Revealed: Massive Chinese Police Database." *Intercept*, January 29, 2021. https://theintercept.com/2021/01/29/china-uyghur-muslim-surveillance-police/.

Greve, Louisa. 2011. "The Future of Uyghur-Han Relations in China: A Dialogue." YouTube video, December 16, 2011. National Endowment for Democracy, UAA, Laogai Research Foundation. https://youtu.be/51GIH81XLE0.

Grose, Timothy. 2013. "The Uyghurs of the Xinjiang Class: Boarding School Education, Ethno-national Identity and the Zhonghua Minzu's Discontented Members." PhD diss., University of Indiana.

———. 2015a. "'Escaping Inseparability': How Uyghur Graduates of the 'Xinjiang Class' Contest Membership in the Zhonghua Minzu." In *Language, Education and Uyghur Identity in Urban Xinjiang*, edited by Joanne Smith Finley and Xiaowei Zang, 157–75. London: Routledge.

———. 2015b. "(Re)Embracing Islam in Neidi: The 'Xinjiang Class' and the Dynamics of Uyghur Ethno-National Identity." *Journal of Contemporary China* 24 (91): 101–18. https://doi.org/10.1080/10670564.2014.918408.

———. 2019. *Negotiating Inseparability in China: The Xinjiang Class and the Dynamics of Uyghur Identity*. Hong Kong: Hong Kong University Press.

Gruenewald, Tim, and Saskia Witteborn. 2022. "Feeling Good: Humanitarian Virtual Reality Film, Emotional Style and Global Citizenship." *Cultural Studies* 36 (1): 141–61. https://doi.org/10.1080/09502386.2020.1761415.

Guay, Joseph, and Lisa Rudnick. 2020. "Open Source Investigation: Understanding Digital Threats, Risks, and Harms." In *Digital Witness: Using Open Source Information for Human Rights Investigation, Documentation, and Accountability*, edited by Sam Dubberley, Alexa Koenig, and Daragh Murray, 292–314. Oxford: Oxford University Press.

Gunaratna, Rohan, Arabinda Acharya, and Wang Pengxin. 2010. *Ethnic Identity and National Conflict in China*. Basingstoke, UK: Palgrave Macmillan.

Gupta, Sonya Surabhi, ed. 2022. *Subalternities in India and Latin America: Dalit Autobiographies and the Testimonio*. New Delhi: Routledge.

Ha, Guangtian, and Slavs and Tatars, eds. 2021. *The Contest of the Fruits*. Boston: MIT Press (copublished with Haverford College).

Hacking, Ian. 2004. "Between Michel Foucault and Erving Goffman: Between Discourse in the Abstract and Face-to-Face Interaction." *Economy and Society* 33 (3): 277–302. https://doi.org/10.1080/0308514042000225671.

Haig-Brown, Celia. 2003. "Creating Spaces: Testimonio, Impossible Knowledge, and Academe." *International Journal of Qualitative Studies in Education* 16(3): 415–433.

Halupka, Max. 2014. "Clicktivism: A Systematic Heuristic." *Policy & Internet* 6 (2): 115–32. https://doi.org/10.1002/1944-2866.POI355.

———. 2018. "The Legitimisation of Clicktivism." *Australian Journal of Political Science* 53 (1): 130–41. https://doi.org/10.1080/10361146.2017.1416586.

Han, Byung-Chul. 2015. *The Transparency Society*. Redwood City, CA: Stanford Briefs, an imprint of Stanford University Press.

———. 2017. *Psychopolitics: Neoliberalism and New Technologies of Power*. London: Verso.

Hancock, Black Hawk, and Roberta Garner. 2011. "Towards a Philosophy of Containment: Reading Goffman in the 21st Century." *American Sociologist* 42 (4): 316–40. https://doi.org/10.1007/s12108-011-9132-3.

Handley, Erin, and Michael Li. 2019. "'Dead' Uyghur Poet Abdurehim Heyit Appears on Chinese State Media, Says He's Never Been Abused." *ABC,* February 11, 2019. https://www.abc.net.au/news/2019-02-11/chinese-state-video-tape-of-uyghur-musician-reported-dead/10798536.

Harrell, Stevan. 2001. *Ways of Being Ethnic in Southwest China*. Seattle: University of Washington Press.

Harris, Rachel. 2005. "Reggae on the Silk Road: The Globalization of Uyghur Pop." *China Quarterly* 183: 627–43.

———. 2007. "Situating the Twelve Muqam: Between the Arab World and the Tang Court." In *Situating the Uyghurs between China and Central Asia*, edited by Ildikó Bellér-Hann, M. Cristina Cesàro, Rachel Harris, and Joanne Smith Finley, 69–88. Aldershot, Hampshire, UK: Ashgate.

———. 2016. *The Making of a Musical Canon in Chinese Central Asia: The Uyghur Twelve Muqam*. SOAS Musicology Series. London: Routledge.

———. 2020. *Soundscapes of Uyghur Islam*. Bloomington: Indiana University Press.

Harris, Rachel, and Aziz Isa. 2019. "Islam by Smartphone: Reading the Uyghur Islamic Revival on WeChat." *Central Asian Survey* 38 (1): 61–80.

Hart, Kevin, and Geoffrey H. Hartman, eds. 2004. *The Power of Contestation: Perspectives on Maurice Blanchot*. Baltimore: Johns Hopkins University Press.

Hart, Tabitha B. 2015. "Analyzing Procedure to Make Sense of Users' (Inter) Actions: A Case Study on Applying the Ethnography of Communication for Interaction Design Purposes." In *Communicating User Experience: Applying Local Strategies Research to Digital Media Design*, edited by Trudy Millburn, 27–56. Lanham, MD: Lexington Books.

Hasmath, Reza. 2019. "What Explains the Rise of Majority-Minority Tensions and Conflict in Xinjiang?" *Central Asian Survey* 38 (1): 46–60.

Hayes, Anna. 2012. "HIV/AIDS in Xinjiang: A Serious 'Ill' in an 'Autonomous' Region." *International Journal of Asia Pacific Studies* 8 (1): 77–102.

He, Baogang. 2007. *Rural Democracy in China: The Role of Village Elections*. Basingstoke, UK: Springer.

Hegde, Radha S. 1998. "A View from Elsewhere: Locating Difference and the Politics of Representation from a Transnational Feminist Perspective." *Communication Theory* 8 (3): 271–97. https://doi.org/10.1111/j.1468-2885.1998 .tb00222.x.

———. 2011. "Introduction." In *Circuits of Visibility: Gender and Transnational Media Cultures*, edited by Radha S. Hegde, 1–20. Critical Cultural Communication. New York: New York University Press.

———. 2016. *Mediating Migration*. Global Media and Communication. Cambridge: Polity Press.

Heide, Dana. 2021. "'Lässt Mich Nicht Kalt': Wie Deutsche Firmen in Chinas Unterdrückter Provinz Xinjiang Geschäfte Machen" ['It Does Bother Me':

How German Firms Do Business in China's Oppressed Province Xinjiang]. *Handelsblatt,* July 15, 2021.

Hesford, Wendy S. 2011. *Spectacular Rhetorics: Human Rights Visions, Recognitions, Feminisms.* Next Wave. Durham, NC: Duke University Press.

Hesford, Wendy S., and Rachel A. Lewis. 2016. "Mobilizing Vulnerability: New Directions in Transnational Feminist Studies and Human Rights." *Feminist Formations* 28 (1): vii–xviii. https://doi.org/10.1353/ff.2016.0012.

Heyit, Abdurehim. 2019. "I Have Never Been Abused" Says Detained Uighur Abdurehim Heyit. YouTube video, February 11, 2019, *Guardian.* https://youtu .be/VYKbI3eZ3io.

Hill, Jane H., and Judith. T. Irvine. 1993. "Introduction." In *Responsibility and Evidence in Oral Discourse,* edited by Jane H. Hill and Judith T. Irvine, 1–23. Cambridge: Cambridge University Press.

Hill, Zahara. 2017. "Black Woman Tarana Burke Founded the 'Me Too' Movement." *EBONY,* October 18, 2017. https://www.ebony.com/news/black-woman -me-too-movement-tarana-burke-alyssa-milano/.

Hjorth, Larissa, and Sun Sun Lim. 2012. "Mobile Intimacy in an Age of Affective Mobile Media." *Feminist Media Studies* 12 (4): 477–84. https://doi.org/10.1080/ 14680777.2012.741860.

Höglund, Kristine. 2019. "Testimony under Threat: Women's Voices and the Pursuit of Justice in Post-War Sri Lanka." *Human Rights Review* 20 (3): 361–82.

Holdstock, Nick. 2015. *China's Forgotten People: Xinjiang, Terror and the Chinese State.* London: I. B. Tauris.

Hollier, Denis, ed. 1989. "Actions, No! Words, Yes!" In *A New History of French Literature,* 1034–39. Cambridge, MA: Harvard University Press.

Holmes, Brian. 2006. "Artistic Autonomy and the Communication Society." *Third Text* 18 (6): 547–55.

Holt, Elizabeth. 1996. "Reporting on Talk: The Use of Direct Reported Speech in Conversation." *Research on Language and Social Interaction* 29 (3): 219–45. https://doi.org/10.1207/s15327973rlsi2903_2.

———. 2000. "Reporting and Reacting: Concurrent Responses to Reported Speech." *Research on Language and Social Interaction* 33 (4): 425–54. https:// doi.org/10.1207/S15327973RLSI3304_04.

Hopgood, Stephen. 2013. *The Endtimes of Human Rights.* Ithaca, NY: Cornell University Press.

Horlacher, Stefan. 2010. "Taboo, Transgression, and Literature: An Introduction." In *Taboo and Transgression in British Literature from the Renaissance to the Present,* edited by Stefan Horlacher, Stefan Glomb, and Lars Heiler, 3–21. New York: Palgrave Macmillan.

Horsti, Karina. 2017. "Communicative Memory of Irregular Migration: The Re-Circulation of News Images on YouTube." *Memory Studies* 10 (2): 112–29. https://doi.org/10.1177/1750698016640614.

———, ed. 2019. *The Politics of Public Memories of Forced Migration and Bordering in Europe*. London: Palgrave Macmillan Memory Studies.

Horsti, Karina, and Klaus Neumann. 2019. "Memorializing Mass Deaths at the Border: Two Cases from Canberra (Australia) and Lampedusa (Italy)." *Ethnic and Racial Studies* 42 (2): 141–58. https://doi.org/10.1080/01419870.2017.1 394477.

Howard, Keith, ed. 1995. *True Stories of the Korean Comfort Women*. London: Cassell.

Howell, Anthony, and C. Cindy Fan. 2011. "Migration and Inequality in Xinjiang: A Survey of Han and Uyghur Migrants in Urumqi." *Eurasian Geography and Economics* 52 (1): 119–39. https://doi.org/10.2747/1539-7216.52.1.119.

Huang, Cindy. 2009. "Muslim Women at a Crossroads: Gender and Development in the Xinjiang Uyghur Autonomous Region, China." PhD diss., University of California Berkeley. https://escholarship.org/uc/item/2gf5512s.

Human Rights Watch. 2020. "China: Big Data Program Targets Xinjiang's Muslims." December 9, 2020. https://www.hrw.org/news/2020/12/09/china-big-data-program-targets-xinjiangs-muslims.

Hymes, Dell. 1964. "Introduction: Toward Ethnographies of Communication." *American Anthropologist* 66 (6): 1–34.

———. 1972. "Models of the Interaction of Language and Social Life." In *Directions in Sociolinguistics: The Ethnography of Communication*, edited by John J. Gumperz and Dell H. Hymes, 35–71. New York: Holt, Rinehart & Winston.

———. 1985. "Toward Linguistic Competence." *Revue de l'Aila* 2: 9–23.

———, ed. 1996. "Speech and Language: On the Origins and Foundations of Inequality among Speakers." In *Ethnography, Linguistics, Narrative Inequality: Toward an Understanding of Voice*, 25–62. London: Taylor & Francis.

Ignatieff, Michael. 2002. *Die Politik der Menschenrechte*. Hamburg: Europäische Verlagsanstalt.

Illouz, Eva. 2007. *Cold Intimacies: The Making of Emotional Capitalism*. London: Polity Press.

———. 2008. *Saving the Modern Soul: Therapy, Emotions, and the Culture of Self-Help*. Berkeley: University of California Press.

ILO (International Labour Organization). 2015. "Counterterrorism Law of the People's Republic of China (Order No. 36 of the President of the PRC)."

December 27, 2015. https://www.ilo.org/dyn/natlex/natlex4.detail?p_isn
=103954&p_lang=en.

International Consortium of Investigative Journalists. 2019. *China Cables Documents*. November 24, 2019. https://www.icij.org/investigations/china-cables/
read-the-china-cables-documents/.

IOM (International Organization for Migration). 2019. *Glossary on Migration*.
IOM: Geneva, Switzerland. https://publications.iom.int/system/files/pdf/
iml_34_glossary.pdf.

Jackson, Cecile. 2012. "Speech, Gender and Power: Beyond Testimony." *Development and Change* 43 (5): 999–1023. https://doi.org/10.1111/j.1467-7660.2012
.01791.x.

Jakobson, Roman. 1957. *Shifters, Verbal Categories and the Russian Verb*. Cambridge, MA: Department of Slavic Languages and Literatures, Harvard
University.

Jenkins, Henry. 2009. "What Happened before YouTube." In *YouTube: Online
Video and Participatory Culture*, edited by Jean Burgess and Joshua Green,
2nd ed., 109–25. Digital Media and Society. Cambridge: Polity Press.

Jenks, Chris. 2003. *Transgression*. Key Ideas. London: Routledge.

Jervis, John. 1999. *Transgressing the Modern: Explorations in the Western Experience of Otherness*. Oxford: Blackwell.

John, Nicholas A. 2017. *The Age of Sharing*. Cambridge: Polity.

Kadeer, Rebiya, and Alexandra Cavelius. 2007. *Die Himmelsstürmerin: Chinas
Staatsfeindin Nr. 1 erzählt aus ihrem Leben*. 3rd ed. München: Heyne.

Kadeer, Rebiya, with Alexandra Cavelius. 2011. *Dragon Fighter: One Woman's
Epic Struggle for Peace with China*. Carlsbad, CA: Kales Press.

Kaiser, Karen. 2009. "Protecting Respondent Confidentiality in Qualitative Research." *Qualitative Health Research* 19 (11): 1632–41. https://doi.org/10.1177/
1049732309350879.

Kalou, Zoi, and Eugene Sadler-Smith. 2015. "Using Ethnography of Communication in Organizational Research." *Organizational Research Methods* 18 (4):
629–55. https://doi.org/10.1177/1094428115590662.

Katriel, Tamar. 1991. *Communal Webs: Communication and Culture in Contemporary Israel*. SUNY Series, Anthropology and Judaic Studies. Albany: State
University of New York Press.

———. 2015. "Expanding Ethnography of Communication Research: Toward
Ethnographies of Encoding." *Communication Theory* 25 (4): 454–59. https://
doi.org/10.1111/comt.12072.

———. 2021. *Defiant Discourse: Speech and Action in Grassroots Activism*. Politics
of Language. Abingdon, UK: Routledge.

Katriel, Tamar, and Gerry Philipsen. 1981. "'What We Need Is Communication': 'Communication' as a Cultural Category in Some American Speech." *Communication Monographs* 48 (4): 301–17. https://doi.org/10.1080/03637758109376064.

Kaufmann, Katja. 2018. "Navigating a New Life: Syrian Refugees and Their Smartphones in Vienna." *Information, Communication & Society* 21 (6): 882–98. https://doi.org/10.1080/1369118X.2018.1437205.

Kay, Jilly Boyce. 2020. *Gender, Media and Voice: Communicative Injustice and Public Speech.* New York: Palgrave Macmillan.

Keles, Janroj Yilmaz. 2016. "Digital Diaspora and Social Capital." *Middle East Journal of Culture and Communication* 9 (3): 315–33.

Khursheed, Ambreen, Syed Karrar Haider, Faisal Mustafa, and Ayesha Akhtar. 2019. "China–Pakistan Economic Corridor: A Harbinger of Economic Prosperity and Regional Peace." *Asian Journal of German and European Studies* 4 (7). https://doi.org/10.1186/s40856-019-0044-2.

Kim, Seung-kyung, and Na-Young Lee. 2017. "Shared History and the Responsibility for Justice: The Korean Council for the Women Drafted for Military Sexual Slavery by Japan." In *Women's Activism and "Second Wave" Feminism,* edited by Barbara Molony and Jennifer Nelson, 193–212. London: Bloomsbury Academic.

Kitchin, Rob. 2014. *The Data Revolution: Big Data, Open Data, Data Infrastructures & Their Consequences.* London: SAGE.

Koch, Natalie. 2013a. "Introduction—Field Methods in 'Closed Contexts': Undertaking Research in Authoritarian States and Places." *Area* 45 (4): 390–95.

———. 2013b. "Technologising the Opinion: Focus Groups, Performance and Free Speech." *Area* 45 (4): 411–18.

Kok, Saskia, and Richard Rogers. 2017. "Rethinking Migration in the Digital Age: Transglocalization and the Somali Diaspora." *Global Networks* 17 (1): 23–46. https://doi.org/10.1111/glob.12127.

Koven, Michèle. 2002. "An Analysis of Speaker Role Inhabitance in Narratives of Personal Experience." *Journal of Pragmatics* 34 (2): 167–217. https://doi.org/10.1016/S0378-2166(02)80010-8.

Kreide, Regina. 2013. "Menschenrechte als Platzhalter: Eine politische Menschenrechtskonzeption zwischen Moral und Recht" [Human Rights as Place-holders: A Political Human Rights Frame Between Morality and Law]. *Zeitschrift für Menschenrechte* [Journal for Human Rights] 7: 80–100.

Kristeva, Julia. 1980. *Desire in Language: A Semiotic Approach to Literature and Art.* European Perspectives. New York: Columbia University Press.

———. 1986. "Word, Dialogue, and the Novel." In *The Kristeva Reader: Julia Kristeva*, edited by Toril Moi, 35–61. New York: Columbia University Press.

Labov, William. 1972. "The Transformation of Experience in Narrative Syntaxes." In *Language in the Inner City: Studies in the Black English Vernacular*, edited by William Labow, 354–96. Philadelphia: University of Pennsylvania Press.

Latina Feminist Group, The. 2001. *Telling to Live: Latina Feminist Testimonios*. Latin America Otherwise. Durham, NC: Duke University Press.

Lavička, Martin. 2021. "Changes in Chinese Legal Narratives about Religious Affairs in Xinjiang." *Asian Ethnicity* 22 (1): 61–76.

Leeds-Hurwitz, Wendy. 2005. "Ethnography." In *Handbook of Language and Social Interaction*, edited by Kristine L. Fitch and Robert E. Sanders, 327–54. Mahwah, NJ: Lawrence Erlbaum Associates.

Lefebvre, Henry. 1991. *The Production of Space*. Translated by Donald Nicholson-Smith. Oxford: Blackwell.

Leibold, James, ed. 2019. "Interior Ethnic Minority Boarding Schools: China's Bold and Unpredictable Educational Experiment." Special Issue, *Asian Studies Review* 43 (1): 3–15. https://doi.org/10.1080/10357823.2018.1548571.

———. 2020. "Surveillance in China's Xinjiang Region: Ethnic Sorting, Coercion, and Inducement." *Journal of Contemporary China* 29 (121): 46–60. https://doi.org/10.1080/10670564.2019.1621529.

Leibold, James, and Timothy A. Grose. 2019. "Cultural and Political Disciplining inside China's Dislocated Minority Schooling System." *Asian Studies Review* 43 (1): 16–35. https://doi.org/10.1080/10357823.2018.1548571.

Leighter, James L., Lisa Rudnick, and Theresa J. Edmonds. 2013. "How the Ethnography of Communication Provides Resources for Design." *Journal of Applied Communication Research* 41 (2): 209–15. https://doi.org/10.1080/00909882.2013.782419.

Leng, Sidney, and Cissy Zhou. 2021. "China Census: Xinjiang's Population Jumps 18.3 Percent over Past Decade as Sprawling CPCC Conglomerate Expands Operations." *South China Morning Post*, May 12, 2021. https://www.scmp.com/economy/global-economy/article/3133228/china-census-xinjiangs-population-jumps-183-cent-over-past.

Leudar, Ivan, Jacqueline Hayes, Jiří Nekvapil, and Johanna Turner Baker. 2008. "Hostility Themes in Media, Community and Refugee Narratives." *Discourse & Society* 19 (2): 187–221. https://doi.org/10.1177/0957926507085952.

Leung, Linda. 2007. "Mobility and Displacement: Refugees' Mobile Media Practices in Immigration Detention." *M/C- A Journal of Media and Culture* 10 (1): 1–5.

———. 2010. "Telecommunications across Borders: Refugees' Technology Use during Displacement." *Telecommunications Journal of Australia* 60 (4): 58.1–58.13. https://doi.org/10.2104/tja10058.

Leurs, Koen. 2015. *Digital Passages: Migrant Youth 2.0. Diaspora, Gender and Youth Cultural Intersections*. MediaMatters. Amsterdam: Amsterdam University Press.

———. 2016. "Young Connected Migrants and Non-Normative European Family Life: Exploring Affective Human Right Claims of Young E-Diasporas." *International Journal of E-Politics* 7 (3): 15–34. https://doi.org/10.4018/IJEP.2016070102.

———. 2017. "Communication Rights from the Margins: Politicising Young Refugees' Smartphone Pocket Archives." *International Communication Gazette* 79 (6–7): 674–98. https://doi.org/10.1177/1748048517727182.

Leurs, Koen, and Saskia Witteborn. 2021. "Digital Migration Studies." In *Research Handbook on International Migration and Digital Technology*, edited by Marie McAuliffe, 15–28. Cheltenham, UK: Elgar.

Li, Huaiyin. 2005. *Village Governance in North China, 1875–1936*. Stanford, CA: Stanford University Press.

Lindskov Jacobsen, Katja. 2015. "Experimentation in Humanitarian Locations: UNHCR and Biometric Registration of Afghan Refugees." *Security Dialogue*, 46 (2): 144–64. https://doi.org/10.1177/0967010614552545.

Lookout. 2020. *Mobile APT Surveillance Campaigns Targeting Uyghurs*. June 2020. https://www.lookout.com/documents/threat-reports/us/lookout-uyghur-malware-tr-us.pdf.

Lowrey, Annie. 2009. "Seven Questions with Rebiya Kadeer." Blog. *Foreign Policy*, August 21, 2009. https://foreignpolicy.com/2009/08/21/seven-questions-with-rebiya-kadeer/.

Lugones, Maria. 2003. *Pilgrimages/Peregrinajes: Theorizing Coalition against Multiple Oppressions*. Feminist Constructions. Lanham, MD: Rowman & Littlefield.

Lynn, Adam. 2018. "App Targeting Uyghur Population Censors Content, Lacks Basic Security." *Open Technology Fund*. August 31, 2018. https://www.opentech.fund/news/app-targeting-uyghur-population-censors-content-lacks-basic-security/.

Lyon, Arabella. 2013. *Deliberative Acts: Democracy, Rhetoric, and Rights*. University Park: Pennsylvania State University Press.

Madianou, Mirca. 2016. "Ambient Co-Presence: Transnational Family Practices in Polymedia Environments." *Global Networks* 16 (2): 183–201. https://doi.org/10.1111/glob.12105.

———. 2019. "Technocolonialism: Digital Innovation and Data Practices in the Humanitarian Response to Refugee Crises." *Social Media + Society* 5 (3). https://journals.sagepub.com/doi/full/10.1177/2056305119863146.

Maitland, Carleen, ed. 2018. *Digital Lifeline? ICTs for Refugees and Displaced Persons*. Information Policy Series. Boston: MIT Press.

Marlowe, Jay. 2019. "Social Media and Forced Migration: The Subversion and Subjugation of Political Life." *Media and Communication* 7 (2): 73–183.

Marquez, Lorena V. 2019. "Recovering Chicana/o Movement History through Testimonios." In *Community-Based Participatory Research: Testimonios from Chicana/o Studies*, edited by Natalia Deeb-Sossa and Louie F. Rodriguez, 91–110. Tucson: University of Arizona Press.

Mathews, Douglas, Lisa Franzen-Castle, Sarah Colby, Kendra Kattelmann, Melissa Olfert, and Adrienne White. 2015. "Use of Wordclouds as a Novel Approach for Analysis and Presentation of Qualitative Data for Program Evaluation." *Journal of Nutrition and Behavior* 47 (4S). https://doi.org/10.1016/j.jneb.2015.04.071.

Mavroudi, Elizabeth, and Caroline Nagel. 2016. *Global Migration: Patterns, Processes, and Politics*. London: Routledge.

McClintock, Anne. 1997. "No Longer a Future in Heaven: Gender, Race and Nationalism." In *Dangerous Liaisons: Gender, Nation, and Postcolonial Perspectives*, edited by Anne McClintock, Aamir Mufti, and Ella Shohat, 352–89. Cultural Politics, vol. 11. Minneapolis: University of Minnesota Press.

McMurray, James. 2017. "The Ethnic as Ethic: Education Choices amongst the Uyghur of Xinjiang." PhD diss., University of Sussex.

McNeill, William Hardy, and Jean W. Sedlar. 1970. *Classical China*. Vol. 5 of *Readings in World History*. New York: Oxford University Press.

Menchú, Rigoberta. 1984. *I, Rigoberta Menchú: An Indian Woman in Guatemala*. Edited and introduced by Elisabeth Burgos-Debray. New York: Verso.

Menke, Christoph, and Arnd Pollmann. 2007. *Philosophie der Menschenrechte zur Einführung*. Hamburg: Junius Verlag.

Merleau-Ponty, Maurice. 1962. *Phenomenology of Perception*. Translated by Colin Smith. London: Routledge & Kegan Paul.

Mezzadra, Sandro, and Brett Neilson. 2013. *Border as Method, or, the Multiplication of Labor*. Durham, NC: Duke University Press.

Mignolo, Walter D. 2007. "Delinking." *Cultural Studies* 21 (2–3): 449–514. https://doi.org/10.1080/09502380601162647.

Milburn, Trudy, ed. 2015. *Communicating User Experience: Applying Local Strategies Research to Digital Media Design*. Studies in New Media. Lanham, MD: Lexington Books.

Miller, Derek B., and Lisa Rudnick. 2008. *The Security Needs Assessment Protocol: Improving Operational Effectiveness Through Community Security.* New York: United Nations Institute for Disarmament Research.

Millward, James. 2007. *Eurasian Crossroads: A History of Xinjiang.* New York: Columbia University Press.

———. 2021. *Eurasian Crossroads: A History of Xinjiang.* Revised and Updated. New York: Columbia University Press.

Ministry of Public Security of the People's Republic of China. 2016. *Order of the President of the People's Republic of China.* http://www.mps.gov.cn/n2254314/n2254409/n4904353/c5548987/content.html (now defunct).

Miracola, Sergio. 2019. "How China Uses A.I. to Control Society." Commentary. *Italian Institute for International Political Studies (ISPI):* 17–19.

Mitchell, Timothy. 2002. *Rule of Experts: Egypt, Techno-Politics, Modernity.* Berkeley: University of California Press.

Monachesi, Paola, and Marina Turco. 2017. "New Urban Players: Stratagematic Use of Media by Banksy and the Hong Kong Umbrella Movement." *International Journal of Communication* 11: 1448–65.

Morozov, Evgeny. 2009. "The Brave New World of Slacktivism." *Foreign Policy,* May 19, 2009. https://foreignpolicy.com/2009/05/19/the-brave-new-world-of-slacktivism/.

———. 2011. *The Net Delusion: How Not to Liberate the World.* London: Penguin Books.

Mote, Frederick W. 2003. *Imperial China, 900–1800.* Boston: Harvard University Press.

Mouffe, Chantal. 2007. "Artistic Activism and Agonistic Spaces." *Art & Research: A Journal of Ideas, Contexts, and Methods* 1 (2). https://chisineu.files.wordpress.com/2012/07/biblioteca_mouffe_artistic-activism.pdf.

Nagy, Peter, and Gina Neff. 2015. "Imagined Affordance: Reconstructing a Keyword for Communication Theory." *Social Media + Society* 1 (2). https://doi.org/10.1177/2056305115603385.

Nayar, Pramod K. 2011. *States of Sentiment: Exploring the Cultures of Emotion.* New Delhi: Orient Blackswan.

NED (National Endowment for Democracy). 2019. "National Endowment for Democracy Responds to Threat of Chinese Government Sanctions." December 2, 2019. https://www.ned.org/national-endowment-for-democracy-responds-to-threat-of-chinese-government-sanctions/.

———. 2020. "Uyghur Human Rights Policy Act Builds on Work of NED Grantees." May 29, 2020. https://www.ned.org/uyghur-human-rights-policy-act-builds-on-work-of-ned-grantees/.

———. 2021. "Xinjiang/East Turkistan (China). 2020." Accessed February 25, 2021. https://www.ned.org/region/asia/xinjiang-east-turkestan-china-2020/.

Newby, Laura J. 2007. "'Us and Them' in Eighteenth and Nineteenth Century Xinjiang." In *Situating the Uyghurs between China and Central Asia*, edited by Ildikó Bellér-Hann, M. Cristina Cesàro, Rachel Harris, and Joanne Finley, 15–29. Aldershot, Hampshire, UK: Ashgate.

Newman, Janet. 2012. *Working the Spaces of Power: Activism, Neoliberalism and Gendered Labour*. London: Bloomsbury Academic.

Nigro, Roberto. 2005. "Experiences of the Self between Limit, Transgression, and the Explosion of the Dialectical System: Foucault as Reader of Bataille and Blanchot." *Philosophy & Social Criticism* 31 (5–6): 649–64. https://doi.org/10.1177/0191453705055493.

Ning, Jizhe. 2021. "Main Data of the Seventh National Population Census." *National Bureau of Statistics of China*. May 11, 2021. http://www.stats.gov.cn/english/PressRelease/202105/t20210510_1817185.html.

Norman, Donald A. 1988. *The Psychology of Everyday Things*. New York: Basic Books.

Nozaki, Yoshiko. 2005. "The 'Comfort Women' Controversy: History and Testimony." *Asia-Pacific Journal* 3 (7). https://apjjf.org/-Yoshiko-Nozaki/2063/article.html.

NurMuhammad, Rizwangul, Heather A. Horst, Evangelia Papoutsaki, and Giles Dodson. 2016. "Uyghur Transnational Identity on Facebook: On the Development of a Young Diaspora." *Identities: Global Studies in Culture and Power* 23 (4): 485–99. https://doi.org/10.1080/1070289X.2015.1024126.

O'Connor, Brendan H. 2017. "Language Out of Place: Transgressive Semiotics and the Lived Experience of Race in Borderlands Education." *Journal of Language, Identity & Education* 16 (3): 127–41. https://doi.org/10.1080/15348458.2017.1283991.

OHCHR (United Nations Human Rights Office of the High Commissioner). 1966. *International Covenant on Economic, Social and Cultural Rights,* December 16, 1966. https://www.ohchr.org/sites/default/files/cescr.pdf.

———. 2007. *Convention on the Rights of the Child*. http://www2.ohchr.org/english/law/crc.htm (now defunct).

Oiarzabal, Pedro J. 2020. "(Re)loading Identity and Affective Capital Online: The Case of Diaspora Basques on Facebook." In *The SAGE Handbook of Media and Migration*, edited by Kevin Smets, Koen Leurs, Myria Georgiou, Saskia Witteborn, and Radhika Gajjala, 246–57. Thousand Oaks, CA: SAGE.

Oliver, Kelly. 2001. *Witnessing: Beyond Recognition*. Minneapolis: University of Minnesota Press.

Ong, Aihwa. 2006. *Neoliberalism as Exception: Mutations in Citizenship and Sovereignty*. Durham, NC: Duke University Press.

Onishi, Norimitsu, and Constant Méheut. 2020. "Once a Slogan of Unity, 'Je Suis Charlie' Now Divides France." *New York Times*, December 19, 2020. https://www.nytimes.com/2020/12/19/world/europe/france-charlie-hebdo-slogan.html.

O'Reilly, Karen. 2005. *Ethnographic Methods*. London: Routledge.

Ozduzen, Ozge, Umut Korkut, and Cansu Ozduzen. 2020. "'Refugees Are Not Welcome': Digital Racism, Online Place-Making and the Evolving Categorization of Syrians in Turkey." *New Media & Society* 23 (11): 3349–69. https://doi.org/10.1177/1461444820956341.

Parham, Angel Adams. 2004. "Diaspora, Community and Communication: Internet Use in Transnational Haiti." *Global Networks* 4 (2): 199–217. https://doi.org/10.1111/j.1471-0374.2004.00087.x.

People's Daily Online. 2005. "'East Turkistan' Major Terrorist Threat to China," September 6, 2005. http://english.peopledaily.com.cn/200509/06/eng20050906_206700.html (now defunct).

Peters, John D. 2009. "Witnessing." In *Media Witnessing: Testimony in the Age of Mass Communication*, edited by Paul Frosh and Amit Pinchevski, 23–41. Basingstoke, UK: Palgrave Macmillan.

Pham, Allie. 2007. "Surviving through the Cape of Invisibility." PhD diss., University of Oklahoma. https://hdl.handle.net/11244/319661.

Philipsen, Gerry. 1987. "The Prospect for Cultural Communication." In *Communication Theory: Eastern and Western Perspectives*, edited by D. Lawrence Kincaid, 245–54. New York: Academic Press.

———. 1992. *Speaking Culturally: Explorations in Social Communication*. SUNY Series in Human Communication Processes. Albany, NY State University of New York Press.

———. 1997. "A Theory of Speech Codes." In *Developing Communication Theory*, edited by Gerry Philipsen and Terrance L. Albrecht, 119–56. Albany, NY State University of New York Press.

———. 2002. "Cultural Communication." In *Handbook of International and Intercultural Communication*, edited by William B. Gudykunst, 51–67. Thousand Oaks, CA: SAGE.

Philipsen, Gerry, and Lisa Coutu. 2005. "The Ethnography of Speaking." In *Handbook of Language and Social Interaction*, edited by Kristine L. Fitch and Robert E. Sanders, 355–79. Mahwah, NJ: Lawrence Erlbaum Associates.

Pollozek, Silvan, and Jan Hendrik Passoth. 2019. "Infrastructuring European Migration and Border Control: The Logistics of Registration and Identification at Moria Hotspot." *Environment and Planning D: Society and Space* 37 (4): 606–624. https://doi.org/10.1177/0263775819835819.

Pratt, Geraldine, and Caleb Johnston. 2017. "Crossing Oceans: Testimonial Theatre, Filipina Migrant Labor, Empathy, and Engagement." *GeoHumanities* 3 (2): 279–91. https://doi.org/10.1080/2373566X.2016.1278178.

Quakernack, Stefanie. 2016. "(Re-)Framing Testimonio on YouTube: Multimodal Performances of Dispossession in Digital Narratives of Undocumented Youth." PhD diss., University of Bielefeld. https://pub.uni-bielefeld.de/record/2902068.

———. 2018. *Political Protest and Undocumented Immigrant Youth: (Re)framing Testimonio*. London: Routledge.

Radio Free Asia. 2017a. "Round-Ups of Uyghurs Continue as Egypt, China Condemned by Rights Groups," July 10, 2017. https://www.refworld.org/docid/5971a893c.html.

———. 2017b. "Xinjiang Police Search Uyghur Homes For 'Illegal Items,'" April 4, 2017. https://www.rfa.org/english/news/uyghur/searches-04042017172301.html.

Rajagopalan, Megha. 2018. "China Is Forcing People to Download an App That Tells Them to Delete 'Dangerous' Photos." *BuzzFeed News*, April 10, 2018. https://www.buzzfeednews.com/article/meghara/china-surveillance-app.

Rajagopalan, Megha, and Bethany Allen-Ebrahimian. 2020. "Asia In-Depth Podcast: Xinjiang under Surveillance." *Asia Society*. Podcast hosted by Nico Luchsinger. August 6, 2020. https://asiasociety.org/blog/asia/asia-depth-podcast-xinjiang-under-surveillance.

Ramzy, Austin. 2019. "'Show Me That My Father Is Alive.' China Faces Torrent of Online Pleas." *New York Times*, February 17, 2019. https://www.nytimes.com/2019/02/17/world/asia/uighurs-china-internment-camps.html.

Rancière, Jacques. 2004. "Who Is the Subject of the Rights of Man?" *South Atlantic Quarterly* 103 (2–3): 297–310.

Retis, Jessica, and Roza Tsagarousianou, eds. 2019. *The Handbook of Diasporas, Media, and Culture*. Medford, MA: Wiley-Blackwell. https://doi.org/10.1002/9781119236771.

Reyhan, Dilnur. 2012. "Uyghur Diaspora and Internet." *e-Diasporas Atlas*. Paris: Éd. de la Maison des Sciences de l'Homme. http://www.e-diasporas.fr/working-papers/Reyhan-Uyghurs-EN.pdf.

Reyhan, Dilnur, and Camille Grin. 2014. "Le Web Ouïghour—Production de Discriminations et d'Altérité: Les Representations Des Femmes Ouïghoures Dans L'Espace Numérique." *Regard Sur Les Ouïghour-e-s* 3 (9): 06–15.

Roberts, Sean. R. 2007. "'The Dawn of the East': A Portrait of a Uyghur Community Between China and Kazakhstan." In *Situating the Uyghurs between China and Central Asia*, edited by Ildikó Bellér-Hann, M. Cristina Cesàro, Rachel Harris, and Joanne Smith Finley, 203–18. Aldershot, Hampshire, UK: Ashgate.

———. 2018. "The Biopolitics of China's 'War on Terror' and the Exclusion of the Uyghurs." *Critical Asian Studies* 50 (2): 232–58. https://doi.org/10.1080/1 4672715.2018.1454111.

———. 2020. *The War on the Uyghurs: China's Internal Campaign Against a Muslim Minority*. Princeton Studies in Muslim Politics. Princeton, NJ: Princeton University Press.

Roth, Silke, and Markus Luczak-Roesch. 2020. "Deconstructing the Data Life-Cycle in Digital Humanitarianism." *Information, Communication & Society* 23 (4): 555–71. https://doi.org/10.1080/1369118X.2018.1521457.

Rotman, Dana, Sarah Vieweg, Sarita Yardi, Ed H. Chi, Jenny Preece, Ben Shneiderman, Peter Pirolli, and Tom Glaisyer. 2011. "From Slacktivism to Activism: Participatory Culture in the Age of Social Media." In *CHI '11 Extended Abstracts on Human Factors in Computing Systems*. New York: ACM. https://doi.org/10.1145/1979742.1979543.

Roy, Srila. 2013. "On Testimony: The Pain of Speaking and the Speaking of Pain." In *Tapestry of Memory: Evidence and Testimony in Life-Story Narratives*, edited by Nanci Adler and Selma Leydesdorff, 97–110. New York: Routledge.

Rudelson, Justin Jon. 1997. *Oasis Identities: Uyghur Nationalism along China's Silk Road*. New York: Columbia University Press.

Ruppert, Evelyn, and Stephan Scheel. 2021. *Data Practices: Making Up a European People*. Cambridge, MA: MIT Press.

Sacks, Harvey, Emanuel A. Schegloff, and Gail Jefferson. 1974. "A Simplest Systematics for the Organization of Turn-Taking for Conversation." *Language* 50 (4): 696–735. https://doi.org/10.1353/lan.1974.0010.

Sankey, Diana. 2016. "Recognition of Gendered Experiences of Harm at the Extraordinary Chambers in the Courts of Cambodia: The Promise and the Pitfalls." *Feminist Legal Studies* 24 (1): 7–27.

Saparov, Arsène. 2017. "Contested Spaces: The Use of Place-Names and Symbolic Landscape in the Politics of Identity and Legitimacy in Azerbaijan." *Central Asian Survey*, 36 (4): 534–54.

Saussy, Haun. 1993. *The Problem of a Chinese Aesthetic*. Stanford, CA: Stanford University Press.

Sautman, Barry. 1998. "Preferential Policies for Ethnic Minorities in China: The Case of Xinjiang." *Nationalism and Ethnic Politics* 4 (1–2): 86–118. https://doi .org/10.1080/13537119808428530.

Save the Children. 2009a. "The History of Save the Children." https://www .savethechildren.org/us/about-us/why-save-the-children/history.

———. 2009b. "Our Programs around the World." http://www.savethechildren.org/ programs/?WT.mc_id=1109_sp_prog_index (now defunct).

Save the Children China. 2006. "Children's Voices." http://www.savethechildren .org.cn/savethechildren/table/view/base_index/index_t emp.php?table_id=93 (now defunct).

Schankweiler, Kerstin, Verena Straub, and Tobias Wendl, eds. 2019. *Image Testimonies: Witnessing in Times of Social Media*. Routledge Series in Affective Societies. Abingdon, UK: Routledge.

Schapp, Allison. 2014. "Variation in the Use of Twitter Hashtags." *Qualifying Paper in Sociolinguistics*. New York: New York University. https://s18798 .pcdn.co/shapp/wp-content/uploads/sites/18562/2020/09/Shapp_QP2_Hash tags_Final.pdf.

Scheel, Stephan, Evelyn Ruppert, and Funda Ustek-Spilda. 2019. "Enacting Migration through Data Practices." *Environment and Planning D. Society and Space* 37 (4): 579–88. https://doi.org/10.1177/0263775819865791.

Schegloff, Emanuel A. 1997. "'Narrative Analysis' Thirty Years Later." *Journal of Narrative and Life History* 7 (1–4): 97–106. https://doi.org/10.1075/jnlh.7 .11nar.

Schluessel, Eric. 2007. "'Bilingual' Education and Discontent in Xinjiang." *Central Asian Survey* 26 (2): 251–77. https://doi.org/10.1080/02634930701517482.

———. 2009. "History, Identity, and Mother-Tongue Education in Xinjiang." *Central Asian Survey* 28 (4): 383–402. https://doi.org/10.1080/02634930903577144.

Schultheis Moore, Alexandra. 2016. "'Dispossession within the Law': Human Rights and the Ec-Static Subject in M. NourbeSe Philip's *Zong!*" *Feminist Formations* 28 (1): 166–89. https://doi.org/10.1353/ff.2016.0020.

Searle, John. 1969. *Speech Acts: An Essay in the Philosophy of Language*. Cambridge: Cambridge University Press.

Sennett, Richard. (1977) 2002. *The Fall of Public Man*. New York: Alfred A. Knopf.

Shah, Nishant. 2020. "The Cog That Imagines the System: Data Migration and Migrant Bodies in the Face of Aadhaar." In *The SAGE Handbook of Media and Migration*, edited by Kevin Smets, Koen Leurs, Myria Georgiou, Saskia Witteborn, and Radhika Gajjala, 464–76. Thousand Oaks, CA: SAGE. https:// doi.org/10.4135/9781526476982.n45.

Sheller, Mimi, and John Urry. 2006. "The New Mobilities Paradigm." *Environment and Planning A: Economy and Space* 38 (2): 207–26. https://doi.org/10 .1068/a37268.

Shichor, Yitzhak. 2010. "Net Nationalism: The Digitalization of the Uyghur Diaspora." In *Diasporas in the New Media Age: Identity, Politics, and Community*, edited by Andoni Alonso and Pedro J. Oiarzabal, 291–316. Reno: University of Nevada Press.

Shirk, Susan L. 2007. *China: Fragile Superpower: How China's Internal Politics Could Derail Its Peaceful Rise*. New York: Oxford University Press.

Shove, Elizabeth, Mika Pantzar, and Matt Watson. 2012. *The Dynamics of Social Practice: Everyday Life and How It Changes*. London: SAGE.

Smets, Kevin. 2019. "Media and Immobility: The Affective and Symbolic Immobility of Forced Migrants." *European Journal of Communication* 34 (6): 650–60. https://doi.org/10.1177/0267323119886167.

Smets, Kevin, Koen Leurs, Myria Georgiou, Saskia Witteborn, and Radhika Gajjala, eds. 2020. *The SAGE Handbook of Media and Migration*. Thousand Oaks, CA: SAGE.

Smith Finley, Joanne. 2007. "'Ethnic Anomaly' or Modern Uyghur Survivor: A Case Study of the Minkaohan Hybrid Identity in Xinjiang." In *Situating the Uyghurs between China and Central Asia*, edited by Ildikó Bellér-Hann, M. Cristina Cesàro, Rachel Harris, and Joanne Smith Finley, 219–38. Aldershot, Hampshire, UK: Ashgate.

———. 2013. *The Art of Symbolic Resistance: Uyghur Identities and Uyghur-Han Relations in Contemporary Xinjiang*. Brill's Inner Asian Library, vol. 30. Leiden: Brill.

———. 2019. "Securitization, Insecurity and Conflict in Contemporary Xinjiang: Has PRC Counter-terrorism Evolved into State Terror?" *Central Asian Survey* 38 (1): 1–26.

Smith, Linda Tuhiwai. 2012. *Decolonizing Methodologies: Research and Indigenous Peoples*. 2nd ed. New York: Zed Books.

Smith Finley, Joanne, and Xiaowei Zang, eds. 2015. *Language, Education and Uyghur Identity in Urban Xinjiang*. Routledge Studies on Ethnicity in Asia 2. London: Routledge.

Soliev, Nodirbek. 2017. "Uyghur Militancy In and Beyond Southeast Asia: An Assessment." *Counter Terrorist Trends and Analyses* 9 (2): 14–20.

Søndergaard, Rasmus Sinding. 2022. "The Contested Origins of US Democracy Promotion: The National Endowment for Democracy and Its Congressional Critics." *International Politics* 59: 187–205. https://doi.org/10.1057/ s41311-020-00267-z.

Spivak, Gayatri Chakravorty. 1984/85. "Criticism, Feminism and the Institution. An Interview with Gayatri Chakravorty Spivak." *Thesis Eleven: Critical Theory and Historical Sociology* 10-11 (1): 175–187.

———. 2008. *Other Asias.* Malden, MA: Blackwell.

Sprain, Leah, and David Boromisza-Habashi. 2013. "The Ethnographer of Communication at the Table: Building Cultural Competence, Designing Strategic Action." *Journal of Applied Communication Research* 41 (2): 181–87. https://doi.org/10.1080/00909882.2013.782418.

Stone, Jeff. 2016. "Scarlet Mimic, Chinese Hacking Group, Suspected of Surveillance Campaign against Tibetan, Uyghur Minorities." *International Business Times,* January 26, 2016, sec. Technology. https://www.ibtimes.com/scarlet-mimic-chinese-hacking-group-suspected-surveillance-campaign-again st-tibetan-2280096.

Strauss, Anselm, and Juliet Corbin. 1998. *Basics of Qualitative Research: Techniques and Procedures for Developing Grounded Theory.* 2nd ed. Thousand Oaks, CA: SAGE.

Sudworth, John. 2018. "China's Hidden Camps: What Happened to the Vanished Uighurs of Xinjiang?" *BBC News,* October 24, 2018. https://www.bbc.co.uk/news/resources/idt-sh/China_hidden_camps.

———. 2020. "China Uighurs: A Model's Video Gives a Rare Glimpse inside Internment." *BBC News,* August 4, 2020, sec. China. https://www.bbc.com/news/world-asia-china-53650246.

Sutkutė, Rūta. 2016. "The Mediatization of New Movements: The Case of 'Je Suis Charlie.'" *Media Transformations* 12. https://doi.org/10.7220/2029-8668.12.03.

Tarde, Gabriel. (1895) 1999. *Monadologie et Sociologie.* Collection Les Empêcheurs de Penser en Rond 1. Paris: Les Empêcheurs de Penser en Rond.

Tazzioli, Martina. 2020. *The Making of Migration: The Biopolitics of Mobility at Europe's Borders.* London: SAGE.

Thum, Rian. 2014a. "China in Islam: Turki Views from the Nineteenth and Twentieth Centuries." *Cross-Currents: East Asian History and Culture Review E-Journal* 12. https://cross-currents.berkeley.edu/e-journal/issue-12.

———. 2014b. *The Sacred Routes of Uyghur History.* Cambridge, MA: Harvard University Press.

Tiberj, Vincent. 2017. "Une France Moins Xénophobe?" *La Vie des Idées,* June 6, 2017. https://laviedesidees.fr/Une-France-moins-xenophobe.html.

Tobin, David. 2020. *Securing China's Northwest Frontier. Identity and Insecurity in Xinjiang.* Cambridge: Cambridge University Press.

Tohti, Ilham. 2022. *We Uygurs Have No Say: An Imprisoned Writer Speaks.* London: Penguin Random House.

Toops, Stanley W. 2016. "Spatial Results of the 2010 Census in Xinjiang." Blog. *China Policy Institute*, University of Nottingham, March 7, 2016. https://blogs.nottingham.ac.uk/chinapolicyinstitute/2016/03/07/spatial-results-of-the-2010-census-in-xinjiang/.

Treem, Jeffrey W., and Paul M. Leonardi. 2013. "Social Media Use in Organizations: Exploring the Affordances of Visibility, Editability, Persistence, and Association." *Annals of the International Communication Association* 36 (1): 143–89. https://doi.org/10.1080/23808985.2013.11679130.

Tsing, Anna Lowenhaupt. 1993. *In the Realm of the Diamond Queen: Marginality in an Out-of-the-Way Place.* Princeton, NJ: Princeton University Press.

Turner, Victor. 1980. "Social Dramas and Stories about Them." *Critical Inquiry* 7 (1): 141–68.

Tursun, Sajide. 2017. "Gender and Urban Aspirations: The Case of Highly Educated Uyghur Women in Shanghai." *MMG Working Paper.* Max Planck Institute for the Study of Religious and Ethnic Diversity Göttingen, Germany. https://www.mmg.mpg.de/61918/wp-17-06.

Twigt, Mirjam A. 2018. "The Mediation of Hope: Digital Technologies and Affective Affordances within Iraqi Refugee Households in Jordan." *Social Media + Society* 4 (1). https://doi.org/10.1177/2056305118764426.

UAA (Uyghur American Association). n.d. "Mission." Accessed June 12, 2020. https://www.uyghuraa.org/whoweare.

UHRP (Uyghur Human Rights Project). 2014. "Trapped in a Digital Cage: Chinese State Repression of Uyghurs Online." https://uhrp.org/report/trapped-virtual-cage-chinese-state-repression-uyghurs-online-html/.

———. 2015. "Uyghur Voices on Education: China's Assimilative 'Bilingual Education' Policy in East Turkistan." http://docs.uyghuramerican.org/pdf/Uyghur-Voices-on-Education.pdf.

UNICEF. 2010. "Convention on the Rights of the Child." https://www.unicef.org/child-rights-convention.

United Nations. 1948. "Universal Declaration of Human Rights." https://www.un.org/en/about-us/universal-declaration-of-human-rights.

———. 1976. "International Covenant on Civil and Political Rights." *Treaty Series*, vol. 999: 171–346.

University of British Columbia School of Public Policy and Global Affairs, Institute of Asian Research, and Simon Fraser University Gender, Sexuality, and Women's Studies. n.d. *Xinjiang Documentation Project.* Accessed January 15, 2022. https://xinjiang.sppga.ubc.ca.

Uyghur Tribunal. 2021. *Uyghur Tribunal Judgement.* December 9, 2021. https://uyghurtribunal.com/wp-content/uploads/2022/01/Uyghur-Tribunal-Judgment-9th-Dec-21.pdf.

van den Bos, Matthijs, and Lisa Nell. 2006. "Territorial Bounds to Virtual Space: Transnational Online and Offline Networks of Iranian and Turkish–Kurdish Immigrants in the Netherlands." *Global Networks* 6 (2): 201–20. https://doi .org/10.1111/j.1471-0374.2006.00141.x.

Vanderklippe, Nathan. 2017. "China Probes Deeper into the Lives of Uyghur Minority." *Globe and Mail*, December 29, 2017. https://www.theglobeandmail.com/ news/world/scholars-shocked-by-changes-in-chinas-xinjiang-comparing-it -to-north-korea-and-apartheid-era southafrica/article37455333/ (now defunct).

van der Ploeg, Irma, and Jason Pridmore. 2016. *Digitizing Identities: Doing Identity in a Networked World*. New York: Routledge.

Vergani, Matteo, and Dennis Zuev. 2015. "Neojihadist Visual Politics: Comparing YouTube Videos of North Caucasus and Uyghur Militants." *Asian Studies Review* 39 (1): 1–22. https://doi.org/10.1080/10357823.2014.976171.

Villenas, Sofia A. 2019. "Pedagogies of Being With: Witnessing, *Testimonio*, and Critical Love in Everyday Social Movement." *International Journal of Qualitative Studies in Education* 32 (2): 151–66. https://doi.org/10.1080/09518398 .2018.1533148.

Volkswagen Group. 2019. "Growth and Change." February 2019. https://www .volkswagenag.com/en/news/stories/2019/02/powerhouse-for-the-mobility -of-tomorrow.html.

Voloshinov, Valentin. N. (1929) 1973. *Marxism and the Philosophy of Language*. Studies in Language. New York: Seminar Press.

Vuolteenaho, Jani, and Lawrence D. Berg, eds. 2016. *Critical Toponymies: The Contested Politics of Place Naming*. London: Routledge.

Waite, Edmund. 2006. "The Impact of the State on Islam amongst the Uyghurs: Religious Knowledge and Authority in the Kashgar Oasis." *Central Asian Survey* 25 (3): 251–65. https://doi.org/10.1080/02634930601022534.

Wall, Melissa, Madeline Otis Campbell, and Dana Janbek. 2017. "Syrian Refugees and Information Precarity." *New Media & Society* 19 (2): 240–54. https://doi .org/10.1177/1461444815591967.

Wayit, Kewser. 2020. "China, Can You Tell My Parents That I Am Still Alive?" Facebook, September 13, 2020. https://www.facebook.com/100005356803973/ videos/1506972449491301/.

Whittaker, Zack. 2019. "Malicious Websites Were Used to Secretly Hack into iPhones for Years Says Google." *TechCrunch*, August 30, 2019. https://tech crunch.com/2019/08/29/google-iphone-secretly-hacked/.

Witteborn, Saskia. 2007a. "The Expression of Palestinian Identity in Narratives about Personal Experiences: Implications for the Study of Narrative, Identity, and Social Interaction." *Research on Language and Social Interaction* 40 (2–3): 145–70. https://doi.org/10.1080/08351810701354581.

———. 2007b. "The Situated Expression of Arab Collective Identities in the United States." *Journal of Communication* 57 (3): 556–75. https://doi.org/10.1111/j.1460-2466.2007.00357.x.

———. 2010. "The Role of Transnational NGOs in Promoting Global Citizenship and Globalizing Communication Practices." *Language and Intercultural Communication* 10 (4): 358–72. https://doi.org/10.1080/14708477.2010.497556.

———. 2011a. "Constructing the Forced Migrant and the Politics of Space and Place-Making." *Journal of Communication* 61 (6): 1142–60. https://doi.org/10.1111/j.1460-2466.2011.01578.x.

———. 2011b. "Discursive Grouping in a Virtual Forum: Dialogue, Difference, and the 'Intercultural.'" *Journal of International and Intercultural Communication* 4 (2): 109–26. https://doi.org/10.1080/17513057.2011.556827.

———. 2011c. "Gendering Cyberspace: Transnational Mappings and Uyghur Diasporic Politics." In *Circuits of Visibility: Gender and Transnational Media Cultures*, edited by Radha S. Hegde, 268–83. Critical Cultural Communication. New York: New York University Press.

———. 2012a. "Forced Migrants, New Media Practices, and the Creation of Locality." In *The Handbook of Global Media Research*, edited by Ingrid Volkmer, 312–29. Oxford: Wiley-Blackwell. https://doi.org/10.1002/9781118255278.ch18.

———. 2012b. "Testimonio and Spaces of Risk." *Cultural Studies* 26 (4): 421–41. https://doi.org/10.1080/09502386.2011.587881.

———. 2021. "Data Privacy and Displacement: A Cultural Approach." *Journal of Refugee Studies* 34 (2): 2291–2307. https://doi.org/10.1093/jrs/feaa004.

———. 2022. "Digitalization, Digitization and Datafication: The 'Three D' Transformation of Forced Migration Management." *Communication, Culture & Critique* 15 (2): 157–75. https://doi.org/10.1093/ccc/tcac007.

Witteborn, Saskia, and Leah Sprain. 2009. "Grouping Processes in a Public Meeting from an Ethnography of Communication and Cultural Discourse Analysis Perspective." *International Journal of Public Participation* 3 (2): 14–35.

Wong, Edward. 2009. "Riots in Western China Amid Ethnic Tension." *New York Times*, July 5, 2009. https://www.nytimes.com/2009/07/06/world/asia/06china.html.

Xinhua. 2017. "Economic Development in Xinjiang on Fast Lane." *China Daily*, July 12, 2017. http://www.chinadaily.com.cn/business/2017-07/12/content_30085544.htm.

———. 2018. "China-Eurasia Expo Opens in Xinjiang," August 30, 2018. http://www.xinhuanet.com/english/2018-08/30/c_137431276.htm.

Yang, Hyunah. 2008. "Finding the 'Map of Memory': Testimony of the Japanese Military Sexual Slavery Survivors." *Positions* 16 (1): 79–107. https://doi.org/10.1215/10679847-2007-012.

Yeh, Emily. 2007. "Exile Meets Homeland: Politics, Performance, and Authenticity in the Tibetan Diaspora." *Environment and Planning D: Society and Space* 25 (4): 648–67. https://doi.org/10.1068/d2805.

Yu, Sherry. 2020. "Beyond the Third Space: New Communicative Spaces in the Making on YouTube." In *The SAGE Handbook of Media and Migration*, edited by Kevin Smets, Koen Leurs, Myria Georgiou, Saskia Witteborn, and Radhika Gajjala, 526–36. Thousand Oaks, CA: SAGE.

Yuan, Zhenjie, and Hong Zhu. 2021. "Uyghur Educational Elites in China: Mobility and Subjectivity Uncertainty on a Life-Transforming Journey." *Journal of Ethnic and Migration Studies* 47 (3): 536–56. https://doi.org/10.1080/1369183X.2020.1790343.

Yuval-Davis, Nira. 1997. *Gender & Nation*. Politics and Culture. London: SAGE.

Yuval-Davis, Nira, and Floya Anthias, eds. 1989. *Woman, Nation, State*. London: Macmillan.

Zang, Xiaowei. 2016. "Socioeconomic Attainment, Cultural Tastes, and Ethnic Identity: Class Subjectivities among Uyghurs in Ürümchi." *Ethnic and Racial Studies* 39 (12): 2169–86. https://doi.org/10.1080/01419870.2016.1139154.

———. 2017. *Uyghur Conceptions of Family and Society: Habits of the Uyghur Heart*. Routledge Studies on Ethnicity in Asia 3. London: Routledge.

Zengerle, Patricia. 2021. "U.S. House Passes Measure Clamping Down on Products from China's Xinjiang Region." *Reuters*, December 9, 2021. https://www.reuters.com/world/us/us-house-passes-measure-clamping-down-products-chinas-xinjiang-region-2021-12-08/.

Zetter, Roger. 2007. "More Labels, Fewer Refugees: Remaking the Refugee Label in an Era of Globalization." *Journal of Refugee Studies* 20 (2): 172–92.

Zuboff, Shoshana. 2019. *The Age of Surveillance Capitalism: The Fight for a Human Future at the New Frontier of Power*. London: Profile Books.

Index

Athanasiou, Athena, 89, 100, 103
automated surveillance, 84, 88, 170
Aydin Anwar (Twitter account), 104
Aygul (interviewee), 91–92
Aynur (interviewee), 74–76, 77, 82, 139, 166
Aziz, Abdul, 168

Bachelet, Michelle, 8–9
Baidu, 116
Baixing Anquan (Citizen Security), 84
Bakhtin, Mikhail M., 127, 143
Bamman, David, 81
Banksy, 113
Baojia system (*baojizahi*), 31–32
Baren uprising (1990), 12
Basic Law of the Federal Republic of Germany, 171
Bataille, Georges, 30
BBC, 142, 162, 172
bearing witness: and testimonios, 122; use of term, 8
Beijing (Kunming), attack in (2013), 9, 80
Beijing Winter Olympics (2022), 177
Bellér-Hann, Ildikó, 51
belonging: as positioning the political subject, 167; as related to unity, 90
Belt and Road Initiative (BRI), 13, 87, 115, 170, 176
Benmayor, Rina, 124
Benson, Linda, 67
Beraja, Martin, 85, 115
Bernal, Victoria, 43, 93
Biden, Joe, 9
biometric borders/bordering, 170, 171
biometric data and data collection, 46, 82, 83
biometric fingerprinting, 85

biometric technologies, 46, 84
Blackburn, Kevin, 38
Black Lives Matter, as challenging received language and social realities, 28
Blanchot, Maurice, 30
Bratich, Jack Z., 30
BRI (Belt and Road Initiative), 13, 87, 115, 170, 176
Brighenti, Andrea, 6, 31
Brophy, David, 80
Buddhism, as part of diverse religious practices, 58
Bunin, Gene, 126, 153, 154, 155, 162
Burgos, Elizabeth, 37
Burke, Tarana, 160
Busdachin, Marino, 96
Bush, George W., 102, 147, 172
Butler, Judith, 89, 100, 103
Byler, Darren, 76–77, 80, 81, 83–84, 170

The Capture of Speech and Other Political Writings (de Certeau), 17
Carbaugh, Donal, 48
CarbonSteal, 116
Cassirer, Ernst, 173–74
Chaplin, Charlie, 17
Charalambous, Constadina, 42
Charlie Hebdo, attack on editorial team of, 157
Chen, Yangbin, 57
Chen, Yu-Wen, 56, 94
Chen Quanguo, 13
Chestnut Greitens, Sheena, 13, 175–76
China: anti-terrorism strategies in, 170; as denying any allegations of violence, 168; hacking of digital

GLOBALIZATION
IN EVERYDAY LIFE

As global forces undeniably continue to change the politics and economies of the world, we need a more nuanced understanding of what these changes mean in our daily lives. Significant theories and studies have broadened and deepened our knowledge on globalization, yet we need to think about how these macro processes manifest on the ground and how they are maintained through daily actions.

Globalization in Everyday Life foregrounds ethnographic examination of daily life to address issues that will bring tangibility to previously abstract assertions about the global order. Moving beyond mere illustrations of global trends, books in this series underscore mutually constitutive processes of the local and global by finding unique and informative ways to bridge macro- and microanalyses. This series is a high-profile outlet for books that offer accessible readership, innovative approaches, instructive models, and analytic insights to our understanding of globalization.

Seeking Western Men: Email-Order Brides under China's Global Rise
    Monica Liu   **2022**

Children of the Revolution: Violence, Inequality, and Hope in Nicaraguan Migration
    Laura Enríquez   **2022**

At Risk: Indian Sexual Politics and the Global AIDS Crisis
    Gowri Vijayakumar   **2021**

Here, There, and Elsewhere: The Making of Immigrant Identities in a Globalized World
    Tahseen Shams   **2020**

Beauty Diplomacy: Embodying an Emerging Nation
    Oluwakemi M. Balogun   **2020**

The authorized representative in the EU for product safety and compliance is:
Mare Nostrum Group
B.V Doelen 72
4831 GR Breda
The Netherlands

www.ingramcontent.com/pod-product-compliance
Lightning Source LLC
Chambersburg PA
CBHW020700270326
41928CB00005B/205